A Border

Shane Connaughton

faber and faber

First published in Great Britain in 1995
by Faber and Faber Limited
3 Queen Square London WC1N 3AU

Photoset by Datix International Ltd, Bungay, Suffolk
Printed in England by Clays Ltd, St Ives plc

© Shane Connaughton, 1995

Shane Connaughton is hereby identified as author of this work
in accordance with Section 77 of the Copyright,
Designs and Patents Act 1988

A CIP record for this book is
available from the British Library

ISBN 0–571–17661–5

2 4 6 8 10 9 7 5 3 1

In Memory
of
Marie Conmee

Introduction

I grew up in a village called Redhills on the Cavan/Fermanagh border. My father was a police sergeant on the southern side of the frontier where Ireland faces up to Britain. The border was a political fact but you could see the line only in people's hearts and minds. Eyes are mere maps – you can't trust them.

In 1991 the Samuel Goldwyn Company came from Beverly Hills to Redhills to make the feature film *The Playboys*, written by myself and a friend of mine, Kerry Crabbe. It starred Albert Finney, Robin Wright, Aidan Quinn and Milo O'Shea, and was directed by Gillies MacKinnon. The film was set in the 1950s and concerned a company of strolling actors who – as happened in Redhills in those pre-TV days – arrive in the village and despite the rickety power of Church and State work their rickety Art. With, of course, the transforming power of Love. Love can set you on the road or knock you off the rails . . . Usually both.

Redhills is two hours from Belfast, two hours from Dublin, in the middle of nowhere. We haven't even got a main road running through us. The making of the film was a sensation. People from home and abroad flocked into the village. There was Albert Finney dressed up as a Garda sergeant, there was Sean Penn holding Robin Wright's baby, there was John James North, our local blacksmith, dressed up as a blacksmith and acting with the lot of them . . . On one never-to-be-forgotten day President Robinson visited us, the first time ever anyone so important had come to our neck of the woods. When they heard the word, natives in New York and Sydney downed tools on the spot and came home for the summer. TV crews from all over arrived to do documentaries. We who were making the film became characters in the film. We were changing lives by the act of story-telling. Changing our own lives. But that was then and this is now . . .

Now I had a novel published, *The Run of the Country*. Like *The Playboys* and also my first novel, *A Border Station*, it too was set in the 1950s. I turned it into a film script and, to give the moneymen a chance and because I was tired of the fifties, I updated it. David Aukin and Channel Four gave us a million and my agent gave the script to Peter Yates and he gave it to Castle Rock in Los Angeles and they gave us the rest . . . and one day Peter came to see Redhills and the surrounding drumlin country and liked what he saw. 'Yes,' he said, 'it's buttery country. I like it. We'll do it. I'll want you on the set every day.'

This was an unusual invitation. Writers are normally barred. They sit fretting on the end of a telephone. I was going to be right in the thick of the action. This was too good to miss. Goodbye London, Dublin – I was coming back home for months and getting paid for it. Getting yet another crack at my own childhood. Or a fantasy of it. Certainly remembered emotions. Atmospheres. The past. And this time I would wrap it up for ever. Precisely how, I didn't know.

The day before we started filming I was having a drink in McMahon's – there are two pubs in the village, McMahon's and McCaffrey's, you can't mention one without the other, you can't drink in one without drinking in the other. It's a village. Loyalties and drinking have to be divided. People in the pub were talking about the film and someone said, 'Are you going to keep a diary this time?' During *The Playboys* everyone from Kerry to Sam Goldwyn kept asking me why I wasn't keeping a diary of all the excitement. Keeping a diary for me meant preserving the excitement for others whilst missing out on it yourself, so that time I didn't. But because that man asked me that question I found myself going into Clones and buying a big notebook. And resolving to fill it from the first 'Action' to the final 'Cut'. I often cursed the man and his question. But over the weeks the pain gave way to monastic ritual. During the lulls I'd retreat to my car and write, or wait until night when I became a thief stealing my own goods away through the minefield of politics, religion, relationships, the countryside, time itself. I wasn't interested in showbiz gossip or stabbings. So as well as thief I was policeman too. The following is my scene-of-crime report.

Day 1: Saturday 13 August 1994

We're across the border at Clogher, Co. Fermanagh. It's a big field in a political no man's land just over the Finn River from Cavan and Monaghan. Every Saturday higglers, hucksters, tinkers and shopkeepers from all over Ulster gather here to sell their wares to thousands of bargain hunters, buying anything from third-hand tools to vegetables, bread, clothes and holy pictures. The field, packed with cars, lorries, vans, stalls, men, women, children, is at the foot of wild drumlin hills and flanked on one side by a swamp of rush and muddy water, and on the other by a laneway leading in from the distant Cavan–Clones road. The nearest villages are Redhills in the South three miles away and Newtownbutler six miles away into the North. The RUC don't police the market for fear of attack by the IRA. There is a British Army checkpoint over the hills along the Enniskillen road. The soldiers rarely leave their post and when they do it is to return to base via helicopter.

The field is strewn with crushed stone to improve conditions underfoot. People crunch from stall to stall. On the hill a bullock stands pissing red water. A shopper, measuring a pair of jeans against his waist, looks up. 'Whoever owns don baste needs to be towld.' He turns to the Pakistani stall-holder: 'How much are you askin' for these here trousers?' Red water is a disease in cattle picked up from bad land. Border land is always bad. Kids run past licking ice-cream cones. A heron rises from the swamp and, skinny legs trailing behind, just manages to crank itself up into the sky. The place is certainly an alternative to Sainsbury's.

We're in a corner of the field shooting a bungee-jumping scene. The entire market focuses on a cage dangling 180 feet above the ground from the end of a crane jib. A stuntman gets ready to jump. The film crew rush about setting lights, arranging extras, keeping the onlookers back. Peter Yates, the director, big cigar in hand, strolls through the chaos speaking to the actors, never raising his voice. He wears a light blue anorak, white trousers, canvas shoes and looks as calm as an admiral on dry land for the day. He's done it all before: *Bullitt, Robbery, The Friends of Eddie Coyle, The Dresser, Breaking Away* . . . He's worked with Steve McQueen, Robert Mitchum, Dustin Hoffman, Dennis Quaid, Cher . . . So what the hell is he doing with me? How the hell did I get into the club?

He spies me peeping at him from the side of the crane. He comes over and we embrace. 'Well, dear boy, this is what you wanted. We're making your film right here on your home territory.' 'Good luck, Peter,' I mumble into his shoulder and I feel my hands flapping on his back, as weak as flippers.

He goes back to the action. Conor, the clapper loader, holds up the clapper-board in front of the camera. On a corner of the board he has stuck a green, white and orange tricolour. Philip, the camera operator, squints into the eyepiece. On the side of the camera he has stuck the word 'Guinness' and, beside that, a little blue plaque of the Blessed Virgin. Simon, the focus puller, adjusts a lens. Mike Southon, the director of photography, sits in front of a monitor. They each have long hair scraped back and tied in buns. They look like a bunch of pirates – especially Conor, who has a Vandyke beard and earrings.

'Roll 1. Slate 1. Take 1.'

Peter, his body tense, his voice full of an energy he wants to communicate, shouts, 'ACTION!' The stuntman drops as gracefully as a hawk, then twangs up and down graceless as a broken doll.

A local man – one of the extras – asks me if the film is going to be a good read. I tell him I hope it's going to be the other way around. Another man sits on the ground. 'I just had a bypass two weeks ago. The oul ticker accounted for me father and two of me brothers. But this is grand. Forty pounds for the day and all the grub you want.' He wears a dark grey suit, the same colour as his hair. He's about sixty, well-built and has a lovely boyish smile. In his eyes you can see the faraway look of someone wondering about borrowed time.

But all our time is borrowed. I see the owner of the field moving from stall to stall collecting his rent money. He looks as strong and craggy as the country. Even though he's fifty-five, his hair is crow-black and curly. I know he's fifty-five, I went to school with his brother. I'm about to go over to talk to him when a man stands in front of me holding out his hands. His fingers are raw and red, and the skin is flaking badly. Dermatitis.

'Looka them. No doctor is any good. You can't wear gloves. I'm a brickie. The sand and cement gets in under any cream. I've tried every man in the country for the cure.'

'Maybe you should try a woman,' I say to him.

He looks at me. 'I'd try the divil himself if I thought it would work.'

Over at the crane and jib they are setting up another shot. The bungee-jumping is organized by Irish Army soldiers stationed in Dublin. They wear white T-shirts and black tracksuit bottoms. For the benefit of the camera, one of them does his normal spiel into a microphone. His nasal Dublin accent overlaid with an American twang gives a rare twist to the Queen's English. 'Is there anyone out there amonk you interested to bungee-jump? Is there not a man amonk you interesting in the trill of a lifetime?'

One of his mates works in the Army museum. He's an expert on the British and German officers imprisoned in the Curragh during the Second World War. 'Look at my wrist, boy. What do you notice? I don't wear a watch, see? Because I love my work. Time means nothing to me. It's a waste of time worrying about what time it is. My wife has to come of an evening: "You know what time it is, boyo? Home. Now."'

In between shots, most of the film crew seem to be on

3

mobile phones. Heads inclined they listen into these black seashells, wandering about in different directions, trying to get the best signal. A Cockney voice calls out, 'What are we? Is this Ireland or England?' It's a good question, but he's enquiring about which code he should dial.

John Phelan, the location manager, whispers, 'I'll be glad to get out of here. If anyone was going to do anything, here's the place they'd do it.' He means the IRA might kidnap Vicki, our leading actress. She's a member of the Smurfit family, Ireland's only multinational company. They're not short of the spondulicks. Vicki's a nice girl and twenty-two, when for the part she should be eighteen.

'If they do kidnap her, John, we can recast and this time get someone the right age. In fact, what's the IRA's number? I'll give them a ring.' I think he thinks I'm joking.

He goes away, his Reeboks crunching the stones as he walks in circles trying to get a good signal on his phone. There are so many of them making calls they're all bumping into one another.

I shake hands with Tom Conlon, the owner of the field. He knows everyone at the market: Protestant and Catholic. He looks at me. He's calm, solid as a rock. 'Don't worry, Shane. Round here both communities pull together. Despite the war going on.'

The field is teaming with people. Clouds scud across the sky. The hills above us are scrawny, overgrown with briar, whin, thorn and bush. A wisp of sun escapes, misses the hills but lies across the market. We are at the end of the rainbow. This old Border field is a crock of gold. Fool's gold maybe. At the back of a stall I saw a man sell for £50 fifty counterfeit twenties.

I hear Peter shouting, 'CUT!'

We're back at Clogher Market finishing the bungee sequence. Our forty extras are doing their best to look like thousands. Apart from us the field is empty. Away in a corner, Saturday's rubbish burns in a skip. I hear one of the extras telling a friend about her mother: 'She went into the mental home with her nerves. They took her in. When she saw the other cases in there she soon got better. But she liked it. She understood the inmates. Didn't the Matron give her a job as a nurse. She never looked back from that day out.' There's no shortage of stories in this neck of the woods. Nor is there such a thing as an 'ordinary' person. I sit talking to Albert Finney. He's not working today, but decided to turn up anyway to have a look. The locals know him from when we made *The Playboys*. Every girl that passes smiles at him.

Albert gets on well in Ireland. He loves horses and people. People love him back. Simon, his son, is part of the camera team. My daughter Tara is a trainee assistant director. Toby Yates is an assistant editor. Showbiz is familybiz . . .

'I prefer to be alone when I'm working,' Albert says. 'Unencumbered by a wife or girlfriend. After a hard day's work you want to go back to your room to relax, prepare for tomorrow. They expect to be entertained.' He gives a Widow Twanky inflection to 'entertained' that makes me laugh. 'No, no, it's true. No, I like this life. Every movie is different . . . New places, new faces.'

John, the location manager, comes for me. He looks edgy. 'Quick.' I follow him out of the field. Across the road from the field is a shop, a house, petrol pumps and a big yard with a hard surface. Most of our vehicles are parked in the yard: caravans for the actors, the make-up wagon, the costume bus, the kitchen bus, the double-decker bus on which we eat our meals, cars, lorries . . . We're bigger than any circus. You can get into the yard only through two big iron gates. I notice these gates are chained up. The shop and the house look dilapidated. Over the last few years they have been bombed by the IRA. They are owned by Ken North, who apparently served soldiers, and his wife does office work for the RUC in Lisnaskea. Not long ago their son was captured and forced to drive a proxy bomb to an Army checkpoint. While he was driving the bomb, Ken and his wife were tied up somewhere. The son managed to untie himself from behind the wheel of the vehicle he was driving and escape . . .

In the past I've had a drink with Ken. As they say around here, 'You couldn't meet a nicer fellah.' But there *is* a war going on. You can drink with your neighbour and after 'last orders' he might be going home to a bomb or, depending on his religion, he might be going home to a house full of British soldiers hell-bent on duty, destruction and revenge. Ken is no longer in business here. Apparently he has leased the shop to a man called McCracken.

Our location manager has rented the yard for two days from this McCracken. He has paid him £250. Deal done. Except now it seems that the deal is about to be changed.

McCracken and his workmate, McKiernan, have chained up the gates so we can't get our trucks in or out. 'Why?' I ask John. They saw Tony Devlin drive our generator truck out of the market field and fill up at a nearby petrol station. Along the border there are dozens of petrol stations, shops and off-licences all attracting trade from the South because of the lower Northern prices. McCracken is insisting that Tony should have filled up at his pumps. 'He says it's a conspiracy. You're from around here. Come on, we've got to confront him.' Holy fuck. Someone told me McCracken shot a farmer's dogs because they wandered into his fields . . .

McCracken and McKiernan are in the tumbledown house. I recognize young McKiernan. He's about twenty-four and weighs twenty stone. He's massive. He lives with his parents and siblings and, until recently, with his grannie. One night the house caught fire and she was burnt to death. Death stalks the land . . .

Young McKiernan leans his massive frame against a damp wall; McCracken leans against the opposite wall. The ceiling is coming in, the floorboards are up, but there's a telephone in a window recess and I'd say it works.

McCracken is middle-aged with a sun-tanned, wiry body. I can see a white slash of flesh through a rip in his trouser leg. John and I stand looking at them. John tries to be reasonable.

'Tony Devlin is from Belfast. He doesn't know the set-up round here. He didn't even think your pumps were in working order, for God's sake.'

'Right,' I say, 'they look broken.'

Young McKiernan, staring at the floor, says, 'Youse were put up to it.'

'What?' says John, 'Put up to it? Who by, for God's sake?'

'Be Tom Conlon,' says McCracken staring out the window. The pair of them won't look us in the eye. Normally if you are in a position of weakness, you are the one with a shifty look, not the ones with the power. And they've got the power because they've chained our vehicles inside the gates. And it's no use calling the RUC because they won't come down here. And if we tried to force our way out . . . a big convoy of trucks and crash the gates, well . . . I keep thinking of dead dog rumours.

I know the young fellow – Adie McKiernan. I've had a drink with him in the same pub that I met Ken North. 'Adie. Why would Tom Conlon put us up to it? Tom went on holidays yesterday. I met him when we were here on Saturday and he told me he was going. He doesn't even know the driver of the generator truck.'

Silence. Adie shifts his great weight from the wall and dials a number on the phone. The phone is the only article not covered in dust. In another room I notice a pool table, the baize ripped, the markings and ball positions crudely drawn with a biro. The dialled number doesn't answer . . . Adie resumes his position and stares at the floor. McCracken hasn't moved a muscle. John and I go outside. Polite as ever, John says, ''Scuse us, gentlemen.'

'What the hell's going on, John? If it's money they want, give it to them.'

As location manager, John's job is to give as little money as possible to anyone. 'No way,' he says, horrified. 'If I give in to one I'll have to give in to dozens. We made a deal. They've got to abide by it, for God's sake.'

My heart palpitating with fury, I rush across the field to see Peter Yates. He and Mike Southon are discussing framing, lenses, lights, angles ... I can't bring myself to tell them what's going on; that we might be trapped here for days ... Holy God, it's crazy. My heart pounding even faster, I run back to John like a demented hen. I'll strangle them ... Well, I won't. They'd knock me over with a feather duster. Not that there'd be one readily to hand here ...

John is back in the house with them. It's a classic situation: Hollywood versus the locals, and the locals always win. Or is it? There must be something else going on that we don't know about. Anyway, I'm a local. A deal is a deal.

McCracken is a tight man in a tight corner. He hasn't moved and stares out of the window. John and I could fit together in Adie's big green anorak. Adie's a Catholic. McCracken a Protestant ... From across the market field I can hear the bungee guy from Dublin doing his spiel for the camera. It's always the same: 'Is there not a man amonk you interesting in the trill of a lifetime? ...'

McCracken is now looking down at the rip in his trousers. You couldn't draw words from him with a pliers. Adie does the talking.

'Them gates are shut and that's it.'

'Well, look,' John says, his arms outstretched, appealing, 'from now on we'll fill up with you. We'll fill all our trucks at your pumps. All the time we're in the area, that's at least eight weeks, we'll fill up here. You've got to take the chains from the gates, lads. This is outrageous.'

'And I'll fill up with you as well,' I chip in.

'We don't do unleaded,' Adie says, for the first time looking into my eyes. They notice everything, even what juice your car drinks. 'But we'll have it in three days' time,' he adds.

'OK,' I say. 'From then on you'll be getting my custom and I never break my word.' While I spoke the words, I'm sure I meant them.

'Shane's a local man, for God's sake,' John says.

'I know,' Adie says, flatly and unimpressed. 'That generator truck holds eighty gallons of diesel. It's a lot of custom you took elsewhere.'

'But we didn't fucking know, Adie!' I shout. McCracken looks up at me. He's taut as a tow rope.

Adie and McCracken are genuinely miffed. There's more to this than meets the eye. Finally we do a deal. When we are leaving tonight all our trucks, cars, lorries will fill up from their pumps – and for the rest of the time we're in the area we'll use them too. All this to get the chains off the gates.

Outside we hear from local people that McCracken and Adie are trying to run a market to rival Tom Conlon's, but their yard and premises just aren't big enough. They do not like to see the teeming multitude going into Conlon's field every Saturday. I say to John his mistake was not putting all our vehicles in the big field. We didn't need to go near McCracken. 'Yeah, but how was I to know there are other issues bubbling away under the surface?'

John is from Dublin. He's about thirty, greying hair, wears Reeboks, jeans and a brown leather jacket, and used to be a science teacher. Now he knows there are no rules along the Border. Tony Devlin, the driver who unwittingly started the whole thing, throws his head back, laughs and says, 'Hate tha'. Love kissin' but hate tha'.' It's his catch-phrase. I go over and sit by the hedge. I can see my shirt button being thumped in and out by my heart. And this is only Day 2!

If ever the Catholics and Protestants do get together round here, London, Dublin and the world better look out.

McCracken's negotiating technique is powerful: just sit and do not speak one word. That way your enemy is forced to come up with ever more appealing compromises.

On the way home our vehicles topped up at the pumps. The bill came to £190. Not bad for chains and silence. Chains and silence – that reminds me of somewhere . . . Oh yeah . . . Los Angeles.

Day 3: Tuesday 16 August

A fellah thumbs a lift. He's got a shotgun. He's in his twenties, with long black hair and a very pale face for a countryman. He sits hunched in the passenger seat and, when he speaks, is quiet and intense: 'Last year I shot 123 foxes. I'll shoot anythin' for sport or to ate. I seen me shootin' an oul scald crow one time. I took a grievance agin her. I knew where her nest was. I'd go to the tree and she'd see me coming. Away with her over the fields. I went out one mornin' and she saw me comin' . . . I lay under the tree all day. She never came near the whole day long. Come evening I see her comin' in, but she wheels and lights on another tree. I'm well down in long grass, but she must sense I'm there. She waits for two hours. I lie with only me eyes blinking. Dusk is coming down like black smoke. Doesn't she fly up and sails over and on to her nest. She couldn't resist longer. Bang. I bags her.'

I let him out of the car, he thanks me profusely and he's away over a hedge into a field. The fox slaughter is one thing but that – 'I took a grievance agin her' – I found frightening. Only man can take such a grievance against a fellow creature. Or fellow man . . .

We're filming at a place called Trehoo Cross in green fields and creamy country. It's a crossroads in the middle of nowhere. All our trucks, vans, cars, caravans are parked along the road for about a mile. Sean Doris, our local Garda from

Redhills, and my daughter Tara are at either end controlling the traffic: surprised farmers on tractors, an old lady on an older bicycle, a creamery tanker, a school bus . . . I hear Peter tell Matt Keeslar, the American actor who is playing the lead, 'This scene is crucial. It's a crossroads in his life.' Massive arc lights on shiny chrome stands are placed along the road and inside the hedges. Cattle come down to the hedges and gawk over at us. Local people gather to watch. Kids on bicycles arrive . . . 'Is there any one famous?' they ask.

Matt the American walks along the road, rehearsing. He's just out of Julliard, the famous acting school in New York. He looks to me four years too old for the part. He's supposed to be eighteen. Once they found the girl they had to find a boy that matched. Matt is ridiculously handsome. He walks along the country road all neat, tight, trim and talented.

'You can tell don boy doesn't come from round here,' a watching farmer says.

'How?'

'Round here people have arses built for the hills.'

The way a film is shot out of sequence is like a nightmare: bits of your life all jumbled up in disorder. Now they're shooting a scene pushing a van up a hill, with Matt and a Dublin actor, Anthony Brophy. Brophy's accent is spot on. Matt works with the dialect coach. All the English accents and Matt's American accent worry me. The English accents belong to the crew, Peter and of course Albert Finney, who arrives in his Garda sergeant's uniform. Whatever the merits of the story, it is culturally specific. It's set around here: Cavan, Ireland.

'Shane,' Peter calls to me, 'we need a line here. What would Prunty say to Danny pushing the van?' Anthony plays Prunty, Matt is Danny.

'Push, yah hoor.' They all look at me blankly.

Peter raises his eyebrows. 'Shakespeare, eat your heart out.' Everyone laughs. 'No, no, only jesting. Good. That's why we have you here, dear boy.'

One of the watching kids asks me what the film is about. 'It's about a teenager who runs away from his police-sergeant father after his mother dies. He teams up with Prunty, a real Cavan character, who shows him the run of the country; gives him the chance to experience life, politics, sex, love.'

The kid looks up at me: 'Is Madonna in it?'

'No. Vicki Smurfit.'

I go to Albert and talk to him about a line he has to say: 'I want it out with you . . . what you said about Mammy.' I talk about the emotion behind the line. I get the feeling he isn't too pleased. I probably shouldn't have done it. God, if Albert Finney can't work it out for himself, no one can. Then I see John Phelan, the location manager, beckoning me up into the back of a truck full of electrical gear. He tells me that P. J. McMahon, who owns the garage in Redhills, will not remove his cars from the front of his premises while we're filming. 'We only need him to clear his cars for two days, one of which is a Sunday when he's shut anyway. Have a word with him.'

John jumps down from the back of the truck. It's started raining. I feel utterly depressed. No way am I going to say one word to PJ. We went to school together, along with his brother Gerry, who runs the pub next door to the garage. My father, who was Sergeant in Redhills, had many a run-in with PJ's father. In fact in *A Border Station* I've based a story on one famous occasion when my father raided the pub for after-hours drinkers. Has nothing changed? Am I going to raid PJ? No way. OK, I'm the local boy, part of my job is to smooth things out. But at times like this I wish I was a stranger, an outsider. I'm not going to get into a fight with old friends. Hollywood is full of money. Let them fork out the extra if that's what it's all about. They can deduct it from my money. Jesus, better not suggest that – they probably would!

When we were doing *The Playboys* we had none of these problems. It was a big carnival from first to last. And PJ let us turn his garage into a studio for weeks on end. He was as good as gold. Something's amiss. I suppose second time round things are never the same.

Outside, the rain falls past the big lights. The grass in the fields curves over, silver droplets hanging from the blades ... A middle-aged woman in a dark suit comes walking down the road. She wheels an empty push-chair. A young girl walks beside her carrying a big baby. The baby is covered with eczema. It's all over her ankles, wrists, fingers. She tries to scratch all the time and the young girl tries to stop her. The baby scratches and cries. Her nails leave red weals all over her suffering skin. The woman is home from, of all places, Los Angeles. On holiday. She's an attorney in LA. 'Family law. Divorces. There's more money in it than showbiz.' She's got a helicopter out there and her boyfriend owns the firm that makes the stands for the lights used in filming – in fact, the very stuff we're using here along this country road, just down from the house in which she was born.

'We all have to come from somewhere,' she says. The young girl and the baby are her nieces. She's a calm, gentle person with a lovely shy smile. 'Once you leave home,' she says, 'the chain is broken. Then it's holidays or home for good in a coffin.'

A man pulls up in a car and complains about being delayed by the filming.

'Only for five minutes,' I say.

'My five minutes, not yours,' he shouts, reeling up his window and roaring off.

The woman and her nieces walk away. She looks over her shoulder and says sadly, 'Ireland is changing. Every five minutes.'

I get back up on to the truck. I notice my shirt button beginning to dance.

Out at Trehoo Cross again. The air is as rich and clean as cream. Torrential rain in the night has soaked the earth and washed the air. The sky is blue. A curlew flies, cries, dives behind a hill. A cock crows in a farmyard. As they say round here, 'A cock can crow on his own dunkill.' Along the roadside in the catering bus the crew are having their bacon, eggs, sausages . . . They look as at home on the bus as at home. A Londoner looks out on to the hills and distant mountain and says, 'At last. An unspoilt part of Europe.'

I see Nigel Wooll, the executive producer, walking down the road towards Peter's caravan. Then the producer, Ruth Boswell, walks up to me. 'Do you think they planned to have an American actor all along?'

'I don't think so, Ruth. It's hard finding a young, handsome, straight type in Dublin. Who is there? Apart from me. No, seriously, Ruth, most actors in Ireland come from the theatre and Irish theatre is still built around characters: Christy Mahon, Jack Boyle, The Covey . . . or their modern equivalent. Peter had to get someone the audience can watch for two hours without puking. Simple as that.'

We change the subject. 'Do you know how much the cars for the stars are costing per week each? £700.' Executive producer . . . producer . . . It was Ruth who took my novel to Channel Four in the first place, but it's Nigel who is actually running the film. The kind of situation that can divide loyalties . . .

Wearing the sergeant's uniform Albert Finney comes on to the 'set' – the country road along which I rode my bike umpteen times when a kid. A bull in a field starts bellowing. Albert looks that strong I think the bloody bull senses a rival. Matt, the young American, is feeling unwell. I wonder if it is nerves. It's the first time he has had to act with Albert. I'd be nervous. In fact I am.

A kid arrives on a bike. He has red hair, freckles and wears glasses with very thick lenses. He lives four miles away, heard we were filming, couldn't resist and wants a job as an extra. He's very, very serious-looking and innocent.

'How much do you get in your pocket?'

'Forty pounds a day if you're over sixteen. Fourteen pounds a day if you're under sixteen.'

'How much if you're under twelve?'

The traffic along the road has been stopped. Mike Southon, the DOP, sits right in the middle of the road looking at his monitor. He looks utterly normal, as if it's the most natural thing in the world to be sitting watching a TV screen slap-bang in the middle of an Irish country road. One of the ADs comes along carrying a tray of tea and biscuits. The actors start acting. Matt and Anthony push the van up the hill . . . Albert drives up in a car . . . They all say their lines . . . How can the reality of all this match the reality in my head?

I turn around at the end of a take and see Ruth lying back against a hedge, her eyes shut in deep thought . . . Good idea. I lie in the hedge beside her, the two of us warming in the sun.

Nigel drives off in his Range Rover. Peter Yates lights up a cigar. I give a chocolate biscuit to the kid with the bike. He looks so pleased you'd swear I'd handed him the world.

Day 5: Thursday 18 August

At last we're filming in Redhills village. Two pubs, one shop, one post office, one garage, twelve houses, a village green in the middle of the lot. On the green, a pump. Behind a high stone wall is the demesne once owned by the Miss Whyte-Venables, now in the possession of the Pattons. Five of the houses are empty. Iron ore was mined round here until the turn of the century. When it rains, the hills still run rusty red. The ore was taken to the railway station for shipping to England. All that remains of the station is an overgrown muddy track filled with bails of silage. The railway bridge with its cut stone parapets still gives graceful entrance to the village from the North. All around are the drumlin hills and the great crow-filled trees inside the demesne wall. The wall was built as a relief scheme during the Great Famine. Now a hundred and fifty years later it's being rebuilt by unemployed locals, this time paid for by the government in Dublin. The village is a relic of feudal and gombeen times. My father was Sergeant here. I grew up here. I recognize all the kids playing on the green. They look just like their parents looked when we were all kids together. They run or kick a ball just the way their parents did. We're not like our mums and dads; we *are* our mums and dads.

Peter is outside the house turned into the police barracks by the art department. He calls me over and, full of charm, takes me by the arm and walks me along the footpath until we are alone. He tells me that Albert had mentioned I'd given him an inflection, a reading on one of the lines he has to say. 'Albert will not take an inflection from anyone. An actor must work it out for himself. He wonders whether you are doing it to the younger actors as well. Now, you may think he's a funny old bugger, but come to me if you think something is not being said right.'

I feel myself blushing. Like a kid getting ticked off. 'Well,' I say, trying to defend myself, 'we're all on this journey together. If I hear an actor say a line wrong, cut the cackle, save time, tell him what was in my head when I wrote the damn thing.'

'No, Shane, tell me. And I'll tell them.'

I have to fight myself to stop myself sulking. Peter looks at me and laughs.

'But it's hard to get to you, Peter, when you're in the middle of a scene. You're surrounded by scores of people, with so many technical things going on . . . OK, OK, I know, I know.'

'I know Albert's playing your father and this is your village, but . . . OK? Now, to much more serious matters. We've already lost two days and we're not even a week in yet.'

I could see immediately what was coming. Cuts. I'd have to cut the script. The production company puts the pressure on at the most intense moments. In the night when you're asleep, calls and faxes zip across the Atlantic. 'CUT.' They buy a story, tell you they love it, then fuck it up. So far, though, I've got to admit Castle Rock have been calm and easygoing.

'If you don't cut it, Shane, they will. Anyway, you know there are scenes you can get rid. We either carry on getting great stuff, somewhat slowly, or we speed up and end up with a pile of shit.'

Peter's so easygoing and smiling, it's hard to get annoyed with him. But I do my best. Off I stomp down the lane at the side of the post office to where all the vehicles are parked. I clatter up to the top deck of the dining bus and sit in silent fury. Ruth joins me. She has a script in her hand and a big blue pencil. There is nothing makes a producer happier than helping a writer cut his script.

It niggles in my mind what Peter said about Albert playing my father. Yes, my father was a sergeant here in the village. Yes, Albert is wearing a sergeant's uniform. But he's playing himself, like every actor. And I'm writing myself, like every writer. I didn't write a documentary. Have I used facts from the past? What I've used is remembered emotions. The engine doesn't go without fire. Emotions = fire. Add imagination and hopefully you've got forward motion.

What niggles most of all though is me making an idiot of myself. Me, whom Albert would consider a failed actor, giving him, whom I consider our greatest actor, a note. And furthermore he's not playing himself . . . . 'like every actor' . That's too glib. Amongst other things actors interpret history, ancient and recent. They have to make decisions. They can do without the confusion of past and present in which I luxuriate. I'll hold my tongue in future. Mind you, knowing me, I can't promise . . .

From the bus I see the gardens at the back of the houses. They run down to the black water of a river which rises in the demesne turf bog. Across the river from the gardens is the Gaelic football pitch. At the back of the pitch are high, smooth, sloping hills. The dining bus is parked beside the changing rooms. A plaque on the wall states that the football ground is dedicated to Max McGrath. Max was a great local character. His memory is more real to me than Ruth, who sits before me pencilling through my script. This is a curse. You wander around in the present and half the time you only see the past. Being back here in the village I suppose it's inevitable my head fills with ghosts. I'm my own ghost.

Ruth and I do a fine surgical job. Her calm, good humour makes the task almost enjoyable. Bodies are erased, heads chopped, tongues cut out for ever. And we're only on the dining bus. God help me when the old crock is finally wheeled into the cutting room.

They're filming up in the barracks kitchen set. I'm going to watch; I'm not going to hide. On the way I meet Anthony Brophy, the Mercutio of the story. He's very unhappy. He's heard that the producers are having trouble understanding his Cavan accent. 'Lose me accent,' he says, 'and I lose me character.' Is accent character? In England, probably.

The kitchen set is crammed with crew, lights, sound gear, props, furniture and, at the receiving end of it all, Albert. I squeeze into a corner. The assistant director, Lisa Mulcahy, tells me that there's no room for me. She's young, bright and right, but I'm not going to shift. I squat down and pretend I'm invisible. She gives up. Peter winks at me. I'm safe.

The scene is where Matt as Danny plucks a chicken. The place soon swims in feathers. Albert as his father comes in and, trying to help, makes matters worse. Albert moves about, growling in his cigar-rich voice, angrily butting his head against the wall of the part until at last he crashes through, taking everybody with him, including, I hope, audiences all over the world. His power is immense. He can be

18

brutal and frightening, then a smile darts across his lips, his eyes suffuse with tears and, watching, so do yours. He still has the same cocky vigour he had in *Saturday Night and Sunday Morning*. As well as great feeling he has great skill. He leaves very little to chance.

The scene ends. Peter and I exchange impressed glances. The crew move out. Albert sits in his chair and, cool as a cube, starts solving the *Daily Telegraph* crossword. No, I don't think I'll be giving him any more inflections. Well . . . not today, anyway. I give a little twitch of a smile in his direction and sidestep out of the kitchen. He doesn't look up from his newspaper. Instantly I get a whiff of past atmospheres – when I was a teenager and my father was Albert's age. The past is always there like an old rut: you have to fight to keep your wheel out.

I walk along the village street. All the doors are open and the children run in and out. Big beardy clouds lift before the wind. The sun comes out. An 'ack-ack' battery of crows fly out of a tree. A young girl carries a bucket of water from the pump. There's not a village in Ireland you'd drive to for a Sunday afternoon outing. Irish villages are not picturesque like English villages. The one exception could be Redhills. If the empty houses were bought up, done up, lived in . . .

I sit on the window sill of McMahon's shop and pub talking to Imelda, the owner's wife. The owner is Gerry, brother of PJ who owns the garage. McMahon's is the kind of place will do you breakfast at seven in the morning or rustle you up a feed at midnight. Great people who look after friend and stranger alike. A man comes up to us and says that the location manager is rubbing people up the wrong way. 'And even the crows know he's tight with the money.'

'He's paid to be tight,' I say. 'He's on a tight budget. It's a hard job trying to please everyone.' It all boils down to money in the end. Last time everything was based in the village, but this time the production offices are at the Slieve

Russell Hotel in Ballyconnell, ten miles away. The art department is in Scotshouse, a village three miles away. Though the heart of the story is Redhills, much of the day-to-day action is elsewhere. I'm pissed off with this myself but it's out of my hands.

I see PJ going into his garage. I decide to have a talk with him, but when I get as far as the door I just walk on, go home to the house I'm living in and into bed until dark comes.

Day 6: Friday 19 August

In the village again. Meet an old friend – Owen Conlon, brother of the man who owns the field at Clogher Market. We went to the same school in Clones – same class, same age. He retired early from a government job in Dublin and now, among other things, has horses which he shows at fairs. His best mare nearly died last Sunday. He fed her fresh hay, took her to a horse show and she lay down and would have died were it not for the intervention of an old vet who saved the day with a bottle of medicine. Apparently fresh hay causes colic.

He tells me that Shamie McCabe, a schoolfriend of ours, died a few months ago. Multiple sclerosis. I last met Shamie in 1991. He was in a wheelchair. He lived just across the Border in Fermanagh. He told me that at the height of the Troubles in the seventies, every Catholic male in the area was lifted, taken to Castlereagh, interrogated, beaten and offered money to name names. I remember him telling me a soldier kicked him in the back. 'I had a desperate pain in me back before I was lifted, but from the moment the soldier kicked me, the pain went and I never had it again for years. That kick was the best thing that ever happened to me.' Human beings are amazing. No matter how rotten the orchard they stumble into, they can still pluck good fruit. But he's dead now . . .

Owen mentions Mickie Nann. He also went to school with us. He's also dead. I get into my car and drive into Fermanagh to see the field where he died. I go down a lane and come to a house I visited when I was a teenager. The man who lived there had an old record, a seventy-eight, which played famous voices and events from the thirties and forties: a mesmeric Adolf Hitler, Joe Louis fighting Max Schmeling . . . The house stands empty now.

I blunder around looking for the field Mickey died in. I come into a field like any other along the Border. I think I see blood but it's only a dock leaf. It's warm now. Cattle sit over by the hedge chewing the cud, staring at me. Mickey Nann was working in this field. It was summer. He was making hay, helped by a neighbour. This neighbour was slightly odd. Born that way. They were making summer hay. Soldiers came into the field. When they left, Mickey and his neighbour were dead. Murdered. Stabbed with their own hay forks. Their blood spurted into the ground. Neighbours didn't know what had happened to them. Was it a feud over land? Did a local Protestant set them up? An army jeep was seen at the end of the lane. A local Protestant was suspected, threatened. The soldiers' regiment covered everything up. For a time. Then later on in Germany a soldier cracked up and confessed to the crime. He and another psychopath had pitchforked Mickey and his neighbour to death. The soldiers were from Scotland. They had come all the way from another country to this old, jaded hay field and murdered a fellow I went to school with. Because of the cover-up the Commanding Officer of the regiment was demoted. So what?

This was one of the cruellest acts of the Troubles so far. There is no more ancient ritual on a farm than making hay while the sun shines. The land is often wet in summer round here. That's why Mickey and his neighbour were using forks. Even in summer a tractor could bog to the axle . . . People say the soldiers had it planned. That's why the jeep was waiting at the end of the lane. I walk out of the field. All along the

Border the land is fertilized by blood. I feel terrible because I can't remember Mickey's face. I can't put a face to the name. He's a ghost of a ghost in my head.

Out on the main road a man rides past on a bicycle. He wears a tweed jacket and grey trousers clipped about his ankles. His brown brogues are shiny clean. He wears a white shirt and tie. His fair hair is trim and combed. The bicycle looks polished, too. He says 'Good morning' as he goes past. He almost pedantically emphasizes all three syllables. I recognize him. He's the brother of the man murdered along with Mickey Nann.

Back in the village they are shooting a scene in the vegetable garden at the rear of the barracks. They've hacked away debris, weeds and grass, and planted spuds, onions, beans and cabbage. Rhode Island Reds peck away in a pen. In between takes, Albert mouths his lines to himself. He puckers his lips, stretches them wide, opens his mouth and licks his tongue around. He limbers his face so the words fit snugly when the moment comes. He wears an open-necked shirt, old police trousers tucked into his woollen socks and big black boots. He leans on a dung fork staring out across the Gaelic pitch at the drumlin hills. He looks the picture of malevolent peasant and policeman trying to relax in his garden. When he does the scene, he's the image of relaxed crankiness. He's a horse of an actor.

We're all handed a document emanating from America. Everyone has to sign it. We must pledge not to harass anyone sexually, religiously or politically. Also we must not make any jokes about Vietnam veterans. Immediately the entire crew are calling each other abominable politically incorrect names. Mary Gough, one of the ADs, says, 'Already this morning I've been called a fat tart. Can I sue?' Mike Southon says, 'Oh Mary, whoever said that is a liar. You're not a fat tart. You're just an old tart.' Signing this document is standard practice in America, it seems.

Peter and I go down to the bottom of the garden. Knee-deep in weeds with rhubarb-sized leaves – no one knew what they were called when I was a kid and no one knows now either – we talk about Castle Rock's reaction to the cuts. They're pleased – surprise, surprise – but they're concerned we're behind with the shooting. Peter is suggesting we do a week of nights to catch up.

Ruth comes down to us looking worried: 'If all we're doing is one and a half minutes a day by forty-two days, we're doomed.'

'We're just getting into our stride,' Peter says. 'We'll do far more than that some days. Relax.'

Lisa shouts for Peter from the barracks kitchen and he goes off to direct another scene. He's gone only a few yards when the guy who has been hired to do the garden asks him how many rotten spuds he needs for a later scene. He solves that one, then is stopped by Rosemary, the costume designer, a very camp English lady: 'Darling, I want to talk to you about frocks.' All costumes, men's and women's, are 'frocks'. I heard her saying to Albert, 'Darling, come and get your frock on.'

'Ruth, let's not panic. It's early days. It takes time to get into the swing of things.'

'You're absolutely right.'

I've always found whether it's a play over a pub in Camden Town or a Hollywood film, almost everything gets done in the time allotted. If you've got half an hour to make love, that's all the time it takes. If you've got only five minutes, you'll manage.

Until the art department temporarily restored this house we're using for the barracks, it had all but fallen down. I seem to remember a family lived here. One or all of them got TB. They left and afterwards the house was boarded up for years. In the fifties, TB was regarded as cancer is today: you were afraid to mention it for fear the very word was infectious. I met a friend the other day who referred to cancer as 'the bad lad'. He wouldn't say the word.

One of the rooms of the house is being used to store props.

A cage of rats sits on a table. We need them for a scene in a bedroom and in the garden. They look tame to me, not like the slimey demons in my mind. This room is damp and tumbling. With the big-leafed weeds at the bottom of the garden it reminds me of Border bigotries: you can patch and cut, but it's the same old rot underneath.

All the villagers know P. J. McMahon isn't going to move his cars. He's certainly made himself the centre of attention. John Phelan wants to involve Sean Doris, our local policeman. He says Sean could order PJ to move the cars if they remain on the public highway. I don't think this is a good idea. Sean has to live in the community. If bad blood is made it could remain long after the film company has gone. I bet it'll all be sorted out, anyway. We're just a bunch of big kids in long trousers. It would be a very boring game if we all agreed with one another.

Friday night at McMahon's pub. We lash the Guinness down. A rock band whacks out the old hits. Lips blow out fogs of smoke. Michael Reilly tells me that McCracken has, on his own bat, filled in a Border crossing blown up by the British Army. Not only is the road now operational, but the British have tarred it right up to the Border with the South. This is amazing. We can't understand it. Normally when locals fill in a road, the Army immediately come out and block it again. McCracken must be doing something right.

At the end of the bar having a quiet drink on his own is Willie Roberts, the leader of the Orangemen on this side of the Border. His son is working on the film with us. Every twelfth of July Willie leads his Orange band up North. His father before him did the very same. I've not met one person in Redhills who begrudges them their day out. The people round here have two religions and two sets of politics, but they live in peace. Maybe that's because the Protestants have no real power this side of partition. Maybe. I ask him why he bothers running the Orange band. 'To give the young folk something to do. Pass on the old traditions. One time every

Orange hall had a dance, but now everybody – Catholics and Protestants – they all go to dances in hotels.'

The pub is hopping with noise, laughter and music. The bar has a low ceiling and is not a big area. But the band has two massive loudspeakers and God help anyone, including Gerry the landlord, who asks them to turn the bloody racket down. I've never met a band yet who can resist battering holes in your eardrums. Why is this? I shout at the guy playing the bass guitar: 'Heh, mate, can you turn it down a bit?' 'What?' he shouts back. 'Sorry, I can't hear you.'

I get drinking with a guy who is going to Cologne, Germany, to open an Irish pub.

'Haven't the German's got enough problems?'

'Looka,' he says, 'the economy in Ireland is dead compared. You know a Rolex wristwatch? Well, there's only one Rolex agent in Ireland. There're eighty-five in Germany. Do you mind Stringfellow's club in London? Years ago I tried to get into it. I couldn't. It was jammed. Two days ago I was in Leicester Square and they were handing out invitations in the street. England is a beaten docket. No, Germany is the place. You see, they got money to spend. In these parts all spare money goes to paying the mortgage. In Germany, ninety per cent rent their houses.'

'The reason they got eighty-five Rolex agents in Germany,' I reply, 'is because the poor bastards are obsessed with time. Here we are enjoying a nice noisy drink and it's two hours after closing.' I look at my watch (not a Rolex), it is creeping up to 2 a.m.

A fellow comes over to me. Out of the blue he says, 'Mickey Nann never went to school with you. It was his brother. And another thing, you were in the wrong bloody field this morning.'

The door opens and big Adie McKiernan comes in. I'm getting out of here.

Our day off. I lie in bed and look out the window on the Whyte-Venables demesne: graceful green hills with grazing sheep; a beautiful copper beech out one window, a massive Californian redwood cedar out the other; through a mass of trees the lake in the morning light shines like polished tin. When I was young, you approached this house cap in hand. Now I'm sleeping in what was the main bedroom. I can't believe my luck. I don't draw the curtains at night so I can see the glory of it all first thing in the morning. In the distance I can see two thoroughbred horses elegantly rump-nuzzling. A great sprawl of galvanized sheds stand in what was once the walled orchard. Time has caught up with the place. In the eighteenth century, the estate was owned by Colonel Whyte. Like all the great families of the time he kept a piper to entertain him after dinner. In his case, every winter he put up the famous *uileann* piper Arthur O'Neill. This tradition changed after the Act of Union in 1800. From then on politics hardened. The last male heir of the Whyte family was born in 1801 and died in 1833. His granddaughter married Edmund Burke Venables. The Revd Arthur Thellusson Whyte-Venables was the last male of the Whyte-Venables. He died in 1929, leaving two daughters. They were the spinsters who ruled the demesne when I played here as a child.

They were walking cliches from a 'Big House' novel. I remember one of them stopped us as we were on our way to the lake to fish. She wanted to see what size hook we were using. She didn't allow big hooks because they hurt the fishes' mouths. Both sisters spoke in plummy English accents and existed not for man, but for their cats. Patsy Flood lived in one of the gate houses. In spring and summer his main duty was to walk the goose, the gander and the goslings to the lake, stay there, and walk them home again in the evening. The sisters visited all the schools in the area three times a year, Catholic and Protestant, and gave each one of us sweets or apples. Some of us took this generosity to be Ascendancy condescension. A sweet or an apple from the wrong hands had political connotations. When they got old, they put the place up for sale on condition they could live in it for the rest of their lives. One of the sisters announced locally that no Catholic need bother bidding. We lived so closely together and harboured such bigotry. Still do. What a waste of time! Weeds and damp – heads and graveyards are full of it. Dorothy died first. Gladys died in 1984 at the age of ninety-four. She ended up in the room I sleep in, infirm, looked after by a local woman. At one period a burglar from Clones lived in the house and Gladys never knew.

People are amazed that I live here alone. They don't know how I dare. I've been asked if I have seen any ghosts. In the pub last night a woman told me she wouldn't stay in the house 'for all the tea in China'. She doesn't realize it's ghosts I'm looking for. Anyway, I'm not in the house alone. Tara is staying here too. We've got the run of the house, the run of the woods. I swim in the lake alone. It is completely surrounded by ancient trees. The branches dip into the water. The water is deep, turfy, frightening. But there are no ghosts: no sign of my father in his uniform, or my mother in her fawn overcoat, a playful look in her eyes, a warm smile on her girlish face; no sign of Gladys and Dorothy driving out in their old Wolsey. The place is now owned by David Patton. He's done up the house and is renting it out to fishermen on holiday. Since it's been renovated I'm the first to live in it. At least I've got a link with the past. But the past is dead.

This evening I went into the other pub in the village – McCaffrey's. I had a drink with an elderly farmer, Willie Cammell. With him was his nephew, home from Birmingham. He helps Willie on the farm and doesn't want to go back to England. The nephew must be about thirty. First thing Willie says to me is, 'I mind your father. A fine man. Aye man, surely.' Then he told me he had a photo of me. 'Aye. I've got it up in the byre.' I let that pass and asked him what kind of farming he was doing. 'Me main crop is spuds. No grain. No grain about this country. Any more. But I always have spuds, gauson. The spring this year was late and we had a drawky summer. With rain and ojus hasky winds.' He uses lots of old words which have their origins in Gaelic. 'Drawky' is from the Irish *driuch*, meaning sickly in appearance. 'Hasky' is from *seasc* which means withering. He also used the word 'lock' which is from *glac*, a handful. Willie is a Protestant, but his ancestors have been here for so long the native language – what's left of it – has stolen on to his tongue. I left Willie and his nephew sitting together at the bar. I sensed there was a silent drama between them: the drama of going back to Birmingham. Willie Cammell gives the impression that he is utterly rooted in the soil – a lovely, gentle, hard-working Irishman. Yet if he lived just half a mile down the road, across the border, he'd be classified as British. Language is the only test. We can own territory, but language owns us.

I went into the street and looked at the moon trailing wedding-dress clouds in the bright sky above the demesne. I didn't want to go home so I returned to the bar, to Willie and his nephew. Willie began to talk about a man called Freddie Jordan. 'John Agnew came to the red bog with two brand new wheelbarrows. Painted blue. I mind them rightly. At the end of the day he hid them under bushes. Man dear, Jordan found them, threw oul fumm atop them and set them alight. For his revenge oul Agnew nailed up all the doors on Jordan's barns and sheds, so when he come home one evening he couldn't drive his cows and pigs and horses in, and was too drunk to know why. I mind the time Connolly chased Jordan in the red bog with a long-handled spade. And it all shiny.' The nephew's eyes danced listening to Willie.

Sean McCaffrey, the pub landlord, held a twenty-pound note up to the light. 'Someone came into the village last night and passed off duds. I was caught for three of them. Sixty pounds. It was a sore blow, I'm tellin' you.'

'Who do you suspect?'

'Now you're talkin'.'

We all fell silent, nursing our pints and our suspicions. Could be anyone.

'Say nawthin', till you hear more.'

Day 7: Sunday 21 August

If they haven't already been on Saturday night, everyone goes to mass on Sunday morning. The chapel is a mile from the village. People drive up there then come down to the village to get the Sunday papers in McMahon's. All wear their Sunday best. Booze, U2, drugs, sex . . . whatever the young are supposed to be into, come Sunday they are into mass. I couldn't name one person around here who doesn't go. In a sense, it's a ritual above religion, the spiritual equivalent of signing on the dole. Because we're filming in the vegetable garden, the traffic is stopped from time to time. Mass has ended. There's a build-up of cars. Some of the film crew asked John Phelan about the possibility of diverting the people returning from the chapel. 'No way. This is Ireland. This is Sunday. We're not diverting anyone.'

After everyone has come and gone with their newspapers I see a handful of Protestants making their way out to their church. That's outside the village as well. In the fifties the vicar was the Reverend Doctor Gamble. He went round on a bicycle or in a pony and trap, wore gaiters and a top hat. The rectory is now owned privately and the vicar is peripatetic, serving a number of churches in the Border area.

I mention religion to Albert and he tells me he can't see the sense in it. 'The first time a man comes back from the dead, then I'll believe. Until then I'll spend Sunday morning with the *Observer*.' He has as sceptical a view on writers. More often than not, when I approach he shouts, 'Oh no, here comes the bloody writer!' He's either joking or taking it for granted I've got a thick skin. This morning I walked across a specially laid lawn at the back of the barracks set. He and Peter were sitting on the edge of it, but not on it. I, of course, walked right across the middle. Albert, when he sees me, booms, 'Keep off the bloody grass! Haven't you read the call sheet? Writers! Go into the parlour and write a novel, will you.' The last is a quote from his own film, *Charlie Bubbles*.

'Where would you be without writers?' I ask weedily.

'With what's his name – Mike Leigh.' Albert gave Mike Leigh money for his first film, *Bleak Moments*. 'He was young, talented. I thought I'd help out. It turned out a bit gloomy though, no? Yah see, yah got to keep it moving.'

'You got to move people's minds,' I reply. 'Not action for its own sake. Mike Leigh's work is his religion. He's got the mental rigour and discipline of a Jesuit. In film-world ortho-doxy, he's the black pope.'

Albert laughs good-naturedly: 'Bit early for this kind of talk, 'nt it?'

'Well it is Sunday.'

We all go down to the bottom of the garden. We're filming the mother's death scene. Separating her husband and son who are fighting, she collapses on to an onion bed, dead. Father and son are crunched with guilt.

It's a beautiful day. The sun is high in a fine sky. Sheep grazing the football pitch are baaing. Cows in a nearby farm-yard are mooing. Dogs are barking. And crowing gamecocks answer each other from their distant pens. Albert crouches over the actress Derbhla Molloy, who is lying on the onion bed. Matt, as the son, stands sobbing beside them. Albert gives the emotions full value. He has to say the line 'We're bucked now, me boyo. She's dead.' Such is the feeling and mood he engenders, he adds another 'dead'. The film crew are silent. All the animals and birds for the moment keep quiet. Albert cradles Derbhla in his arms. He looks so power-ful, yet so emotionally vulnerable underneath it all. It's a bleak moment done with such simple truth that people stand still for a few seconds after Peter shouts, 'Cut!'

Then I walk up the garden, sit down and, against the evidence of what I'd just seen, wonder why Albert had added the extra 'dead'. A bleak moment is the soul up against a blank wall. The emotions are not elasticated. You are unable to say one extra syllable. The line in my novel was the end of a chapter. 'We're bucked now, me boyo. She's dead.' Just that. No more. *Finito*. A bald statement of abject loneliness. But then Albert isn't acting the chapter of a novel. He's trying to bring a scene to life, trying to lift dead words on a page and inject blood into them. Resurrection is what it's all about for the actor. I feel cranky, none the less. I hate excess, even though I'm full of it. You need only one bullet in your gun.

Peter sits down beside me and I know by the way he's smiling that he's got something important to say. By the time he's finished I'm shocked. There is a crucial scene where the father breaks down the door into his wife's bedroom. They sleep apart because childbirth would risk the wife's life. She has a weak heart. For religious reasons they don't practise contraception. Out of passion, frustration, he breaks down her locked door. His son witnesses this and from that moment on there is an Oedipal time-bomb ticking between them.

But Albert doesn't want to break the door down. He thinks it would make the man a rapist. I detect from Peter that the producers are afraid of the scene too. In America they'd certainly look upon the whole thing as an act of rape. The feminist lobby would picket the cinemas. We should be so lucky! What codswollop! Am I going to allow political correctness to emasculate the moment? It's a brutal moment, but as far as I'm concerned a true one. I find the script.

INT. ROOM. NIGHT
Danny peeps out through the barely opened door of his bedroom. He sees his father, in pyjamas, knocking on his Mother's bedroom door.
MOTHER (*OOS*)
Who's there?

FATHER (*Loud whisper*)

Who do you think?

MOTHER (*OOS*)

What do you want?

FATHER

Ask me an easy one.

Danny bites his lip. He winces, frightened, as his Father puts his shoulder to the door and bursts it in with a wood-splitting shatter.

'What's wrong with that, Peter?'

'Well, have another look at it. Albert might be right.'

'We have to have the scene. If the boy doesn't see the father breaking the door down, half the film flies out of the window. The boy has to see this.'

'Calm down. Relax. There might be another way of doing it. Go away, think about it.'

Peter has the ability to stay calm at all times. He puffs on his cigar, leans back in his chair. He has a sun tan that he could have got only in California. I feel my face has gone all pale and flinty with anger. What about Othello? I think to myself. Pretty nasty what he does to his woman.

'Well, what if we hear him saying, "I'm lonely for you," as he breaks the door down. And he hits the door with his head. Bangs his head against the door. Such is his pain. And the boy doesn't hear him say, "I'm lonely for you." So he can keep his obsession about his father.'

'Now we're getting somewhere. And there's all sorts of ways I can cut the scene. Think about it some more. Don't rush. We're not doing it for some time yet.'

I wander off and sit on the window-sill outside McMahon's. It's nothing to do with feminism or political correctness. It's Albert. But what if he's right? He's the one who has to make it work. If it doesn't work for him, it won't work for an audience. If he's not happy, there must be something wrong. If the script stands up when pressure is brought to bear on it, it's a good script. If not, change it. Make it better. A film script is written three times: once at home, again when it's being shot, and finally in the cutting room. So . . . Make it better. Come up with something new.

Two men come out of McMahon's and stand talking. One says to the other, 'The film crowd aren't good spellers. I seen a sign pointing and it says "loc". L-O-C, instead of L-O-C-H.' 'No,' says the other man, 'it's L-O-C all right. Short for "location".'

Brendan, one of the caterers, drives up with an urn of tea and tins of biscuits. He puts them on a table along the village street. We stand around drinking and flapping at scores of wasps attracted by the sugar and biscuits. Someone gets stung on the arm. Penny, the nurse, rushes to deal with it.

Ken, the sound recordist, comes out of the yard from the vegetable garden and grabs a cup of tea. He is very tall, urbane and handsome. He wears a thick padded jacket and trousers tucked into his suede boots. Styrofoam cup in hand, he looks at the village. It is dazzling in the sunshine. Two girls play with a puppy dog on the green. Ken, a Londoner, surveys the idyllic scene. Very quietly, as if thinking aloud, he says, 'How much would property set you back round here?' Without having time to listen to a reply, he rushes back down the yard to the garden.

Writers are wasps: they swot at us, but we're on the other side of the glass.

Day 8: Monday 22 August

I lie in bed looking out at a grey wall of teaming rain. The leaves on the copper-beech tree look like clots of blood. The sheep on the hills stand with their steaming rumps to the angled downpour. Nothing moves but the rain and the revolving black mouths of the ruminating sheep. I take bad weather to be an attack on me personally. Someone is always bound to say, 'Is it always like this round here?' And I always reply, 'We don't come for the weather.'

I look down along the Grand Walk to the lake. Half-way are two cut stone pillars. A stone eagle stands guard on top of one and an eagle hidden in an age of ivy is atop the other. The Miss Whyte-Venables loved the Grand Walk. It took them straight from the croquet lawn along a drive, flanked on one side by trees and on the other by a hilly meadow, to the lake where on summer evenings they fed the ducks or their pet grey heron. I don't know why neither of them ever married. Perhaps it was a genetically inherited disinclination to perpetuate the line. Their looks didn't help. They were as plain as pounders. Men came from England to court them, but they never stayed long. One man got off the train, went to the house, took a look, fled straight to McMahon's where he stayed the night drinking double whiskeys, until he caught the eight o'clock train in the morning. 'God help us,' I heard my mother say once, 'the poor creatures are so ugly they can see in the dark.'

They weren't that bad at all. What man could guarantee a life as gentle as feeding ducks and a pet grey heron? Walking through the lovely tousled trees, picking roses, playing croquet, twice a day setting out fifty saucers of milk for all their well-loved cats . . . Dorothy Alice and Gladys Caroline didn't do much harm. They let us play in the woods. For that alone they deserve praise. These days children aren't allowed inside the walls. This is, in part, owing to the legal oddity that allows people to go on to someone else's land without the owner's knowledge, have an accident and then sue the owner for thousands. When you're young, to run softly through regiments of sun-blotting trees is to be alive in the page of a fairy-tale. In the fifties, thanks to Dorothy and Gladys, we lived whole books.

The rain eases. I get up, go outside on to the balcony. The air smells damp and timbery. Cattle move out from under a sheltering tree. A sheep, back legs straight, front legs kneeling, speedy teeth clicking, rips out the long wet grass. In the village the film crew stand around in the wet and mud of the vegetable garden. Albert sits in underpants and vest under a big coloured umbrella, waiting to do a scene. 'You look so at home there, Albert,' I say to him, 'you could be on holidays in Scarborough.'

Peter, when he sees me, shouts so everyone can hear, 'Oh good morning, Squire. The lord of the manor has arisen. What time do you call this, Squire?' His blustering banter always makes me laugh. It's when he goes quiet and says with a quick smile, 'Could we have a word?' that I worry. He tells me he wants to discuss the breaking down the door scene with me and Albert. I insist it's a pivotal moment for the boy. He accepts this but says, 'I want it done in such a way that it won't appear as if a rapist is on the loose.' I tell him I'll keep thinking about it.

I meet Ruth Boswell in the street. She has discussed the scene with Peter and told him how important she thinks it is. 'Believe me, I emphasized to him that the father must break the door down. You know, here we are in this beautiful village, with beautiful intelligent people, but underneath is this utter violence.' Ruth is a good person. An intelligent person. But like many others she has this idea that we Irish are charming geniuses, but unfortunately bloodthirsty underneath. 'There's been one violent death in this village in a hundred years,' I say. 'More than can be said for Muswell Hill.' Ruth was being complimentary in her own way and instead of being rude I should have shut my mouth. But such is paranoia . . .

I sit in my car reading the *Irish Times*. It's full of 'Who are we? What does it mean to be Irish?' stuff. It even creeps into reports on football and hurling matches. National self-analysis is the obsession: the 'who are we? we don't know, therefore we're not who we think we are, therefore partition is not only understandable but also acceptable' kinda thing. I think that's the drift. We're one big mess, anyway – North and

South. I go back to the film set. Albert and Matt are acting a scene where the father, as he shaves, reminisces and talks about his hopes for the future. 'One good murder, that's all I ask. And me the only one able to solve it.' Because of the crime-free backwater they live in, the son knows his father's prayers will never be answered. The way Albert plays it is touching and amusing, but then he turns and winks to Matt, I think to let us know that his desire for a murder is only a passing moment's fondness. I edge my way through the crew, sidle up to Peter and, making sure Albert doesn't see me, whisper, 'He'd never wink. He is absolutely serious. That's why it's both sad and funny.' 'OK, don't worry. I can cut before we get to the wink,' Peter replies. He gives me a smile sharp as a scissors and lights his cigar. He is a buffer between me and the material. Only for him I think I'd be carried away in a strait-jacket. I can see the headline: 'Frustrated writer tries to strangle himself.'

The father is a tough character, rough and cruel even, but full of hurt and a love he can't express. How do you play this without making the man appear brutal and unsympathetic? Albert is conscious that he has to search for lighter moments, otherwise he'll come across as a crashing bore. He's also conscious of the fact that he played the police sergeant in *The Playboys* and wants to make sure there is no echo of the one in the other. When he first read the script of *The Run of the Country*, he phoned me and said, 'Yes, it's good, but I've played the sergeant in Redhills before, haven't I?' 'Same part never worried Sean Connery,' I joked.

They're not the same parts. Albert is seeing to that. And I'm sitting like an invisible hawk on his shoulder, and on Peter's, and on everyone's including my own, ready to pounce if I see something I think is wrong. It's torture. I've turned up hale and hearty at my own funeral. I see myself as a kid walking through the village, going to McMahon's for milk, going to school barefooted in summer, making hay on McManus's hill which dominates the village; on Christmas Day walking with my father and brothers in the demesne, the fir trees stiff under ice and snow, my father saying, 'Look at that. You wouldn't see better on a postcard.' Sometimes I go from the vegetable garden we're using in the film 200 yards up the road to the real garden at the back of the real barracks where the ten of us lived in a kitchen and three damp rooms. I go to check on detail, knowing there are no details I haven't checked a thousand times. In my head, when I see Albert acting the part, I can't help comparing him with another ghost patrolling round the village in full uniform of shirt, tie, trousers, boots, great coat, cap, whistle, baton, bicycle . . . The connections are tenuous, but they are there. In my head.

It's confusing, but it's better than being on the dole. I wrote a script and it's getting made. Someone's paying for it. Someone is paying me to stroll around on my own turf, sit with Seamus Kelly in his grocer's shop chatting about gone times, lie in bed each morning looking out on the lush woods, hills and memories. Seamus used to own McCaffrey's pub. It was in his family for 100 years until recently, when the years caught up with him and he sold it. My father drank with him, drove to football matches with him. My father and mother were at his wedding when he got married to Deirdre Duffy from Belturbet. Deirdre has a photograph of my parents at the wedding. In it they are young, strong and smiling . . . Unlike me, Seamus never lives in the past. The past is beyond resurrection. He lives for today. But in a sense he stands in the past every day, because his shop has hardly changed since the fifties. This is why I love going into it. Children come in and buy liquorice or sweets. In one corner are spades, shovels, wooden handles; in another, boots or wellingtons. He sells food, milk, fishing tackle, treacle . . . The other day he said to me, 'You're horrid like him. Your father.'

I leave the film set, go back to the car and finish reading the paper. I love reading the newspaper but as soon as I've finished I'm cross that I've wasted my time reading it. The rain starts tumbling down. The glare of the film lights is the colour of wet straw. From one end of the village to the other, young ADs shout 'Cut!' or 'Rolling!' It all seems so important. It is. For now. Like a story told to a child in bed. The moment is all. The now. Forget the bloody past . . .

I see my brother Brian walking towards me. He comes out of the rain like I'm dreaming. It is him. He's come down from Dublin. He is the image of the old man. Not as tall, but a dead ringer. The rain stops. We go into the demesne and out on to the lake in the boat. We row right past the spot where we caught our first fish – a tiny perch. Our rod was a long ash plant with a reddish-brown line, a small hook and worm. We landed the fish on the side and, because it was muddy, decided to wash it. We washed it, all right – in the lake. The fish swam away . . . The two of us walk in the woods, along the dark avenues leading to the land of memory and regret.

Later I go to the pub. We're auditioning a band for the dance-hall scene. Me, Nigel the executive producer, Mark Geraghty the art designer and Tara. Except for Tara, we're of a stone-age generation and have proven cloth ears. Mark and I joke with Nigel: he likes the band because (a) they're cheap and (b) they're cheap.

There's a friend from school drinking with his wife. He still looks as strong as an ox, still sings sweet as a thrush. For the last week, as part of his job, he's been driving thirty bale-loads of straw a time from Co. Louth to Redhills. 'If you hadn't got into films you might have been doing the same, lad.' He and his wife tell me that when they got married in 1971, they had only £40. 'That much? In 1972 when I got married I had considerably less.'

'Did you know I did a month in prison in 1959 for being in Sinn Fein?' he asks.

'No, I didn't.'

'I doubt, lad, there'll ever be peace in this country. Aye man, surely.'

Driving home along the avenue to the house, smoky mist sits on top of the trees like the whole wood's on fire – a sign of bad weather. Frogs jump out of the puddles along the way. I swerve to avoid them. The Guinness helps.

Day 9: Tuesday 23 August

First thing this morning we're back down in the muddy vegetable garden. Every inch of ground is wet and messy. I've never seen so many trendy wellingtons moving about in the one space. Matt is sorting through rotten spuds. Albert is up the garden, hoeing at weeds. Conor, the clapper loader, holds up the board: 'Roll 49. Scene 169. Take 3.' Snap and we're away. I always saw the two actors together, on their knees, hoaking like badgers through the rot and stink. Spuds . . . famine . . . survival. But no, they're yards apart. So what am I going to do? Sneak up to Peter and whisper, 'Peter, don't you think . . . '? No, forget it. It's too early in the morning.

Into Clones to get rain-proof gear for Tara. She gets £120 per week and no expenses, and every penny she earns will go towards paying her overdraft at university. So I have to pay for the gear. How can she run up such debt? All students do is learn how to drink. Clones is a real Border town. It's had its economy wrecked and has been bombed by Loyalists during the Troubles. The roads from the North are cratered, so people who once came here for the shopping have for the last twenty years gone elsewhere. It's a neat town on two hills, joined by one long, narrow street – Fermanagh Street. On one hill is the Catholic church, on the other the Protestant. Fermanagh Street is all small shops and pubs. Covered alleys lead into backyards. The once exotic Luxor Cinema stands shut and empty. The railway station is no more. The meat factory is part-time and seasonal. When I was at the secondary school it was the main town of the region. My mother did her shopping here. She never went to Cavan town. Now Cavan is thriving and Clones is trying to awaken from the nightmare. Someone's just started a petrol-pump business – the first petrol pump in the town for twenty years. The EEC is beginning to make a difference. Prices on either side of the border are equalizing. The Customs and Excise have withdrawn, but the roads are still blown up . . .

Today being Tuesday, the shops are closed all day. Don't ask me why. Except they are not quite closed. 'Closed' signs hang in the windows, but the doors are ajar. The shops are, for the most part, quaint. Family upstairs, business downstairs. Old ladies seem to be in charge. Well, not that old. My age. A big-boned woman sold me a pair of wellingtons – big gnarled fingers with raw red knuckles – on her own behind a counter, surrounded by stacked boxed shoes from another age.

I look in the window of another shop. A woman's very-white hand reaches into the display from behind the partition and repositions a silk bra and knickers. You can't see the rest of her body. Just the hand. It's like a magic show. It's a desperate hand. As if by moving the articles, however slightly, they'll sell. Right enough, two women and a child with a Liverpudlian accent stop and look in. I can't cope with the tension – I walk on. I go into a draper's. An elderly man and his daughter are doing the accounts. The ledgers are open on the counter and they are leaning on the counter looking at them.

'Sorry, are you closed?'

'Yes. But we're open.'

I buy an anorak. I walk back up Fermanagh Street to the Diamond. Two men shout at me. 'Many's the time you come up that hill on a push-bike to school.' No idea who they are.

After the Great Northern Railway was axed, we rode the nine miles to Clones. I was useless on a bike and always arrived late, with my vest and shirt sticking to my clammy back. My brother Brian loved the bike. I can still see him head down, pounding on the pedals, a rapidly disappearing curly-haired dot in the distance. It was no surprise when, years later, he won the Irish equivalent of the Tour de France.

One of the men turns out to be Mickey Carron, now an

estate agent. He's a live wire, witty, direct. Very Clones. They don't care what they say or how they say it. 'I just this mornin' sold a house to a man out the country. You'd know him. Nichol. Fellah with the sign above the eatin' house.' 'Sign above the eating house?' I had no idea what he meant. Mickey explains – a moustache. On top or struggling, no Clones man will render the ordinary ordinarily. Their tongue is quick, their thoughts coiled. They like words. Words pass the time. We stand in the Diamond, talking in the sun. The Diamond is a fine wide stretch of cobbled ground, surrounded by pubs, shops and banks. It's dominated by the Church of Ireland and an ancient Celtic cross. One of the shops is Matthews's.

'You went to school with John Matthews, didn't you, or am I incorrect there? Poor John, the best of a fellah. Comin' back from a Chamber of Commerce meeting in Armagh, just outside the town out the road there, heart attack. Crash. The car caught fire. At least I hope he had a heart attack. It was a cruel way to die. Now he was one man, I can't think of any others, who gave to the poor.' John never married. He lived with his very old mother. She died not long before he died himself. On his own at last, freedom, he never lived to enjoy it.

The only trophy I've ever won John put it up. It was for winning a push-penny tournament played in break-time on top of a smooth surface in the physics lab at school. The trophy was a cup two-inches high and not as wide as an egg-cup. John had to buy the thing in his own shop. In those days his mother ran the place, his father having died when John was very young. When I brought home the cup, my mother was waiting with a bottle of red lemonade. She, my father and the rest of the family celebrated my victory. They did it out of a sense of fun and half-seriously in the hope of greater things to come. My mother knew that when she filled that tiny cup with lemonade, she was filling us up with dreams. We had little to shout about. However trivial a triumph, in a depressed world it had to be blown sky-high . . . I still have the cup. It's the only thing I've kept from that past. I keep it on my mantelpiece, with a die in it always showing six . . . Poor John.

Beside John's shop is the Ulster Bank. An impressive, tall stone building, it has a red hand of Ulster carved in a slab high up on the front wall. In the fifties there were quite a few of these slabs. If you hung about on corners, chances were you spent a lot of time on the Ulster Bank corner on the Diamond. A slab broke free one day. Down came the red hand of heavy stone hitting two youths idling on the corner. One of them was badly injured, the other in Mickey Carron's description was 'killed stone dead'. The dead man's name was Billy Hand. 'He had a hand-to-hand existence,' Mickey added with deadpan delivery. 'Death's an oul trickster.' Another man comes and joins us. Straight out he asks me, as he rubs the fingers of his right hand together, 'Have you piles of dibs?' 'I'm only the writer,' I reply.

Back in Redhills they're still down in the vegetable garden. Everything is set up to go, but Mike Southon doesn't give the word. He's peering up at the sun, calculating how long we've got before the next cloud passes over. Everyone is patient, except me. We don't want the sun. Right now we need cloud. Making films is like farming – you want rain in one field, sun in the other. Peter Yates has cut the son throwing the garden fork up on the shed in anger. My idea was that, after a pause, the fork slides down and sticks in the ground at the father's feet. A good image . . . but we haven't got time to make it work. Albert, hands dangling by his side, crouching, alert, waits for action. He's wearing a torn brown pullover and dark trousers tucked into his boots. He juts his chin out, puckers his lips, glances up at the approaching cloud. He's like an old prize fighter ready to slug out another round. Matt, the young American, stands tall and nonchalant. He's got a calm, introverted talent, well-suited to films. He looks like a cross between a young Gregory Peck and Michael Douglas. He and Albert are from completely contrasting backgrounds and cultures. So am I. So is Peter. But here we are in this old garden, waiting for a passing cloud. Misery or films make strange bedfellows.

I ask Simon Finney what it's like working with his father. 'All right. Once you get used to the mordant wit.' He smiles and looks over at Albert. Albert catches his eye and winks at him. Then Albert as the father looks at Matt as the son . . . His face tightens. Matt looks at him, emotionless to the point of insolence. Mike Southon shouts, 'Go! We'll just get it if you go now.' Peter shouts 'Action!' and Albert is tearing down the garden at Matt: father and son at each other's throats, words and spittle flying, the ground churning under their angry feet. Looks good to me.

Later I sit with Peter in his caravan. Lunch. Toby, his son, joins us. The two men are so alike in manner it's uncanny. They even laugh in the same way. It's unfair when we get older and our sons come up on our heels, reminding us of how we once looked. Our children are mirrors on legs.

'Editing,' Peter says, 'is like having a pencil with a big rubber. You can do anything you want. You can rub it all out, put it back in.' Peter is like a very experienced old circus clown. He makes you laugh and, before you know it, you're in the ring with him, helping him out. The crowd laugh, go silent. You hear a devilish chuckle, turn round and there he is smiling, an eyebrow raised observing you, an 'Everything all right? Relax' expression on his face. You relax, get out of the ring and wonder why on earth you agreed to go in in the first place. He never cracks a whip. His charm makes all the tigers jump through hoops of fire.

'Relax,' he says. 'We're here for a couple of months, the money is poor, the work is hard, but if we don't enjoy ourselves we might as well be down a coalmine. Or we might as well have not left home, hm?'

'Why did you cut the garden-fork bit?'

'Pardon?'

'The graipe? The fork thrown up on the shed roof?'

43

'I knew something was troubling you. We haven't got a shed. The fork is still there between the two men. The boy does grab it. That's the important thing. Threatening his father with it sparks the death of the mother.'

'When I was sixteen I was sorting through rotten potatoes with my father. Instead of getting on with it I was hanging round the kitchen window with my mother. She was inside cooking an apple pie. My father got really angry. I was a sweaty, raging teenager with nowhere for my passions to go. He hadn't much outlet for his passions either. I didn't understand it at the time. He grabbed hold of me round the neck. I reacted as if he was really choking me. My mother came running out to separate us. The garden fork was stuck in the ground. My father walked away. I grabbed the fork, knowing my mother would stop me using it. I was spluttering with rage. I felt so angry that he had attacked me that I was catatonic for a minute or so. My mother calmed me down. Life went on. It was only years later I realized the passions burning up the lives of men and women. My father had to put the bread on the table for eight children and his wife. My parents slept apart. It was, in part, an Irish contraceptive stratagem. I slept in the same bed with my mother until well past the age of reason. It was a classic explosive set-up. We didn't know about Freud in those days. The only Freud we had was fried bread. You see where the scene's coming from?'

'The feelings you describe, I hope we've got them in. I know we have. You're suggesting we build a shed? For one shot?'

'No.'

'Well then. We can't get everything in. Don't worry.'

I had to get it off my chest. A good action makes a good image. But ... Anyway, at the time I didn't throw the fork up on the shed. My mother kissed my tears away. I stuck the graipe back in the ground. No kisses – madness. I still hear the shouts in the garden, especially when I shout at my own son, Tom. He's staying in the village on holiday

44

with friends. He's fifteen. He watched a bit of the filming the other day. It was Albert and Matt in the bloody garden. He laughed at Albert's shapes and shouts. 'He's just like you, Dad.' It convinced me that Albert's on the right path. And I'm not.

I crossed the border into Fermanagh and recrossed it again into Cavan. If you know the road surface you can tell where you are; if not, you won't have a clue. No map can help. Signposts are twisted. Shiny tar – Fermanagh. Rough tar – Cavan. If your ear is good you can tell by the accents. Across the Border the Cavan drawl shakes off the dust and picks up a biblical clip. 'Howya? How's she cuttin'?' becomes 'Are ye rightly?' Cavan, Fermanagh, Monaghan – they're as tangled as bushes. Monaghan land, like a uterus, runs deep into womby Fermanagh. The land is watery: lakes and the Rivers Finn and Erne. The Erne splits Fermanagh right the way up her stomach. In summer, the Erne is in Fermanagh. In winter, Fermanagh's in the Erne.

Along the Border, here at Leggykelly, it was, is and always will be smugglers' paradise. All the Border people drink in the Leggykelly Inn. It used to be owned by a Catholic. It's now owned by a Protestant. Property doesn't often change hands round here. Religion runs in the soil. The Leggykelly changed religions. And the old post office at Cloverhill, two miles away. That was Protestant and is now Catholic. A local scrap dealer, Seamus McArdle, bought it and has turned it into an upmarket restaurant. Seamus is also a banjo player. After the coffee he'll play you a tune. George Farrelly, the landlord of the Leggykelly Inn, is unmarried and lives on his own. He's getting on in years now and lies resting on his bed in a room just off the public bar. His pub is used by detectives, spies, informers, operators, smugglers, travellers, sportsmen, horsey folk and the rest of us. Any trouble and George rises from his bed, adjusts his hat, points to the door and the offending person has to quit the premises pronto.

I sit with a total stranger having a drink. I ask him how he thinks the Troubles are going to end up.

'The hardest row to kill is a row in the family. The inlaws and the outlaws. I was caught up in the Troubles meself. I was blown up be a bomb in Enniskillen.'

'That must have been . . . terrible.'

'It was nothin'. I was unconscious all the weeks of the pain.'

As I am leaving I shake hands with him, hoping I can steal some of his strength. The world is full of saints. Miles from the nearest chapel.

Not far from the Leggykelly Inn is a cottage lived in by a brother and sister – Shamie and Cissie Connolly. They've made few concessions to modernity. Cissie still cooks on an open turf fire. Kettle, skillet and iron pots sit on the naked fire or hang on hooks from the crane. She keeps flour, sugar and salt in a big wooden bin the size of an old dealer's desk. They have a dresser, a press, a table and chairs. On either side of the fire are two armchairs. The fire is never out. The house is never empty of people. It is the centre of hospitality in this part of Ulster. There is always tea in the pot. The kettle is always steaming. Bread is always baking. The table is never without an apple pie. Talk and argument never cease. The language is rich. When I called today, Cissie told me about a young child who'd broken an egg in the kitchen the day before. 'I pretended I was cross. Oh, she didn't give a rap. She stared me out of countenance.' Shamie, describing a tall, fine woman, said, 'I'm telling you she was as neat as pins in paper.' It's a fairy-story of a place. Time moved on and Time's the loser. The blazing hearts and turf defeat the clock.

Shamie and Cissie live along the Cavan–Derry road. All day cars beep going past the house. The old leather armchair is the one I sat in when a boy. It hasn't moved. And when I sit in it I don't move for ages. Shamie used to work in England. Each day it's on he listens to *The Archers*. Not in a million years would you guess he was an *Archers* fan. Today I sat eating bread and blackcurrant jam. The news was on . . . The Reverend Doctor Paisley bellowing out his blood-curdling litany of doom . . .

Dusk crept down the drumlins, smothered the backyard. Out of the door I could see a gamecock and hens making for the byre. I could hear them flutter and fly up on to the rafters. They roost there till dawn.

Day 10: Wednesday 24 August

We're enacting a cockfight in a place called Derryleague. This is wild country which is approached up a winding lane bordered by tall, thick hedges of bramble, blackthorn, whin and ash. The hills are so steep you wonder how the cattle can graze them without falling over. When you finally reach the top, the views are breath-taking. Behind are the Cuilcagh Mountains in West Cavan and Fermanagh. Below is the Annaghlee River, winding its way through lush meadows and old fields thick with ragwort and thistle. Going down to the river, the land falls away so slanty that you have to run to keep upright. An abandoned Volkswagen car sticks out of a hedge. A horse-drawn potato digger is eaten to rust by weeds and grass. It's been raining heavily – the ground is mud to the knees. All the film trucks are in an adjoining field: the whole carnival of lorries, buses, vans, cars, jeeps and toilets. There's even a marquee set up for the extras.

The river is in full spate. She's risen six inches overnight. The marker is an old paling post hanging with barbed wire. On a rope stretched between two poles hang hessian sacks. In each sack is a gamecock. Their muffled trumpetings blare through the mayhem and dark morning light. People gather by the river. A ring is mown in the tall grass. Posts are driven in. A rope is slung around. The extras as cockfighters gather. Weighing scales are produced, scissors, spurs . . . It is at this pit of death that the boy meets the girl, Annagh Lee. Peter decides he's going to build up the fight stage by stage, as if shooting a documentary. The extras – men, women and children – are the real thing. They know the game.

Mary Gough, one of the ADs, shouts, 'three men this way, please, with cocks!' Every man in the place steps forward. Much laughter. 'No,' Mary shouts eventually, 'three cocks in sacks!' 'Cavan condoms!' someone else shouts. More ribald laughter. Big drops of rain slap down. The extras make for shelter. In a queue for the toilet, a man carrying a hessian sack says, 'Hold me cock while I take a piss.' If the rain continues we'll never get out of this field. The vehicles will never make it up the hill to the lane.

'Brave slap of country this. Don river's full of trout.' The Tourist Board don't know this place exists. They couldn't find it. When you see such lost beauty you know why wars take place. It looks like a land worth fighting for. There have been brawls over women, usually in pubs. Land wars are all fought sober. The Trojan War was over land and cattle, not Helen. I can see a small field up a hill, 200 yards from where I shelter. It's just a daub of green surrounded by elderberry, bramble, ash, nettle, whin, fern and thorn hedges. It's at such an angle the grass is almost lying flat from the roots. The hedges are so tall the ground is dark for months on end. But for a moment the sun comes down and fills this tiny hillside field with light. For a moment it is not a field at all. It's an old bucket full of shillings, hidden by a miser at the bottom of a ditch. I'd fight for that territory myself: 'a plot whereon the numbers cannot try the cause . . . ' The land round here has been fought over for centuries. There's a fort on every hill. Not for Helen, not for religion – for land! A cloud scuds over and the patch of ground returns to what it is – a drumlin purgatory for man and beast alike.

At the catering wagon one of the kitchen girls gets stung on the breast by a wasp. She screams. Dozens of men eagerly go to her assistance. 'Stung at the nipple – there's no worse spot,' a man says. Shamie Connolly is one of the extras. He tells everyone he was stung yesterday all over the arms and face. He rubbed vinegar on to the stings. 'I got a thick skin. Divil the hate harm done.' The wasps are laden with sting. They land only to sting.

The rain falls thick and fast. It hits into the ground like shotgun pellets. Everything comes to a halt. We haven't one shot in the can yet. And it's noon. For this day I prayed for good weather. An early lunch is called. We all sit in the marquee. The cocks in their hessian sacks are brought in as well. They crow all through the meal. You can't help laughing. Here we are in this muddy field, sitting having our dinner in a big tent with all these fucking cocks crowing. It's like a mad party without rhyme or reason: no one knows the host; no one knows why they've been invited. 'What are you talking about?' Shamie says to me, 'Man dear, this grub's the best. Relax, yah hoor. This is better nor ploughin'.'

Ruth thinks we should cancel the rest of the day and move back into the village. Work indoors. The rain is caning into the canvas over our heads. Ruth and the ADs go to Peter in a panic. In surprise he looks up from his dinner: 'No decisions will be made until I've enjoyed my lunch.' We watch him eating, relaxed as though he's at a wedding. He has his pudding, his coffee, then he lights up his cigar and beams at us. 'To cancel now, we'd never get the vehicles up out of this field. It's hard enough walking through the mud. We wouldn't get back to Redhills until nightfall. We go on. Here. We shoot in the rain. When lunch is over, of course.' He's the calmest man I've ever met.

Lunch over we go outside. The downpour gives way to squalls, then drizzle. 'A soft class of a day,' someone says. The river is rising visibly. The water comes sweeping round a bend, rushes straight on, swells out into a belly of overflow and in the distance, having disgorged into a field, flows on faster, deeper and just a little slimmer. It's like someone's emptied out a skyful of Guinness at your feet. But at last: 'Roll 59. Scene 158. Take 1.' Slap. 'ACTION!' In the middle of all the

49

weeping chaos Peter stands as calm as an old admiral in a stormy sea. Both ends of his cigar are wet.

As I drive home along the demesne avenue, a badger runs before me. The headlights pick him out, imprison him. Because of sheep fencing at either side he can't escape left or right. He runs on in front, bobbling up and down like a strange clockwork toy.

Day 11: Thursday 25 August

The river has risen another notch on the barbed-wire post. But at least it isn't raining. Noel Bartley, the man who owns the fields, wanders around chatting and taking photographs and trying to remain calm at the sight of his churned-up land. Overnight the vehicles seem to have sunk to the axels in the mud. Only the four-wheel-drive jeeps and two massive tractors can move. They have gouged deep ruts up and down one side of the hill.

Across the river, just barely visible, is the remains of a house and farmyard. Noel knew the two old ladies who lived there. Sisters. Aunts of Field Marshall Montgomery. 'He visited here. Didn't they have an eye for the right spot? That bungalow way in the distance there – that's owned by the Jehovah Witnesses.' They've always had an eye for the right spot . . . 'The two ladies were dedicated to keeping old donkeys alive. One fell down and couldn't get up again. A local man was called to see what he could do. He looked at the oul ass lying there. "What seems to be the matter?" asks the ladies. "Nawthin' much," says your man. "He just needs four new legs".'

The place is now owned by a family called the Mundays. They live in a house over the hill. The Munday girls come over and back to see us filming. They have to row across the river. The family dog accompanies them, sitting up in the front of the boat. It's a fine sight to see those lovely girls coming across the flood, rowing, laughing, in the middle of this paradise, like there's no tomorrow.

Peter is directing the extras. One of the men has a woman's handbag hanging on a strap from his shoulder. In it are kept the scissors and spurs for the gamecocks – an innocent-looking handbag containing the instruments of war. When the fight is filmed the spurs are removed. The actions of the cocks are so quick the camera cannot tell. The cocks rise in fury at each other, their vicious, pecking beaks full of enemy feathers. Peter is shooting the fight through the legs of the spectators, so it looks worse than it is. It's all a flurry of feathers, for the most part hidden.

Many of the people are talking about a man who last night committed suicide. He entered the ring of death on his own. I can't make out who it is and I don't hear a name being mentioned. The men talk in a matter-of-fact way about the event. Then I overhear a man say he was a brother of the former featherweight champion of the world, Barry McGuigan. Having gone to school in Clones, I knew the family. Barry's uncle gave my sister Marie a teaching job in a school outside Redhills back in the fifties. Barry's aunt was a girl called Angeline Rooney. I remember being smitten with her and trying to pass notes to her until my sister put a stop to it. I fell for the name – Angeline – and her dark, curly hair. I was at Loftus Road on Saturday 8 June 1985 when Barry beat the great Pedroza to win the world title. Later I met him and his family in their London hotel. He knew Redhills and remarked about me growing up there: 'You had the run of the country.' The expression hit me like a well-timed jab. He'd just won one title and given me another.

A man told me it was Barry's brother for certain who was dead. Dermot. 'He'd just bruk off with the girlfriend.' The pain and the pain left behind . . . I went to the river, picked up a lovely-coloured feather, put it on the water and watched it sail away. That was my prayer for Dermot.

Another man mentions a man in Belturbet who a few

weeks ago put a shotgun in his mouth and pulled the trigger: 'Why are so many young people killing themselves?'

'They weren't young,' I reply.

'Aye. But all the same . . .'

We all sit around drinking tea like we're at a wake. Someone mentions a man called Tierney who goes to all the cockfights and, though crippled, runs the toss-pit from his chair. I've seen him doing this myself. 'Don boy's no daw. He sells Bingo tickets and no one'll go by him without buying. He's ropes of money. Slaps of it.' As we sit and talk by the river, a trout leaps in the turfy water.

Later I stand with an English technician watching the filming. The extras are marvellous, because they are the real thing. 'Look at them all,' I say. 'Now guess which of them did time in prison for the IRA.' He searches the faces for clues. Faces are masks. He gives up. I decide not to point out the man. I simply say, 'I'll only say arms were found on his land.'

'Oh how awful. The real criminals always go free.'

'What's your definition of a criminal? What's your definition of a freedom fighter?'

'Hm, I see. I don't know Irish history as well as you.'

I go back to Redhills. The day is drawing to a close. On the village green I meet a very old man leaning on a stick and his daughter's arm.

'What are you up to this time?' the man asks me. 'Your father was a grand man.' I know what's coming. Every time I meet him he says the same things.

'How would you know? Did you ever live with him?'

'I read your book. It's a dirty book. I don't mind telling you – I burnt it.'

'You got to keep warm somehow.'

'Never mind him,' his daughter says. 'He only burns good books.'

Going in past the gatehouse at the entrance to the demesne, Mrs Rudden, who keeps an eye on things, calls me. 'Your son Tom is in the woods with Fintan and a load of girls.

52

They're shouting and screaming and scaring the pheasants. They went out on to the lake as well, in the boat.'

I roam the woods looking for them. The pheasants are pecking around in their pens. They'll be released eventually for slaughter. And I hope someone gives me one. I can't find Tom. All the secret places I once knew are now in his possession.

Day 12: Friday 26 August

Today the sky is blue, high, wide and handsome. The last day of the cockfight. Instead of sitting in the marquee we take our breakfasts outside and sit along the river. People are still talking about Dermot McGuigan and the man who used the shotgun on himself.

'No he nivir put the gun in his mouth. He put it to his throat.'

'Aye, and the wife and childer in the room below at the time.'

'The boy in Clones hanged himself.'

'Those men must have been in ojus torment. For when the thorn is in your brain you can have no rest.'

'Any of us would do the same if the oul head was tormented sore. Aye man, surely.'

'Aye man, surely.'

A wasp lands on a man's wrist and walks up under his sleeve. I watch and wait for it to come back out. I don't want to tell the man in case he panics and gets stung. Another man has seen the wasp and me looking at it. We exchange smiles. He doesn't want to panic the man either. But the man feels something and looks up his sleeve. At that moment the wasp stings him, and flies out and away. The man slaps at his wrist and then sucks the red weal. 'Well fuck the hoor from a height.'

A man lying back on his spread-out coat, arms behind his

head, looking up into the blue, says, 'One day I was sitting on the edge of a flax hole with a girl. Hadn't I a slit in me trouser leg. And wasn't I sittin' over a feckin' wasps nest. They got in me trousers and stung the balls off me. Oh, I ended up in hospital.'

'Well the girl didn't get a sting from you, anyway.'

'That's a sting takes nine months to come out.'

'Oh, Holy God,' says an elderly man, 'a sting from a wasp is a quare thing. I was one time stung in the ear. Holy Jazus.'

His statement of pain remembered is so trenchant we all laugh.

Over by a tree I see a woman crying. I go over to see what's the matter. She explains that she was given a non-speaking part in the film, but now it has been taken from her. She was so happy to get the part, but now the tears are rolling down her cheeks. The ADs try to explain to her that the director didn't think she was the right size and age for the part, and that is why someone else has been asked to do it. She can still do a walk-on. I see the woman who has been given this non-speaking part. She is smiling and laughing with her friends . . .

It is getting towards lunch and still we haven't shot a thing. Because of the weather. Today it's too good. It doesn't match the last two days. We need clouds. The sun I thought a gift from the gods is now a monster. There it is up in the sky, right over the field, burning down on us. Any clouds that appear seem to take fright and blow off to the left or right. There are wisps of clouds low down and mackerel ones high up, but when they drift anywhere near us the sun repels them.

All the technicians, the crew, a steady-cam team from Germany and, of course, the extras are sitting or lying down in a field or along the river. It's as if we're all on a picnic. By now we have lost four hours because of sun. On Wednesday we lost four hours because of rain. That's one whole day in three.

I ask a man lying beside me, 'What do you do when your heart starts beating like mad?'

'Reach for the Silk Cut. I seen me one night I woke up the heart pumpin' in me chest I thought someone was outside knocking on the wall with a hammer. The wife hit me some dunt, I'm tellin' you. She hates gettin' woken in the night. A fox cryin' at the back door woke her and she blamed me. The ticker's only a clock. And she's countin' down all the time.'

Peter is sitting in the middle of the field in his director's chair. He stands up, looks at the sky and calls an early lunch. Wasps have already stung six people. Big insects dart everywhere. Midges swirl. Frogs jump through the grass. The grass is mashed by feet and sweet-smelling. It invites you to lie on it. We do – scores of us. Shamie Connolly tells the story of a man he knew who hanged himself from the top of his staircase. 'He hung himself by a chain. The wife come in from Bingo that evenin' and she left him danglin' there in the hallway and only called the RUC in the mornin'. She went by him on the stairs goin' up to bed.'

'Well there's a woman and you're lookin' at her across the field there now and her poor man walked into the lake and was found drowned standin' up in the water.' 'Gone to the lake' is a Cavan expression for suicide.

We all go silent. A man walks by us carrying a hessian sack with a cock in it. He's talking to another man: 'This cock of mine bate the King of Ireland.'

Country people take great interest in all sorts of odd and ordinary things. We begin to discuss door hinges. Then someone talks about a cobbler's last he bought at an auction. 'I took it home, slotted me wife's shoe on to the heel piece, gave it a whack with the ball end of me hammer and didn't the heel piece, you know the bit, bruk clane off. That was a poor last.' We all go quiet again and people start looking at me. They're worried that I'm worried by the weather. They are having a powerful day out along the Annaghlee and getting paid for it and fed, while I'm in bits about the day going and nothing getting done.

Peter Reilly, who is lying full out, opens an eye and says, 'There's a laddie-buck comin' up now.' We all look up. Sure enough a cloud is daring to cross the field. In seconds everyone's going mad and filming commences.

We do twenty-one set ups in four and a half hours. The last part of the day is hilarious, with the extras jumping in the river and fleeing from Albert as the police sergeant. The cockfight is over. The river is full of men and women. In places it comes up to their necks. Eileen Little carries the woman's handbag containing the spurs and scissors high above her head. She's under strict instructions not to get the bag wet.

John James North comes by me. 'That was one powerful day. Thank you.' John James used to be the village blacksmith. He still makes horseshoes, but only for tourists. He has a great calmness within him. Round here if you sprain your ankle you go to him. He's got the cure for ankles and knees. I twisted my knee, I went to him. He lives in the village beside the old forge. In his front room I sat down and he knelt on one knee before me. He's elderly now, with a head of silvery hair. I rolled my trouser leg up and he put his hands on my knee. It was visibly swollen. He drew his hand in the sign of the cross on my skin. He made a sign of the cross on the skin at the front, back and sides. In the kitchen the radio was broadcasting the news from London, Dublin and the world. He stayed for a moment on his one knee and I think in silence he said a prayer. That was it. 'Now you'll come back again to me twice more. You have to do that now. There won't be a bother on you.' I went back. Such is his utter sincerity, belief and gentle strength that far from being cynical, I felt humbled by him. I could have sat there for an hour. But I was in the chair only for a minute at most.

As I leave the field, when I reach the top of the hill I look back down and see a long line of the extras queuing up to get their day's pay. I can see John James, his silvery hair clear in the dusk. The river from the distance lies as still as misty glass. Shamie Connolly and Paddy Kelly are laughing as they line up. They've talked and laughed the whole day through.

Day 13: Sunday 27 August

We're along a narrow country road skirting numerous lakes. It's the middle of nowhere. County Cavan *is* nowhereland. You can rattle around empty lanes and roads, rarely meeting a soul. It's the last undiscovered part of Europe. There are over three hundred lakes and three grand rivers – the Erne, the Finn and the Annaghlee. Up in the north-west of the county the longest river in the British Isles rises – the Shannon. The spot is known as the Shannon pot. I drove up there into the Cuilcagh Mountains and the only people I met were two Germans in leather shorts flying down on bicycles. It's magnificently lonely. All you have for company are birds and sheep. The views are spectacular, especially in the evening when the sun's going down. The light then is gold and green, the mountainy shadows slender and dark. The leathery Germans were disconcerting. Further down the county they are moving in, building holiday compounds, houses and restaurants. Adrian Dunbar, an actor friend of mine from Enniskillen, says the only weapons we have are the bad winters and the potholes on the roads. He thinks we should be going round *making* potholes, not filling them in. Nothing will deter them, though. They'll come well-wrapped against the cold and, if necessary, on tractors. Potholes won't worry them. The EEC is opening up the county. If the Loyalists and the IRA ever agree to peace, then we're banjaxed. Round here will be full of tourists in no time.

This morning I met a friend in Milltown village. He was delighted we were filming nearby. We were bringing a bit of life to the place. 'We get few tourists round here and most of them are German. The English are supposed to be this and that, and what they did and didn't do to this country. But if

57

you ask me, they are the only ones. They spend money. They love the pubs and the crack. And any fish they catch, they put them back in the water. The Germans don't spend a penny. They even bring their own cornflakes. And the fish they catch, they put them in fridges and smuggle them back home. Look. Look.' We watch a Volkswagen van drive slowly through the village. On the roof is a boat and a canoe. Strapped to the back are bicycles. 'I betcha,' my friend says, 'if we could see the back seat it's packed with cornflake packets.' None the less he gives the van a cheery wave. Fatal that. They'll be back in droves next year.

The scene being shot is where Albert as the sergeant comes upon what he hopes is a murder. There is a headless 'corpse' in a ditch. Disappointingly for him it turns out to be a grisly accident. The location is a ditch along a thick overgrown hedge near a lake. Between the hedge and the lake are swampy fields of rushes and ragwort. The lake is bottle-green in the cold light and whipped up by a bitter wind. Across the lake on the other side is the remains of the fourteenth-century Drumlane Abbey. The old walls stand in the middle of a cemetery. The light glints off the modern black-marble headstones. Shafts of light come out of the clouds and imprison for a moment a field, a stretch of water, a tree, a herd of cattle. The camera crew stand looking at the light and shadows. Mike Southon, the DOP, says, 'I can't get over the purity of Ireland. And somehow the people are the same.' 'Yes,' says Ken, the sound man, 'can you imagine a group of English extras being asked to hang around in a field for three days and wait until the crew have been served dinner before they can have any? They'd riot, the bastards.'

'For English extras it's work,' I say. 'For the locals round here it's a day out. Three days at a mock cockfight is three days of fierce excitement.' The women extras love the work. It's not work to them. The best thing of all about it is they don't have to cook dinner. Someone serves them dinner. Most women here cook dinner every single day of their lives.

When the women queue up at the catering bus, they beam from ear to ear. I think it's the women who keep the country going. My daughter Tara, who helps out with the casting of extras, is phoned up all the time by women trying to get work for their husbands. The men have not worked for years because there is no work, and what there is is seasonal or casual. For a man to get £40 a day on the film is manna from Heaven. But it's the women who always make the call. Men feel ashamed phoning a slip of a girl for a job standing around and getting paid for it. Men need work. Even if they've land they need extra. The land in Cavan is poor. It can't sustain its people. The young are still emigrating. They abandon their nowhereland for London or Birmingham.

Everywhere we go there are rotting cottages and their overgrown, lost gardens. Windows are boarded, doors are chained. You can feel the damp as you walk past. Where we are today, there is such a cottage just along the road. The place is slowly crumbling into the earth. It overlooks the lake and Drumlane Abbey. Surrounding mature trees are eaten with ivy. Apple trees covered in moss stick out above monster-high nettles. Red apples hang in the morning light. You'd get stung trying to reach them. The house walls are cracking apart. A local man says it belongs to someone working as a porter in the hospital in Cavan. 'It was left to him. By his uncle.' Memory is an old black iron kettle, a cracked blue and white mug. A crow comes out of the chimney. A black, feathery ball of smoke. The wind comes up off the lake and through the hedges, nettles and trees, making a deep, weird noise like it's blowing at an angle into the neck of a big bottle. The outhouses at the rear of the cottage are stone built. But the cold and ivy are prising the stones apart. Through a crack I can see the shafts and skeleton of a cart lying flat on the floor, congealed in the hard mud like a fossil in rock. Hanging on the wall is horse harness – the britchin, the collar . . . They are rotten, eaten by age and damp. It takes only a few winters for the decay to devour an empty house.

Along from where we're filming in the other direction is an amazing building. It is a long, low corrugated-iron shed with the hint of a gospel hall about it. It is almost covered to the roof with nettles, ivy and big scars of rust. I get into it through a rotten door at the back. At one end is a tiny stage. The people who stood on it must have touched the roof with their heads. The stage is utterly rotten and ready to fall. The floor of the hall is covered with old fifties television sets and wirelesses. They are all smashed and without their electronic guts. A local entrepreneur used the place after it ended its days as an Orange hall or the meeting-place of some biblical sect or other. Tall, skinny, pale thistles grow up through the TV sets. The sets are piled higher than my head. I can smell the black-and-white fifties and stark days of conspiratorial prayer on bare floorboards to a God stripped of Romanism and Southern Irish superstition. The place reeks of the severe mercy of the Lord. There are still plenty of gospel halls along the Border – on either side; spiritual fortresses where on Sunday afternoons young men in dark suits pray for deliverance from earthly plots and political dangers. First they meet outside for a chat, then they go inside to pray. It all has a hint of a sunless Alabama. I remember the fifties version – a Bible in one hand, a B-Special rifle in the other.

Coming out of the place I can hear the Angelus bell ring in Milltown. I drive back to Leggykelly and call on Cissie Connolly. She has an apple pie baking in an iron pot on the open fire. It looks scrumptious. We talk about the land, the people. 'Oh,' she says, 'round here we take it or leave it. Here a thing lies where it falls.' Another thing she said was, 'Oh, all the Protestant women were great cooks. The best.'

Back at the filming Albert is down in the ditch dealing with the headless 'corpse'. His playing of the scene gives it a farcical touch, which in one way it is. I do my usual walk through the chaos and whisper to Peter, hoping like mad Albert doesn't see me: 'The father is far too reverential towards a dead person to make a joke of it. He's an Irish country sergeant full of religious fear and awe.' 'It needs the humorous touch. He's very moving at the end of the scene,' answers Peter. I see everything only in immediate bits. The actor has to build the part over a longer span. He has to make it all add up ... eventually. I want to see the sum done in front of my eyes. As it is done in my head. It's odd to see someone as famous as Albert Finney down on his knees in this Cavan ditch. He's our leading heavyweight actor bar none. Hamlet, Macbeth, Tamburlaine, Luther ... *Saturday Night and Sunday Morning*, *Tom Jones*, *The Dresser* ... Yet here he is wrestling with a part of my own story, in my own neck of the woods. All that experience and great talent ... for me ... for Hecuba. It's weird the struggle actors have to make sense of it all. They have a hard, cranky contest with themselves.

The hedges are full of local kids watching him acting. They lie on the grass and nettles and poke their heads through the hedge, impervious to the cold.

The sky clouds over and the rain squalls down. The drumlins disappear, the country goes dark. Across the lake the abbey becomes invisible. And then, as is typical, one field lights up. It's as if the sun is being held in a giant fist with a little light escaping through the knuckles. This lit field dazzles. Although on the other side of the lake you can easily pick out the brown clumps of rushes. More light escapes and soon the land is gleaming all over, except for one small field hedged by tall trees and dense bushes. This field remains in the dark, as though the giant fist holding the sun has opened, but a thumb tip still casts a shadow.

The lake is crowded to the edge by reeds and bullrushes. They shiver and part, and out sail two swans. They glide to the middle of the water and, facing each other, neck to neck, remain motionless. Like ballroom dancers awaiting the music.

Today all the vehicles are parked outside my old primary school: St Brigid's, Killoughter, a mile from Redhills. The school is down the brae from the Catholic chapel and grave-yard. The chapel and graveyard, planted on top of a huge outcrop of rock and whin, dominate the view. As you come along the valley, way above you can see the yew tree by the graveyard gate. It is the only tree that has flourished on that barren hill. From the graveyard the scenery is fantastic. You look right down on top of the trees in the demesne, on the Orange hall along the Cootehill road, on Shannow Wood, on the tiny fields and, in the distance, the mountains. And on to my old school.

School was a penance in my time there: the cane ruled; girls wet the seats with fear; hair was pulled out, ears twisted, flesh and bone punched and beaten. A favourite sermon at Sunday mass was 'spare the rod and spoil the child'. Beating children had official sanction. It wasn't a sin to thump a de-fenceless girl or boy. Any father who stood up to the system was considered odd. In revenge, the teacher wouldn't teach that parent's children. For that reason, very few complained. Round and about I sometimes hear people say beatings should be brought back into the classroom. It's crazy. It's akin to beating a woman until she loves you.

We eat lunch outside the school gates. The kids are on holi-day, but the school is open for painting. I take my courage in my hands and walk into the old classrooms. It's a futile exer-cise. The old voices aren't there.

Coming out of the gates, along the road I see two county-council workers with shovels and brushes cleaning the gul-leys. One of them is Sean Rehill. We were at school together. Sean sat at the back of the class and was never spoken to by the teacher from one end of the year to the other. He was bigger than we were and most days, I think, he came to school in wellingtons. He could run like the wind. In the playground he was never tagged when we played tig. As soon as school finished he'd run out, jump clean across the wall at the rear and hare off home into Shannow Wood. Even when we played tig he rarely spoke. I often envied him his isolation at the back of the class. We'd be getting near-murdered, the teacher sweating with fury, and Sean would simply sit there, as still as a dozing horse. There was always an old jotter on the desk in front of him, but he never opened it. He had a head of thick, blond curls, and was big and raw-boned. He was a big, shocked innocent, in his own world. Not even the teacher would lay a hand on him.

Sean works for the county council now and prefers to work alone. I meet him at all times of the night walking the roads. He travels great distances. Someone saw him in Kells recently, leaning against the Celtic cross in the middle of the town. Kells is thirty miles away. Although now he's about fifty-five, wears dark-blue council overalls and pushes a big sweeping brush, he's still the same boy who sat at the back of the class. The difference now is that he's full of chat. I love meeting him along the road. He asks me about the ins and outs of making films. For instance, he asked me the other day how it was possible to be watching a man on the television who is sitting in a room having a drink, then the next second that same man is driving along in a car. 'How is that done? What happened to the in-between?'

A few weeks ago tinkers came to Sean's house and he agreed to let them paint the whole house. They fiddled him so badly he lost £10,000. The Garda are trying to get it back. 'It was me own fault,' he told me. He has never married. He sticks out, and is as solid as a rock and whins. I wave to him now from the school playground. He looks up from his sweeping and for a moment stares at me. Then his face lights up with a smile. His head is ablaze with smiling. Sean is still a boy and, in that smile, so am I. I think the two of us live in the in-between – maybe we all do; in the moments alone when we're lost from the earth.

Peter and I walk up to the graveyard where we're filming Albert and Matt. When I mention Albert's great experience and fame, Peter says, 'He never thinks about it. It's past. Gone. It's *now*. For us all.' As far as the filming is concerned my past is now. I remember funerals here where the coffin could only go two feet into the ground, and then only sideways, because of the rock. I served at funerals as an altar boy. I know the names on the old headstones. There's Bill Fay's grave. Bill, an ex-policeman, was married to Mrs Fay, the infant-school teacher. She was a massive woman. She was kind enough to her charges until she deemed they needed a good beating. Then she'd send them into the male teacher. He'd wallop these infants. In those days education in Ireland was a madhouse.

At the time the priest was Father Traynor. He was a Doctor of Divinity. One day from outside his parochial house he heard us in the playground swearing like troopers. Down he raced and made us all kneel until the guilty ones owned up. No one admitted anything. He then marched us up to the chapel to confession. It would take him ages to hear us all individually so he absolved us collectively. He did this regularly, absolving us all in a bunch. We simply said our sins to ourselves, he absolved us and it was all over in seconds. Mighty.

One day Fr. Traynor caught Bill Fay drunk and beat the lard out of him with a blackthorn. Bill had a great thirst. He'd collar us going home from school and slip us a few pennies to bring him whiskey from the village – without, of course, the wife knowing. When he died, we school kids went to the wake. They didn't have electricity in the house, just candles and tilleys, or oil lamps. The room where Bill was laid out was shadowy dark, lit by guttering candles. A few of us went in to pray. We were giggling nervously. I was on my knees at the end of the bed. Bill was a big man. I decided to be serious, pious. I bowed my head in prayer. Bill's big toe went right into my mouth. In the darkness I hadn't noticed his feet sticking out. I had tasted a dead man's toe. I fled out of the house and for years after my mother had a light burning beside the bed.

Every Easter we came to the graveyard to pray at the grave of an IRA man killed in the War of Independence. Beforehand, Republicans made speeches. It was so exciting up on top of that hill, the six counties in the distance, listening to the fighting talk. We'd be so fired up that if ordered to do so we'd have marched on Stormont with our bows and arrows and catapults. Maud Gonne spoke here one Easter. This rocky cemetery, this wild hill so near to Heaven, links death and romance. It's full now. They've opened a new one on the other side of the chapel. That's built on rock, too. Now it's weird seeing the actors and technicians moving about through the headstones. They've built a scaffold tower and set the camera on top. There's more of us than you'd see at a funeral.

I drive across the Border and fill up at McCracken's pumps. He's not there, but young McKiernan is. He's got unleaded. The entrance to Clogher market is blocked off by two massive corrugated gates. Why anyone would drive down here to fill up is a mystery. I go into the dilapidated house. It smells of damp.

'Well, Adie, how's the form?'

'I appreciate your business.'

He writes out a receipt. Ken North's name is on the heading. Because of his great weight, he moves very slowly. He writes the receipt on top of the pool table. The slate is visible under the torn baize. He sits back on an old settee. The house is a shambles. It's amazing it's standing at all, having taken the force of at least two bombs. Why do the place up when it could be bombed again any night? Adie's complexion is as pale as the thistle growing up through the television sets in the abandoned gospel hall. Though barren and blasted, life sprouts, clings. McCracken and McKiernan are hardy men struggling to get bread in a world coming down around their ears. Bordermen.

One of the bombs that went off here killed a soldier. He was defusing the bomb which had been placed in a creamery can. When he first looked into the creamery can he thought the job was an easy one. He was too relaxed. The real bomb was right at the bottom. It went off . . . Locals say that when the soldiers first arrived on the scene they took drink and were merry. So that when the bomb specialist set about his work he was careless. I can't believe this rumour. Rumours run wild along the Border. This shop is a knot in the body politic. Mrs North worked for the RUC, an office job. Therefore the shop is a target. She still works for the RUC, she won't give in – and therefore puts lives in danger, her own included. The IRA won't give in either. Until Mrs North stops working for the police . . . But she won't stop working for the police. Why should she? So the wheel keeps turning. However the Norths no longer run the place. So I suppose for the moment it's a draw. Political bitterness runs red as blood. How are we going to live in peace? There must be a better way than soldiers, bombs and bigotry.

'Do you think there'll be a ceasefire?' I ask Adie.

'You'd never know. There might . . . and there mightn't. It's hard to tell. Like the weather.'

The soldier killed defusing the bomb was an Irishman from Limerick. He'd emigrated to England years before, joined the Army . . . A hay field, a creamery can – though familiar, rural and homely it can kill you. A creamery can full of milk, awaiting collection, shining in the sun, was once upon a time innocence itself. Now they're full of Semtex or the middle classes buy them in antique shops. And when you think of it a creamery can with its strong slender form and tight-fitting lid is a perfect canister for a bomb. How would you set about defusing one? For a start how would you get that long-lipped lid off and live to tell the tale?

Outside, an Army helicopter flies across to the checkpoint near Wattlebridge. At the Finn bridge a man fishes from the parapet. Down below, cattle stand in the water and go in under the bridge. A dragonfly darts out and zips along the river just above the surface. Its gossamer wings sparkle blue and gold.

The other side of the bridge down off the main road is the blasted remains of the Nicholls' shop. It used to be a fine two-storeyed building with sheds. People came from all over the South to purchase goods for smuggling back across the Border. I remember Mrs Nicholl. We came from Redhills to buy butter. The Customs were always trying to catch you, and often did. All they had to do was lie in wait on the Southern side and nab you as you cycled past. The Nicholls were Protestant. Opposite the shop up on the roadside is a smaller house. The McAdams live here. I went to school with Pat. He was a pocket dynamo, very cheery, played football. Needless to say, his nickname was 'Tar'. The McAdams are Catholic. In the seventies a bomb was planted in the Nicholls' shop. One of the young McAdams worked in the shop. He and Mrs Nicholl had time to get out. Rumour said that Mrs Nicholl mentioned the cash register and young McAdam ran back in to get her money. Whatever, the bomb went off and the young boy was killed. His sister who was near by was blind-ed. Mrs Nicholl, over seventy at the time, was flung twenty yards across a wall, but she lived. The shop was wrecked. Mr and Mrs McAdam were out at bingo that evening. They ar-rived home to devastation: a dead son, a blind daughter. But they were lucky. Seconds before the bomb went off another daughter and son were in the shop. But they walked off up the road before it exploded. More rumours spread. Someone in the Nicholl family had planted the bomb, because the busi-ness was going badly. This rumour was quickly scotched. Next day the IRA claimed responsibility. Why hadn't they given a warning? They did. Unfortunately it was a shop some distance away that got the warning.

Pat McAdam was working in Belfast at the time. At first the RUC notified the wrong man that his brother had been killed.

Oddly enough this man's brother was killed later on in the Troubles. Mrs Nicholl is still alive. She's over ninety now. The McAdams, cheery as ever, get on with life. The shop is crumbling back to earth, a ghostly monument to the invisible war.

It's funny the way we talk about a bomb being 'planted'. Like it's a vegetable. Ulster was 'planted' in the seventeenth century. And because of that bombs are 'planted' in the twentieth. The other day someone said to me, 'Make hay whilst the sun shines.' It made me think of Mickey Nann. The secret war is full of secret meanings. Along the Border language is a double-edged sword.

When I return to the graveyard the filming is in full swing. They have laid tracks down for the camera the whole way along the laneway, from the graveyard gate to the chapel road. When Albert sees me coming he gives me a look. Then a wink. I listen to all the English accents: Cockneys, Mancunians, Home Counties ... The English have been in Ireland for 900 years, millions of Irish live in England, yet the gap cannot be bridged. We cannot live in someone else's head – so far. Maybe all this will help.

A grey stone wall surrounds the graveyard. Over the wall the land falls sheer away – all rocks, whins, fluffy thistles. Two calves are at a strand of barbed wire. Stuck to the wire is a sack. The calves eat the sack, pulling at it, ripping it. On a clump of rock a white pony stands, his weight on three legs. He's asleep, the lucky bastard.

I make for home and bed. Going through the village I see a Gaelic football match is in progress. I call on Seamus Kelly and gingerly we walk down the garden backs and watch the match, while leaning over the fence that runs around the pitch. Annagh are playing Drumgoon. Annagh is the parish name. It combines Redhills and Belturbet. It's an under-sixteen match. Seamus shouts at the referee over some crime or other committed by a Drumgoon player. Blow me if the referee doesn't shout back at us: 'What the fuck would you know about it?' At this the two of us bellow after him like lunatics but he runs away down the field keeping up with play.

There's a lad playing for Annagh and he scores six goals. He's blond headed and built like a young bull.

'Who is he?' I shout to Peter Reilly, who is team mentor.

'Aubrey Shaw. He's a Protestant out of Belturbet.'

Protestants rarely play Gaelic. Each time he pulls on the jersey, I wonder if he realizes he's debunking history. Maybe things are changing. At last.

Day 15: Tuesday 30 August

I lie in bed and look out on a thick mist tented over the demesne. Trees and sheep are invisible. The sun will come through in a little while and fry it all away – I hope.

I drive up to the chapel. There is the usual circus of cars and trucks outside the school and the chapel itself. Father Browne has closed the chapel for the three days of filming. He's celebrating morning mass in the parochial house. John Phelan tells me the priest has had complaints from some women for letting us near the place. One of the women tells him I'm a basket case and need treatment, my book's filthy and I need my head examined. They've obviously read the novel. They might even have read the film script. We're shooting the scene in the chapel where the hero goes to the vestry and tries on the vestments in order to test his priestly vocation. He's egged on by his friend, Prunty, who makes free with the altar wine and unconsecrated hosts as he watches. They are disturbed by an old farmer who comes to the chapel to have his pig blessed. Prunty persuades our hero to pretend he is, in fact, a young priest, fresh out of Maynooth . . .

Before the filming commenced, well before, there was a meeting between the producer, the film company and all the villagers where everything was explained and agreed. The blessing of the pig was mentioned and no one objected.

Anyway, Father Browne has removed the Sacred Host from the tabernacle so, technically speaking, while we're filming the chapel is not a chapel at all. It's just an empty building. Besides which, none of the crew are going to treat the place with anything other than respect.

Apparently the objecting women belong to a group devoted to Our Lady of Medjugorje in Yugoslavia. Things have changed since the fifties, when there were no such groups to the right of an already conservative church. We all believed the same things, nothing extreme or way out: just Hell, Heaven, the Pope and Emigration. Nowadays, I was told, some women pray when they go to have their hair done. They are led in prayer as they sit being permed, or they are given holy leaflets. Sometimes they meet in their front rooms and sing hymns. Like hairdressing, plumbing and plastering, religion is becoming DIY. Maybe things haven't changed that much. Only on the televised surface. But things have developed. The DIY Brigade – that's definitely new.

Whatever, I feel shocked by the objections. Betrayed. After all, why am I here? To celebrate. To celebrate old places, old faces. Kick-in-the-pants time has arrived. Peter Yates and the crew are unaware of any of this. Even if they were, they wouldn't comprehend. Peter and I sit on the chapel wall looking at the spectacular views. It's a glorious day now. He's heard from Castle Rock in Los Angeles. They want Danny's central dilemma to be the passing of his exams. Danny is the hero, but Peter says his son Toby has a better idea. Toby thinks that the turning-point for Danny should be the realization of the truth behind something the father says earlier in the story: 'It's the living have to resurrect themselves and not the dead.' Before I go off to think about it he says that Castle Rock have no problems with the accents. Relief all round. Gerry Grennell the dialogue coach will be pleased. The way Albert does the accent is interesting. Having a good ear for the accent *per se* is no problem to him. But underneath the words is the down-to-earth tone of Lancashire. There's no hint of Synge-song. The words come out of his mouth newly minted. Thought. Not just emotions.

A tractor and trailer sweep up to the chapel. It is John 'The Scud' Rudden delivering his sow for the pig-blessing scene. We crowd around to look at the sow. She's massive, with two rows of tits, pink and startling. She's lying on straw in the trailer. The raw smell of her clogs the throat. How on earth are we going to get her to stand long enough to do the scene? Still . . . not my problem.

John Rudden is a remarkable character who lives with his sister, Babs, on an isolated farm outside Redhills. He's in his sixties now and has never given two hoots for social convention. He wears wellies, old trousers, a torn cardigan and shirt. His receding hair flies back off his head. His face is unshaven. A few teeth are missing. He looks impish, ready to do or say the first thing that comes into his head. He sees one of the crew, a nifty female. He looks at her with boyish lasciviousness and says aloud, 'Holy Jazus, yon one would soon run down your battery.' When 'The Scud' is around, there is never a dull moment. He's marvellous with animals. He and Babs have lived closely to them all their lives. He understands them. He's in the trailer with the sow, slapping it gently, stroking it, talking back to her when she grunts.

'A mad sow, begob, she'd ate the wheels of a bus. Mind out there, stand back.'

'John, there's a big rip in the leg of your trousers.'

'Oh rip, be damn, when have I time to notice? A poor man like me has less money than a tinker's wife. Away, be damned. Could you lend us a few quid but?'

The crew gather round John mesmerized. A steam of stink rises from the straw. We have to get the sow into the chapel porch and make her stand still while the scene is played around her. She's never been outside her sty before. The chapel, the massive lights shining at her, dozens of strangers . . . Help! I go and sit in my car, even though it's boiling. I stick on the radio. It's like having a nervous tic. Something must be happening in the North. Paisley is thundering like a bull, booming and threatening. He's a Siamese twin who pretends he's not. His twin has the same colour, same language, same home, but he tells everyone the twin doesn't exist and, anyway, it's a foreigner. On the edge of the twenty-first century, religion is no longer an excuse.

A stuntman from London turns up. He's going to arrange the fights when we get to them. He has a broken nose and says he was a professional boxer. 'Well, as it 'appens I had only the two fights. And me optic nerve got damaged.' We talk about the Thomas à Becket pub in South London.

'Do you know, funny thing, all the guvnors, five of them, of that pub, they all died of cancer.'

'Something in the beer?'

'I don't know about that.'

'What do the customers die of?'

'Funny thing, that's never been discussed.'

He refers to the death of 'that boy in whatsit – Clones? I sees it in the paper. As it 'appens, I knew a family in Surrey. Real well-off. The kids at public school, everyfing. But one day they come in and the muvver has hung herself off of the stairs in the hallway. When you do that, when you do it that way, wiv no one around, it's not a cry for help. You mean it.' His sound is different, but his meaning bang-on all the same. So when it comes to pain, there *is* no difference. And when it comes to pleasure, there's no difference. So where's the difference?

The Revd Dr Paisley is on the radio again. He's like a bull charging into a lake. He can bull and horn and bluster till his own sweat blinds him and, though he can make waves, he cannot shift the water out of his road.

Pig time has arrived. Everyone gathers around as the sow is led down from the trailer. John Rudden has tied a rope round its snout and leads it towards the chapel porch. A vet is in attendance: a young guy with a stethoscope hanging from his neck. Turns out he's German. It's amazing the smell from the poor beast. Tony Devlin, the generator truck driver, looks at it, whiffs it. 'Hate tha'. Love kissin', hate tha',' he says. John hands the rope to the actor playing the farmer. This actor is Declan Mulholland. A massive man is Declan, who regularly demolishes plates of bacon for breakfast and I fear now he's going to pay for it. He tugs at the rope, but the sow stands her ground. We haven't even got her inside the porch yet. My idea was to film the scene at the vestry door, where the sow would have been outside and the religious amongst us couldn't object. More importantly, the pig would have no trouble standing upright on the rough gravel. The porch looks very shiny to me. An AD calms me: 'Don't worry, she'll stand no bother. I know animals.'

Peter wants to shoot the scene in the porch because it is more dramatic and looks better. The farmer and his sow will be caught between the dark light of the church and the natural light behind them. John 'The Scud' pushes the sow on the rump, the vet lugs her forward, Declan, already sweating with fear, heaves on the rope and into the porch the sow goes. First thing she does is slip on the tiles and the second thing she does is piss all over the floor. They manage to get her to her feet. Immediately she shits. She hasn't been in the porch ten seconds and already the place is stinking to high heaven. I look outside and notice a swarm of elderly women looking in. They do not look pleased. They are standing back, outside the wall, and the only reason they are not coming closer is because the ADs are stopping them and Fr. Browne is there as well, chatting and talking, and keeping up a pretence of normality. Fr. Browne has spent years in Africa and has seen it all. The vet assures us all the pig will behave after he sedates her. He injects her to make her sleepy. We wait.

Meanwhile inside the chapel itself, on the other side of the doors, are Peter, the camera team, the whole brigade and the blasting light. The heat is intense. Peter, of course, sits in a pew, cigar in hand, waiting for the word. The camera is in position, all set to go. They have been waiting for an hour to do the first shot. Outside in the porch all you can hear is grunts – most of them coming from Declan and the ADs trying to get the pig in position. All the damn sow has to do is stand beside Declan and look piggish. I go out of the side door and round into the porch. The injection has been so effective that the sow cannot stand up. She looks drunk, out of her mind. The place is awash with piss and dung. The smell alone would clot your veins.

Someone suggests we put straw down. The pig will be able to hold her footing on straw. I shoot that down. Straw in a church? Only in the crib at Christmas. They all get around the sow and heave her to her feet. Everyone is perspiring and white-faced. At last the pig is standing but, of course, in the wrong position for the camera. The vet and Declan move her sideways, but she crashes over on her massive tits and sends Declan reeling. 'Holy fuck,' he gasps, 'I'm getting out of here.' I follow him outside and he drinks a gallon of water to cool himself down. 'Acting with fucking animals! Don't worry, Shane, it'll be all right on the night.' Then, typically for an actor, he starts on about the costume the wardrobe people wanted him to wear: 'A fucking tweed hacking jacket and corduroy trousers. Fuck me, I says, I'm an Irish farmer not a Home Counties gentleman. Can you get over that?'

I notice one of the women coming forward. She's middle-aged, grey-haired, in a smart tweed suit. I ask her what she wants and at first she says she's looking for a leaflet announcing forthcoming church events. All the time she's squinting into the porch. She's a fine-looking woman.

'Disgraceful,' she says to me, 'that animal in the chapel.'

'So? The stable at Bethlehem was full of animals.'

She looks at me. I have taken the wind out of her sails – for a moment. 'There wasn't a pig in the stable,' she says angrily.

'That's only because Jesus was Jewish. And being an Arab country the farmer who owned the stable wouldn't have had pigs anyway.'

She looks at me, then, lifting her chin, she stares past me

and walks off. Out on the road a car drives slowly up and down, the occupants straining their necks as they try to see what's going on each time they go past. They're all part of the hymns-in-your-front-room DIY Brigade.

Declan goes back in and an AD enters the chapel via the porch and walks dung into the carpet covering the aisle leading up to the altar. I am now practically fainting with the tension. At least my shirt button isn't dancing, but only because I'm wearing a T-shirt. I go to the side of the altar, light a candle and pray that the blasted sow stands on her proper spot, so that we can shoot the scene and clean up the chapel before I'm lynched.

The power of prayer is wonderful. The sow stands in place. The camera turns over, the actor opens the porch doors and there stands the massive Declan with the massive sow. 'Action,' Peter whispers. The sow is mesmerized by the lights and the strangeness of it all – and the effect of the injection. But not for long. Wham! She whacks the door with her snout, shuts it then falls over. 'Fuck me, and I gave up a beer commercial for this,' says Declan. Peter and the crew are breaking their hearts laughing. 'Don't worry,' Peter says, 'we got something that time. The pig banging the door is great. And don't forget we can get close-ups later on – on a special set elsewhere where we won't need the chapel in the background.'

I'm amazed how practical that man is. And I'm amazed how scared I am of the religious women. I'm scared of them because I wonder are they really religious? The good souls are quiet people. They don't try to force everyone to dance to their tune. We have a good person today – an extra. She has to pray at the back of the chapel during all the pig shenanigans. Her name is Rose McEntee, a very old lady who lives in a thatched cottage painted rosy red, down from the chapel and in a lovely long drive. She's eighty-five, gentle, full of good humour. She smiles and prays for real with all the chaos going on around her. 'It's great, the film, it's great. I never thought I'd live to see the day.'

75

Declan, the ADs and the German vet get porker back on her spot and for a moment she stands motionless – long enough for the camera to get something. The vet says, 'That vas a wery close thing. I nearly lost her.' 'Holy God,' I say to John Rudden, 'what if your sow had died of a heart attack?' He looks at me like I'm mad: 'She didn't but.'

The happiest sight of my life to date is that of the pig being led up the ramp and into the trailer. *Finito*. That poor creature. If she wasn't mad before, she's mad now. Mind you, she'll have a fine tale to tell to all her little ones when they arrive. All twenty of them. I counted her tits. 'Did I ever tell yiz about the time I starred in a film, oink-oink?' As John Rudden drove that great pregnant animal down the hill, I resolved there and then never again to eat bacon for breakfast. It was the least I could do.

The stink she left behind in the chapel porch was awesome. It can be cleaned up. It's the metaphorical stink she's left behind in the parish that worries me more. I came home to give people a good time, help them make a few quid, not upset anyone. Naïve me.

I jump into the car and, half an hour later, am in Cavan General Hospital visiting Nellie Cassidy, an old friend recently admitted. She's seventy-five now and since she came back from Glasgow during the war has lived all her life right on the Border. She lived with her brother Jimmy who died a few years ago. Jimmy was famous all over Ulster for his involvement in cock fighting. He trained them, fed them, in a shed beside his house. Those who had gamecocks handed them over to him a few weeks before a battle and he fed them a brew with secret ingredients known only to himself and Nellie. When he died, the secret was revealed to John James North. John James will not tell a soul until he feels his end is near. It is not illegal to own gamecocks or train them. It is illegal only to fight them. I've seen Jimmy Cassidy train them. Instead of fitting spurs to the cocks' legs he fitted 'boxing gloves': tiny rubber knobs which can't cause injury. The particular breed of cock along the Border was introduced by an Oxford professor who gave Jimmy hatching eggs from game-fowl in Derbyshire. Jimmy was a Republican all his life. His near neighbour was Johnny Roberts, a lifelong Orangeman and father of Willie, who heads the Redhills Orangemen today. Jimmy and Johnny were poles apart politically, had many a bitter row, yet were friends to the end of their days. When Jimmy died, Johnny visited the funeral parlour and was heard to say, 'I won't be long after you, old friend.' Within a week he was dead and buried himself.

Nellie was a Republican like her brother. After we made the film *The Playboys* she wrote me a letter calling me all the names under the sun and accusing me of selling out to the 'Yankee dollar'. I was furious with her and wrote a stinker back. That was in 1992 and I never clapped eyes on her again until this visit to the hospital. When she sees me walk into the ward she greets me with a big grin. We're friends again and ever more shall be so. She's had a stomach operation and has had the stitches out today, but she's cheery as a young laugh-ing girl. 'Do you want a corpse in the film?' she jokes. She lowers her voice and asks me what I thought was the matter with her. 'They'll tell me nothing.' 'The bad lad' springs to mind, but I mumble something about an ulcer. She looks very ill. There is only one other person in the ward with her. This turns out to be Willie Roberts' wife, Ivy. Ivy and Nellie, who live so close together, end up in hospital together. Ivy was a schoolteacher. She is just as cheerful and friendly as Nellie, a person of infinite goodness, always with a twinkle in her eye. Here the two of them are in hospital, in the same ward, on opposite sides of the religious fence, united by a common decency of character and sense of humour. They restore faith in humanity. I was dreading this visit, but now I'm glad I made the effort. To live simply, justly, all people want is a level playing field.

Finished off at the chapel this morning. Met Fr. Browne. He told me the DIYs had reported him to the Bishop. 'Let them,' he said. 'The Bishop is only one man.' In a small community it takes only one or two to stir the pot. One stone dropped in a lake can spread ripples right across the water. Every water-hen in the place wakes up and has a chirp. In fact Redhills is like the world in microcosm: there isn't anything happening in the world that isn't happening in the village. You see the village green and you think, 'This must be the most idyllic spot on earth.' In many ways it is, but underneath the surface all the usual universal conflicts are there: love divided, love unrequited, conflicts of business, politics . . . Why should we be any different? I somehow don't think the Bishop is going to get involved with the pig in the porch. And neither does Fr. Brown.

The chapel has been cleaned up. Professional cleaners from Cavan did the job. The porch is smelling sweet, the tiles are clean, the carpet . . . I sit in my car and turn on the radio. A ceasefire has been announced in the North. All the lads from Belfast on the film unit crowd around and we listen in silence. The Belfast boys are predominantly Protestant. We all look at one another and smile – smile cautiously, but smile we do. Peter Yates comes and listens to the announcement. 'If it's true, which I doubt, do you realize our film is now a period piece?' 'So is Hamlet,' I say. 'Anyway, it's a ceasefire. It doesn't mean the Border has disappeared, does it? The film isn't about the political situation as such. It's a story about a father and his son.'

I drive off to the next location. Down from the chapel some kids are playing. John Phelan told me they weren't let out while we were filming in case we contaminated them. I can't believe this. The kids look at me as I drive by. I give them a wave. A little girl sticks her tongue out at me. It is like a dagger in my heart. She must have heard someone tearing me apart. Religion in Ireland is still raw, still wounds. On the day of the Ceasefire, it's not the IRA Paisley should be worrying about. It's little girls who stick their tongues out . . .

The new location is a derelict farmyard with yet another abandoned house. It was originally owned by Alfie Kells. A fine two-storeyed stone building with substantial outhouses, it must have been a lovely place to live. It's up a short lane off the Cootehill road with drumlin hills to look out on at the front and rear. The slates are slipping off the roof. Many of them have broken into pieces on the ground. The floorboards are rotten. The stairs up to the floor above are blocked by the spring base of a double bed. The guts of a piano lie in one room. The keyboard sticks out the broken window of another. The harmony of lives, the house voices are shattered. Outside, nettles reach up almost to the gutters. Old farm machinery crumbles to rust. A mowing machine sticks out of a clump of weeds and nettles. It looks as though it's in the last stages of being swallowed by the earth. The shed roofs have fallen in. Old cattle dung, as hard as hooves, covers the ground. Torn black-plastic silage bags litter the yard. In this abandoned place, the crew set up their Arri's and standards, monitors, the camera, sound equipment – the entire paraphernalia. 'Give me a quarter CTO!' someone shouts.

I overhear one of the Belfast boys, Tommy Hamilton, saying to Tony Devlin, 'Do you think will it last?'

'I think it will.'

Easy to guess what they're talking about.

Then Tony says, 'Will we have a celebration drink tonight?'

Tommy replies, 'We do every other night. Why break an old custom?'

Day 17: Thursday 1 September

Nothing abandoned about the place we're in today. It's a nineteenth-century mansion owned by Johnny and Rosaleen

Clements. They farm 200 acres, with an additional 100 acres in timber. The Clements speak in the plummy, clipped accents of the Home Counties. When I ask Rosaleen how long they've been here she replies, 'Since the Ulster Plantation – 1675, I believe.' We're using one of their hay barns for a scene where an IRA man is shot by the SAS. The IRA man is played by the stuntman from London. Apparently he dies wonderfully.

The Clements are getting on in years now and work the place themselves with a minimum of help from locals. This morning they were up at five, milking the herd of Aberdeen Angus.

The house is stylish, grey cut stone, lovely chimneys, big windows facing the rising sun and surrounded by hills, graceful lawns and, flowing sweetly at the rear of the house, the Annaghlee River. On the other side of the river is an old walled garden and orchard. To get to it you have to cross a very rickety bridge consisting of frail planks held together by wire and nails. In grander times there was a grander stone bridge. You can see the remains of it in the water. The garden is one of the oldest in the country. It is full of plum trees, apples, roses, cabbage ... It is on a number of levels all leading up from or down to the river. This morning the trees are full of pecking blackbirds. Singing birds are everywhere and the air is sweet with the delicious perfumes of various flowers. It is simple, frugal, uncluttered ... 'People say to me, "Why don't you get a herbaceous border?" Ugh.'

The owners of these big houses work hard. But the children won't stay. They go off and make their own way. Fathers and sons – the old tale maybe and who can blame either of them? 'We keep it up as best we can,' says Rosaleen. 'If we sell, you see, it will look good and we'll get a good price.' The struggle to keep up appearances is too much. The work is too hard. Finally, time has reached into these dark, delightful corners of Ireland and is slowly crushing the brickwork in the orchard, choking the paths with weeds, slowing down human limbs, heaping debts in the bank. They've had a good innings: 300 years not out. But now, suddenly, the pitch is turning, the wicket's getting sticky. I tell Rosaleen to hang on to their Garden of Eden. The EEC are bound to come to their assistance, or the Irish–American Fund. Maybe Disney will turn it into a theme park, paying them a fortune in the process. In the Ceasefire era, tourists will flock to see fairies at the bottom of the garden and Darby O'Gill and little Cavan people cavorting on the front lawn. Sooner or later in our Gardens of Eden a snake appears. Usually ourselves.

The day is so grand – the sun shining, the sky blue, the air creamy, horses nuzzling in the paddock, trout leaping in the river – it is a treat to sit and watch the actors doing their bit. Vicki and Matt are acting a scene in which they discuss their characters' dilemma – the boy has made the girl pregnant. Annagh, the heroine, wants an abortion. He's reluctant. She says, 'What's the alternative? We have it adopted by strangers? We get married? And bingo – you're a daddy? Like your daddy?' Vicki, as they rehearse it, is hitting the 'your' in the last question: 'Like *your* daddy.' It's sounding a bit gobble-degookish – to my ears, anyway – so I tell Peter how I think it should be said. By the time I've said it a dozen times quietly into his ear, the whole thing sounds gibberish even to me. Words constantly repeated soon lose their meaning.

Peter explains to Vicki, she repeats the words, but isn't hitting them right and he won't give the intonation, the inflection to her. She seems to be nervous this morning. Probably because this is the first bit of serious acting she has had to do since the film started and after this she has to go into a hay barn with Matt to do a love scene. There'll be only about twenty pairs of eyes watching them. She tries the line again and fucks it up so badly that they cut it. Why didn't I keep my big mouth shut? Often actors and directors cut a difficult line, not realizing the difficult line is often the key. Pressure of time . . .

Later I manage to catch Vicki on her own – Peter isn't

around. I explain to her just for the record what was in my mind. I'm talking away when a barn door opens and out steps Peter.

'Is he confusing you?'

'Yes,' she says, landing me right in it.

I try to slither out of it. Deep down I'm raging. I explain to Peter exactly the way the line should have been said and he gets angry because that was the way he was trying to get Vicki to say the damn line in the first place. Words are greasy, like snakes – especially your words in someone else's mouth.

I go off and sit by the Annaghlee. Rosaleen Clements comes along, and referring to a horse in the paddock, says, 'When he came here he shook and sweated with fear. He'd been raced and afterwards thrashed if he hadn't done well. Poor chap was so scared.' She talks gently about the horse as if he were a person. If horses had the vote, the Anglo-Irish would still be in the political saddle.

Because we're using real guns today, there are armed Garda Special Branch men on duty. I discuss the Ceasefire with them. One of them insists the whole war in the North is a criminal conspiracy. It has little to do with politics or an unjust society.

'Would men go to jail, die on hunger strike, risk death, if it was simply common criminality? They wouldn't,' I say. 'You're talking nonsense.'

'They would. They have to do what they're told,' says a Garda in his thirties, strong, with a big head of jet-black curly hair. He believes every word he says. He leans up against a barn door cradling his Uzi sub-machine-gun like it's a baby. He tells me he knows for a fact the British want to leave Ireland.

Politics is full of paranoia and conspiracy theories. When I ask him why, if the British want to leave, are they reinforcing and building new state-of-the-art checkpoints costing millions along the Border, he replies, 'That's funny you should mention that. We were on Border duty one night, we met up with some of the RUC lads and I asked them the same question you asked me. They weren't exactly joking, and they says, "They're for you, lads. When the time comes." What they meant was when the Brits leave it's down to us. "Jazus," I says, "we don't want it, lads. Not even South Fermanagh."' South Fermanagh, according to this man, was a good posting for the British Army: 'The people are quiet there. The regiments feel safe.'

A few minutes later I'm sitting on a bail of straw looking at the grand Georgian house when two of the crew from Belfast join me. One of them says, 'No way are we going back to be second-class citizens. And we're still getting a raw deal, believe me.'

The other man says, 'Do you know it was Loyalists killed Brian Faulkner? You know, the former Prime Minister . . . His own people did it. Because he was doing deals with Catholics.'

'But I thought he was out hunting and got thrown from his horse?'

'Aye. But they were lying in wait and frightened the horse. It came out on the road and they scared it and he was thrown to his death.'

He says this in such a way as to convince you honestly that it was a conspiracy planned and craftily executed. You can imagine a coven of Loyalists sitting around plotting when one of them gets the bright idea. 'I got it, lads. When he's on his horse. We'll hide in a hedge and wait for him to come riding up to the spot. Then we'll jump out and go "BOO!" . . . Bingo, the horse goes buck mad . . . Bingo, your man's dead.'

The Garden of Eden is full of conspiracies and snakes. And scared nags.

Johnny Clements drives into the yard on a tractor. 'You see,' he says, 'the house is two-storeyed and when you look closely is not actually that big. So it is comparatively cheap to heat in winter. The winter. That's the thing.' But today is summer. Driving home, the sun slung low and golden over the hills and lake is a silver sword sinking slowly into its golden scabbard in the west. Thistledown comes over the hedges from the fields, covers the road. Before the on-rushing car it scoots sideways and sails up into the air and the dying light. Just the kind of day fatal for your prose.

Day 18: Friday 2 September

Last night I had a drink with Shamie Connolly in Mc-Mahon's and I'm still paying for it this morning. Shamie had spent the day with another man digging a grave – a neighbour's. Shamie is seventy-three. It took them five hours. They went down five feet. It was in Drumalee, not Redhills. I'm amazed that at his age he can still do such back-aching work. 'It's the last thing you can do for your neighbour.' I had no answer to that. The answer is not to be found in big cities. Cities are for the questions. 'The best man to dig a grave in the whole of Cavan is oul Hewitt out of Crubany. He's over eighty-five, yah boya. He gives you the full six-be-two. He laves it neat as a letter-box. And all for £80.' Shamie has a fantastic relish for words. He invests them with the same energy he uses to dig graves. Talking about a friend passing him on the road, driving very fast, he says, 'Collins went by me today like a ball of wind.' He mentions a woman he knows: 'She's neat now. She looks like she's been shot out of a bottle.'

Listening to him in a pub, time passes quickly and you soon lose count of the bottles. He loves argument: 'Love it better nor me tay.' Someone in the pub was talking claptrap. Connolly said to him, 'Are you goin' to talk rubbish all night or is a respectable body not allowed get a word in?' Gerry McMahon asked me how the film was going and if the young actress had star quality.

'Why would anyone want to be a star?' Connolly said.

'Sure the sky's full of them. Besides which, stars are only cinders.'

'I wasn't asking you, Connolly.'

'Be thankful, you got a free answer.'

'Do you know what it is you'd fight with the nails on your toes.'

'Only when I'd be done stamping on yours.'

From laughing and drinking the night shot past. Mickey Reilly, Philip Brady, Ollie Brady and Hughie McInerney let neither the drink nor the talk cease. Gerry handed round sausages on sticks in a vain effort to sober us up and get rid of us. When the plate was passed to Ollie Brady, he looked at it and, utterly deadpan, said, 'No thanks, Gerry, I'm driving.' By the time I drove Shamie home, the sky was full of potential actresses.

This morning the world looks blurred around the edges and invisible in the middle. Apart from that, my brain has gone out with the empties. We're in the village shooting the opening scene – the wake. All the people taking part are friends from school, friends of my parents. I chatted with Pat Smith, who has spent his life buying and selling horses. He is over eighty now, but still looks lean, loose-limbed, weather-beaten. He has tramped all over Ireland for horse flesh. He has gone miles to make sixpence on a deal. I told him Owen Conlon and I were going to visit him one evening. He looked at me. Long years of buying and selling have given his eyes a judgemental look. He gives you a quick once-over, searching for flaws, scanning you from under the peak of his cap. He is devoid of any trace of sentimentality. 'Owen come up a few evenings ago. He brung me a video of horses in Australia and them training them. No way would I do it the way they showed. And it never showed you how they caught them. It was no addition at all.'

Peter and I discuss the end of the film. Again. Sixty extras, all the crew, an Electric Press Kit unit from the UK doing publicity stuff, lots of folk watching the filming – and the two of us in the middle of it all, worrying about the end. 'Definitely the key is, "It's the living have to resurrect themselves and not the dead."' I'm too knackered to bother much. Worried, yes. Hang on till lunch and hope by then the head clears.

Sitting on a beer barrel outside McCaffrey's pub, a woman sits on a barrel beside me and tells me about her mother. 'Something happened to her. She started wandering about and when I'd come home from the convent I'd find her down staring at the lake, the dinner not cooked, nothing done. We couldn't put a finger on it. We took her to all the doctors. One doctor was in a worse state than we were. His wife had left him. I used to dread the nights, in case I heard her stirring and going off into the dark. In the pitch black. You remember mammy, don't you? She's dead these twenty years. But I puzzle at it every single day. Why? What was in her mind?'

I tell her mental illness is an illness like any other – diabetes, cancer . . . No one asks to be mentally ill. It could be genetic, or biological. It could be caused by a virus. Family or environment could spark it off, but it's unlikely. No one is to blame. If a loved one gets cancer, do we blame them? No, of course not. A sickness in the mind or the brain is the same.

'We stuck by her all the years. We never put her away.' This woman is gentle as she talks. I wonder if I had been in her situation, how would I have coped? I'd wilt, I know I would, if . . . I don't know, no one does, until it happens. This woman was tested and survived. She gets up and, laughing, goes off to watch the filming.

Wandering around the rest of the day I hear stories about parents and children at odds: old folk abandoned, young people fleeing. The most fundamental relationships are ropes that bind us. None of us escape. The stuff we carry round in our heads! The mind is in the brain. The brain is the field; the mind, the clay. Some fields are drowned in water or grow only whins and rocks.

Day off. Went to the All Ireland Drag Hunt Finals in Mickey Mullvaney's field outside Redhills. Beagle hounds chase the scent of a dead fox dragged over a three-mile course through hedges, ditches, drumlins, valleys, finishing in the field from which they started. First dog through a gap in the hedge is the winner. The locals pronounce 'beagle' as 'bagle'. Very confusing if you're like Lisa, a friend from Los Angeles. She's staying with Ann, my wife, and me and Tara for a few days. To get to the field we had to drive in a long muddy lane and then park on the side of a hill, skidding and skittering on the soaking grass with all the other cars. Most of the cars towed dog boxes. In the morning it rained so much that the organizers nearly cancelled. We all wore wellies and waterproofs. The crowd wasn't a large one because of the conditions. Those there were the hardy hundreds who'd watch dogs hunting in hell. It's the rawest country I ever saw: hills and valleys covered in wood, hedge and scrub. Some of the fields had been cleared of whin and ragwort and reseeded, and the green of these fields stood out fresh from the others. We were on top of a central hill from which we could see all about us: behind us, Shannow Wood; before us, the Cuilcaghs; off one way, the graveyard outside Redhills with the yew tree growing by the gate; off the other, Bruce Hill near Crossdoney where Robert the Bruce camped on an excursion into Ireland; down in the valleys, a few modern houses built beside the remains of the old. It teemed rain for most of the day. Gerry McMahon set up a very rudimentary tent and served beer. The tent covered Gerry and two of the village boys helping him. The customers were under the clouds. 'My back is near broken from bending up and down lifting cans and bottles.' Gerry told me. 'You wouldn't think it, but this is one of the best days of the year. The huntsmen are fierce drinkers.'

Shamie Connolly was there, John James North, Francie Gilsenan, Paddy Kelly, Francie Dolan and Tommy Hobson . . .

They never stopped making cuts at one another and laughing. 'Is that a dog or a cat you've got there?' 'He's got a licence to be out anyway, not like yourself, yah mad hoor yah.' Referring to the muck and mud Shamie said, 'Ah now, it's a long go through and clatty dirty.'

The sun and clouds chased each other all day. The rain bucketed down, but the dogs hunted regardless. Heats were run off, the best qualifying for the final. When they were lined up for the final, men, women and children milled around to watch. The beagles were strung out in a long line, each owner hanging on to their leads until the 'Go' was given. The leads were lengths of binder twine around the necks. The baying of the dogs before the off was amazing – so intense and urgent and desperate, it was almost visible. It was like being inside a hunting horn. The barking of one merged into the other, so that the entire hillside blazed with deep bugle cries. One owner was pulled off his feet by his straining dog. The hounds look lean, but are very strong. When the 'Go' was given, the crowd cheered and down the hill the dogs went chasing the non-existent prey. The looks on the owners' faces as they peer across the countryside after their hounds is almost touching. If you owned a horse in the Epsom Derby, you couldn't be more excited. I saw one old man looking through binoculars. He was so excited his hands trembled and he couldn't watch further. He handed the binoculars to his son and, turning away, he said a prayer. In one of the heats a dog came hurtling down to the winning gap a hundred yards ahead of his nearest rival, but a foot from the gap he stopped and, sniffing about, wouldn't come through. Other dogs went by him. The owner was distraught. 'He's beaten every dog in the land but won't finish. We've tried everything. He's so damn clever he can sense he's going to be caught at the end and the lead put round his neck. Fiendish, he is, fiendish.' He's the canine equivalent of the boy in *The Loneliness of the Long Distance Runner*.

I met an old hunting man who pointed out his house to

me. He wore glasses on his weathered face and an old blue plastic mac around his shoulders. He struck me as a very quiet, sensitive man. He was full of the gentleness country people possess. He told me he had been married twice. 'And both my women died at thirty-seven.' I asked him how he had coped with such sorrow. 'You got up every morning and just carried on. What else can be done?' These people are stoics. They stand on any hill, facing into any wind, rain or sorrow and carry on regardless. The people on top of Mullvaney's field were the hard core of the community. It would take some plague to knock them over. They have a rare, undiluted spirit.

Being on holiday, Lisa had a camera with her. It was the only one there. They made her official photographer for the day and she managed to photograph the winning dog coming through the gap. The fact that nobody had organized a camera to take snaps shows how unpretentious these hunters are.

When the drag hunt was over, everyone went down to Duggan's pub, a short distance away. There they drank and sang of hunting glory and famous dogs from Fermanagh, Cavan and Monaghan. The prize was presented to Ned Crudden from Newtownbutler. He is a massive man with a massive girth. Strength oozes from him. That his dog had won the All Ireland made him cry with happiness. 'I've niver in me whole life said words in public afore. I'm a happy man tonight.' It was a moving moment to see a huge man cry like a child. He cried more when someone sang a song in which his uncle is mentioned.

> There were huntsmen gathered there that day from Kilridd to Carnmore
> Back through Magheraveely and from Lough Erne's shore
> Here's a health to bold Ned Crudden of sportsmen he's a star

> For with 'Wee Comely' he did bring the cup to old
> Loughgare.

That was the last verse, anyway. The other fifteen I can't remember. The Garda raided the pub at one in the morning. Before driving away we stood in the dark and looked up at the stars hanging over the hill where we had stood earlier in the day. On the damp air we could still smell the fresh mash of grass and clay.

A man said to his daughter, 'Don't fret about the hounds. The hounds are home in the straw. They don't know a hate. Winners or losers. Where did I put the feckin' key?'

'I think Mammy should drive, Daddy.'

Day 19: Sunday 4 September

I have breakfast on the catering bus beside the football pitch. John, one of the drivers from Belfast, sits reading his *Sunday Times*. He's a middle-aged man, with glasses and silver hair, and has an air of quiet dignity in everything he says and does. He's a solid Unionist. He's not given to florid language. He always says what he means. He spends hours hanging round the set, waiting to be called to drive Vicki here and there. 'I just shut up and do what I'm told. It's war, making a film. You sit around bored for hours and eventually you get five minutes' excitement. Eventually. I grew the best ever crop of early spuds this year. All floury. You can't get them in England.'

'What do you think of the Ceasefire?' I ask.

'Funny you mention that. I'm reading about it in the paper this minute. The Troubles. It's like making a film.'

The All Ireland Hurling Final is on TV this afternoon. I watch it in McCaffrey's. The pub is shut, but inside a few hard drinkers murder pints. They are leftovers from the drag hunt who haven't yet made it home. One of them is eighty years of age. He takes my hand. His face is strong, square, with a blue-red tinge to his skin.

'Eighty. Eighty.'

'Wha' – a hundred and sixty?' someone mutters.

'No. Eighty. All the walkin' after me dogs.'

Another hunter says, 'So they're making a film about your life?'

'No. It's not about my life. Touched, maybe, by my life. A fantastic wish that it *was* my life. My life was repressed.'

'We all were them days.'

A man in the Gents buttons up his fly. He stands in front of me and burps. 'There's three ways of making money in this country: the Church, drugs and pornography. But don't coate me.'

The hurling was on the telly in a corner of the bar. We only watched it out of the corners of our eyes. I drank lemonade . . .

When darkness falls we shoot a night scene. A huge crane with two massive lamps on top is positioned along the street. The lamps are higher than the trees. They shine down like night suns: piercing cold light. An old man, Ownie Brides, makes his way home from the pub. He stops and stares up at the lights. 'I've got to have two eye operations. I got a coma in one eye and a cataract in the other. What about it, sure? I'm over eighty.' He walks off into the light and out into the shadows. His cap, his sharp face and gentle eyes still linger in the dark. The fatalistic strength of the people continuously surprises. I said to Tara, 'Look at those people. Take strength from them.' She replied, 'I've got my own strength.'

A woman comes up to me and, laughing, says, 'Has she appeared yet?' She means Miss Whyte-Venables' ghost. I tell her she hasn't appeared. 'She will. She will. And when she does, we'll be able to tell from your face.'

Filming in Clones. Parked on the Diamond and walked down Fermanagh Street and out the Roslea Road to my old secondary school. I stepped into the entrance hall. The tiled floor is still the very same: light-coloured tiles, except the six brown ones in the shape of a cross by the entrance. I recognize the shape of the place, but that's all. It's a big coed comprehensive now. Munch and Toulouse-Lautrec prints hang on the walls. Never heard of them in my day. I look into the cloakroom. We used to have bars with hooks for coats. The bars were great for hanging on upside-down. One afternoon in 1957 I was hanging there like a bat when Gerry McMahon came in and told me that the Man. Utd team had been killed in a plane crash. Upside-down I hung, looking at his shocked face. I came to earth with a bump, but there's a part of me that will hang on those bars for ever.

I walk out of the school and into the cemetery. A few teenage schoolboys come in and stand among the headstones smoking, dragging deep, just like we used to. The school was St Tiarnach's. Recently the name has been changed in an amalgamation with another school. St Tiarnach's is no more. My mates and I have been erased from history.

Back in the town I meet Tony Tighe, one of the all-time great Gaelic footballers. His era was the forties and fifties. I saw him play for Cavan in the 1952 All Ireland Final. I ask him what it was like winning a final? 'Coming home from the match a fellah says, "There's a cockfight in Mullagh." I went with him and didn't land home for two days. My wife nearly threw me out. It was the first time I'd seen a cockfight. And the last. In them days you could celebrate all night and not feel it next morning. Not any more. Not any more.'

The Angelus bell rings out from the Catholic church. A minute later the clock on the Protestant church in the Diamond answers. It's a two-timing town. Even the crows around each church caw differently. Most of my teenage time I used up hanging around the railway station. I gawked at the convent girls who were well-wrapped even on a summer's day – brogues, thick woollen stockings, cardigans, blouses, coats and mysterious nether garments even more restrictive. I practised words that would somehow unlock the lot. A few of us would walk into town and stand near Chapman's the Chemist. Mr Chapman's daughters were Protestant and stunning. No chance there, but the sight of them was good for sore Catholic eyes. Alone I'd watch the woman working in the kiosk on the station platform. She sold newspapers, sweets, cigarettes. She was over thirty, I was sixteen. I'd go into the kiosk and try to kiss her, somehow get warmth from her. The Ladies' was at the end of the platform. She'd lock the kiosk and walk down there into the shadows. I'd follow her and try to kiss her ... She must have thought me a right pest. She never protested too much, though. A big burly fireman off the Enniskillen train began paying visits to the kiosk. He wore a black railwayman's cap and smoked a pipe. I couldn't compete with a pipe. I turned my attentions to Angeline Ronney – always from a safe distance.

Clones is my teenage town full of lost voices. We're shooting a dance-hall scene here, in the Creighton Hotel. The hotel is a mazy confusion of equipment, crew and locals recruited for the dance. To begin with the extras are excited, then it dawns on them: this is going to go on all day long. A girl wears a white crocheted top and a short white silk skirt. There's flesh bouncing everywhere. Ken, the sound recordist, says, 'We're only thirty years too late.' Tony Devlin, says, 'No fool like an old fool. But I'm not going to be suicidal about it. I'm going to be mature. I'm not going to look at her again. I'm going outside for a pint.'

Next door to the hotel is Liam Nicholl's butcher shop. I went to school with his brother Harry. Liam is a neat, kempt man, with dark hair groomed back off his forehead. He moves briskly round his sawdust-covered shop, eager for

93

distraction. He has a taste for life. Being the eldest son he inherited the family business. His world had to become the bottom of Fermanagh Street. In a cubicle in his office he shows me a collection of old twenty- and hundred-pound notes. Wads of the stuff. They are in mint condition. He found them out the country under a relation's bed. The relation didn't believe in banks. He gave me a 1955 twenty for the modern equivalent. A lovely big, fresh, red note from the year I started school here. He told me he'd just had a visit from his bank manager. He is trying to get a loan for a new slaughter house. The manager, to secure the loan, took the deeds of his house, the shop, the existing slaughter house and wanted the deeds of a cottage Liam owns out in the country. 'They crucify you. They'd teach the Romans how it's done.'

Sheep carcasses hang on the walls. A bloody joint of beef sits alone in the fridge. Next door the film rages. Here in this small shop, lives seem small but the drama is intense. We are all in the grip of men in suits who know about money: the fax men, with undertakers' smiles.

I drive out of the town to Lecky Bridge. The bridge has been blown up by the British Army. Huge blocks of concrete and steel girders are in place to prevent entry to the North. Locals have tried to reopen the road umpteen times. Clay is piled up, boulders have been shunted and repositioned, but each time the road is opened the Army comes and, with massive earth-moving equipment, blocks it again. The land on either side of the Border is exactly the same. Old fields with high, thick hedges and ragwort, dock, and moist, deep ditches. It looks so banal that you can't imagine this rural spot arousing feelings as intense as those aroused by the Berlin Wall. Men with a bulldozer opened the road yesterday. Last night the Army moved in and closed it again. They piled more massive concrete and steel slabs in place, making the crossing impassable. The locals will not reopen it today. A man has died in a nearby house and, out of respect, they are delaying retaliatory action.

A young man comes along. He thinks I'm from a news-paper. 'There's a ceasefire. So why don't they open the roads?'

'How do they know the Ceasefire is going to last?'

'They know well enough. Peter Robinson and other Paisley-ites went to Israel to study the electrified fences they've got there. You know, keeping out the Arabs. They want the same here. They're mad.'

Looking at the slabs of stone and steel, and the weeds grow-ing through them, I know this is a Kafkaesque world. There is no such thing as ordinary lives, ordinary places. Any old blade of grass can be fought over.

Another man says, 'Clones is a troublesome town. We were born out of the Troubles.' A British Army helicopter flies up and hovers at a distance. On the Southern side a Garda squad car arrives. I know the driver. He's married to a Redhills girl. We exchange jokey chat. I feel guilty simply for being here. The wind shifts the thistledown and the river gurgles against the concrete and steel. The whole dismal picture is enough to make you cry. This is the politics of spite.

Back in Fermanagh Street I meet the man who for thirty years was the projectionist in the Luxor Cinema before it closed. 'In all that time the only day off I had was Good Friday. The one day the pubs are shut.'

In a tiny window a notice reads: 'Barber's Shop. Opening Soon.'

A man comes and stands directly in front of me. 'I went to school with you.' He looks up at me, grinning. He is short, slight, grey-haired, wears glasses.

'I give in,' I say.

'Me lookin' at you, you lookin' at me. A crazy mirror we make. Stan Kelly.'

'Jesus, yes, Stan. That twinkle, how could I forget?'

'Who'd have thought, Shane, you endin' up a wordsmith?'

'Never thought it at the time anyway, Stan.'

'What sort of job is it?'

'About as entertaining as hearing your own confessions. Or

prison without bars. Sometimes though, not bad. Grand in fact.'

'Aye?'

'Aye, Stan.'

There are twelve pubs in Fermanagh Street – tiny bars. A few customers huddle in each. Stan and I dart into one. Over a nice smooth pint old voices, faces, swim out.

'Jim McCarney's dead you know?'

'Poor Jim. He had real style, that bloke. And music. And smart clothes.'

'Aye. Dead.'

'Probably happen to us one day, Stan. Or night . . . in the middle of nowhere, no telephone and it's raining.'

Day 21: Tuesday 6 September

In Clones still. We're on Roll 117.

When you're bored, go to church. I went to the Diamond and into the Church of Ireland. The church is on top of the Diamond which is on top of the town. At the back of the church is the cemetery. When you look over the wall you can see directly down on to the rooftops. The building itself is locked on all but Sundays. The headstones stick up like pages from an old directory of Ulster families: Cochrane, Averell, Lee, Bevis, Gray, Pogue, Nicholl, Armstrong, Robinson . . . There are more dead Protestants than living ones in Clones today. A woman told me that in O'Neill Park, a public-housing scheme, there are 181 houses and all but one of them Catholic. 'Mind you,' she added, 'no Prod would live up there.'

Protestants moved because of the Troubles. The closed Border roads maimed the town economically. The merchants didn't hang around. The rectory stands empty. It has a fan light over the front door shaped like a rising sun. At the back of the rectory are stone-built, slated outhouses. They are falling apart, caving in with age and rot and neglect. In one outhouse are old jam jars and a 1940s perambulator. This pram is crumbling to rust on its wheels. Rust and cobwebs . . . The graveyard is the only dilapidated, overgrown Protestant graveyard I've ever seen. Usually they are spick and span. Here, though, nettles, weeds and grass are as tall as the head-stones. The shut-off Border has choked the town and every-thing in it.

Back in the Butter Market the filming carries on. There isn't a market in butter any more. The area is just a car park for the hotel. One of the townspeople in the dance scene today is Catherine McGuigan. She is a young, dark-haired girl with the family warmth and vitality. I asked her about her brother's death. She said that Barry's boxing career had been Dermot's life, but Barry lost his title and eventually retired. Then their father died. Then their mother went to America to live with a daughter. These were blows to Dermot. Superficial blows but, allied with the personal demons we all have, he could no longer stand living. He stopped the torture in his head the only way he could . . .

As we were talking, down Fermanagh Street came Ned Crudden. He looked to be still in celebratory mood after his triumph in the Drag Hunt finals. He was coming from a funeral and was making for the Creighton Hotel. 'Next day I got beat in Arva be the dog that came second.' It amazes me that they could stand up next day, never mind go hunting again. But Crudden has amazing strength. It oozes from him. He looks at me, licks his lips. 'Will you come in for a wee one?' I know when I'm out of my depth. 'Some other time.' He goes into the hotel, as slow and stately as a laden ship.

A woman comes up and mentions the day a man drove his car down Fermanagh Street with two passengers on board. He had a heart attack, crashed and all three were killed. 'I don't know,' the woman adds, 'it's a very unlucky town, Clones.' I don't think so. It's a town with people who live dangerously. They have survived economic disaster and

Loyalist bombs. As we talked, I could see a man I went to school with going round his supermarket holding on to the shelves for support. He had been blown up in the bombing. And in the middle of it all Barry McGuigan won a world title.

In the hotel I watch them shooting the scene where our young hero is picked up by a girl. Matt, instead of being shy and stumbling, plays it like he's been pulling girls all his life – New York girls. I'm about to tell Peter that the boy should look as if he's never been with a girl before when I see him going up to Matt and whispering in his ear. The lights dim, the band plays, the extras dance and the girl comes up to Matt for the ninth time. Eventually it looks something akin to the image in my head. What a desperate business this is!

I drive out to Lecky Bridge. It's bucketing rain. A local man is securing a chain around a concrete block. Another secures an end round the tow bar of a tractor. The tractor eases forward through the mud . . . The chain slips off the concrete. They try again. The rain is teeming down so hard I can hardly see the men. It hops off the concrete and steel and lashes back up in a thick spray. The man with the chain wears only jeans, runners and a white T-shirt. Men, equipment and land are soaking. Eventually they manage to move the concrete. The Queen's Highway is clear again. Tonight it will be blocked again by her servants. A car sweeps up from the Fermanagh side and drives straight through and into Clones. It saves going round twelve miles. The Garda squad car arrives. I suppose it's too wet for the helicopter . . .

Back in the hotel, the scene carries on. The camera moves along tracks, smooth as a well-oiled piece of artillery.

Day 22: Wednesday 7 September

This morning we're filming in what used to be the Luxor Cinema. The art department have discovered the three-dimensional sign, minus the neon tubes, and have stuck it above the entrance. I always thought the Luxor the most exotic name ever. It suggested luxury, warmth, sex, Eastern promise. It was an occasion of sin and the priests looked on it that way. Men sat one side, women sat the other. But up on the screen were the false gods of Hollywood and we worshipped them faithfully. But now the place is a ruin. The roof leaks, the seats rot, the damp cuts your nostrils. Old cans for rolls of film lie rooted to the ground with rust. The rust has eaten through the tin. In the box-office, inches of rot and water lie on the floor. The ticket machine is still in position. Tickets, 2/6, 3/6 and 4/-. The cinema staff who were the last to work the place scrawled their names on the box-office wall. One person wrote: '11/1/'78. I hope you feel proud for closing down the last place of entertainment in the town.'

Today we have exhumed the corpse, stuck a gaudy dress on it, a lick of paint . . . People flock around to see it. Schoolgirls lark about in the entrance. One of them keeps up a feigned Scottish accent. She has slightly goofy teeth in a pretty face and makes all her friends laugh constantly. She shouts after each boy who walks past, 'Hallo, MacDuck.'

A businessman bought the cinema for £25,000. It has been shut ever since. Other buildings along the street are in a bad way. Paint peels from the walls, weeds clog the guttering, crows disappear down chimneys. The place is dead on its feet, but if the Ceasefire holds . . . A local man, returned from America, has paid £20,000 for a pub. He's spending £200,000 on it to turn it into a pub-cum-restaurant . . . 'It's a good idea,' someone says, 'for there's no place decent to eat in this town.'

At the top of Fermanagh Street is McDonald's drapery. Into the shop and down steps at the back there is a tea room. You can get cream teas, home-made cakes and pies, and quiche. It's like a place you'd find in Guildford. It's a retreat for the middle-classes. I share a table with the Revd Nigel Balor and his wife from over the Border in Newtownbutler. They are about to pack up and move back to a parish in Belfast. Mamo

McDonald, who runs the place as well as being a glorious cook, organizes workshops on lace-making, sits on various town committees, travels the country setting up women's organizations and writes poetry. She has enough energy to pull a train.

Out on the street again, it begins to rain. We all huddle up the covered alleys between the buildings. Children scoot up the entries and, minutes later, shoot back out again. The rain is hopping into the street, crackling against the surface like lips kissing. In a tiny pub a drinker tells me he has been 'celebrating' a funeral. Another drinker accuses me of stealing his wellington boots.

'I had to go home last night in a woman's slippers.'

'Was she wearing them at the time?'

Night falls and it's still teeming. In a shop doorway I am joined by a young girl in school uniform. I ask her if she has done her homework. She hasn't. 'I know my spellings anyway. And anyway she never asks them anyway, so she doesn't.'

The door behind us opens and her mother joins us. She straightaway launches into a story about her own mother. 'She used beat me with a sally rod in the yard and my father watching from the window, tears running down his face. She was a great businesswoman though.'

'Why didn't your father stop her beating you?'

'Because she'd beat him too.' She looks a bit like Mia Farrow: short blonde hair, nice clothes, a pearl necklace. She is very intense and troubled by love. 'I was married twenty-seven years. My husband left me. I didn't know it was going on until I come in and found him with another woman. It's terrible to say it, but I want him back. I've children and am on Social Welfare. He's living across the Border. He'd never tell me the truth. I met a man and he told me to read the Old Testament. I couldn't. For three days I tried. Then on the phone he told me to read the New Testament. From that moment on, magic entered my life. I know magic is the wrong word, seeing as we're talking religion. That man God is the man I love. He has entered me from that moment. My husband, you see, I mean he was, is, a good fellah. I told him never to bring the woman he's living with into town or I'll smash their place up.' The little girl beside us listens totally unconcerned.

A boy comes out of the door behind us. 'We need a loaf of bread.'

'Run up to Benny's and put it on the slate.'

When the kid comes back with the loaf he tells his mother they owe Benny £19.75.

One of the extras walks up the street. She wears a tartan skirt and a straw hat and is not unlike the woman I'm talking to. 'That one – he had an affair with her as well.' She says it so simply I believe her. Her children look at the woman walking up towards the Diamond. They are unconcerned. They've heard it all before. I'm gripped by it, though. Love isn't blind. Love is wild-eyed with terror. There's a volcano exploding behind every closed door.

Later on, when we're in the Diamond filming, the woman in the straw hat asks to have her photograph taken with me. One of the crew lines us up and snaps us. By standing beside this lovely woman I feel I am betraying the woman down the street. In small towns everyone knows what's going on. All the betrayals, all the emotions, are common property. It's tough.

Someone looks up at the Ulster Bank and recounts the tale of Billy Hand and how he was killed. 'The boy along with him got fifty-eight stitches in the side of his head. He was never right in the head after. He went to Chicago and joined the police force.'

'I'd say the head bang was a requirement.'

Food is served up to us and while I'm eating, leaning against a gable end, a friend from school comes past.

'You heard about Jim McCarney?'

'I did.'

'Often I stood on this spot with Jim. If two girls came along they'd both go for him. Two for him, not one for me. We went on to be priests, the two of us. Jim jumped ship after a month. Got out without anyone knowing. I stuck it a while longer. Never regretted it.'

'What do you think of the Ceasefire?'

'I mind the time of Bobby Sands and the hunger strike. I wouldn't close my pub. I got a threatening phone call in the night. I found out who made it. I went to him. "You touch my effing family and I'll effing kill you," I says. He says to me, "You don't understand. My two brothers were murdered by the Brits. They were hanged in a freezer." A big fridge, you know. No one tells me to shut or open. Is this a democracy or not?'

Every doorway in this town has a story. Love and loathing lurking everywhere. Small town, big lives.

Day 23: Thursday 8 September

Sit in my car in the Diamond out of the rain. It's screeching down hard as nails, banging into the paintwork on the houses and parked cars. Yet the sun is shining. It lights up McDonald's drapery, Wilcar Parts, Nicholson's Pharmacy, Slowey's Fabrics, Jewellers and Bicycles, John Matthews, Groceries, Newsagent and Stationery. It gilds the grey, blue and purple façade of the Ulster Bank and smiles high up on the Red Hand of Ulster carved in stone. Guttering overflows. Water cascades down the front of a building. The sun dazzles, turns the old paintwork new. A peck, a goodbye sigh and the rain stops.

We are filming in the Tower Bar. We've taken it over for the day and filled it with extras and actors. Peter and Mike Southon rehearse the action and discuss the shots: where to place the camera, where to move it, the background lights, close-ups . . . When the crew swing into action to set it all up Peter calls me to one side. Castle Rock want an 'up' ending.

'Examine the endings of the great plays – Shakespeare, the Greeks.' They usually end with a massive explosion, fall-out, then calm.

'Has *Hamlet* an up ending – in Hollywood terms?'

'Just contemplate them. *Othello, Romeo and Juliet. Oedipus.* Your daughter is doing Classics, isn't she? Go and ask her.'

I go out into Fermanagh Street. Tara is near by, directing traffic. I nip over to her and ask her about the endings of Greek tragedies.

'Oh fuck off, dad, I'm busy. Come back later.'

I knew that was a mistake.

A man shows me into a pub he's bought beside the pub he already owns. This pub is tiny, with one bar and a gorgeous snug in which you and friends could get drunk privately. He only opens the place one day a year – the Ulster Football Final, which is always played in Clones. That day the town is packed with thirsty people.

'Can I book the snug for next year? If I'm alive.'

'Aye. Done.'

It's raining again. The gulleys run with water down Fermanagh street from the Diamond. The cobbles are quivering riverbeds. The rain lies lush as long hair down the whole length of the street. In every doorway and alley people shelter. You can just see their noses and bellies sticking out.

A crowd gathers on the corner opposite the Creighton Hotel. It looked at first as if they were waiting for a bus, but there's too many of them. They wear ordinary clothes and, though it's still raining, few have umbrellas. A hearse comes down Fermanagh Street, just managing to manoeuvre its way through the film vehicles parked on either side. Two black cars follow the hearse. Beside the crowd of people the hearse stops. Children and adults get out of the cars. Then the hearse crawls slowly up the steep hill to the Catholic church. A woman wearing a red cardigan and supported by two younger women walks behind the hearse. The older woman is sobbing pitifully. She seems crippled by her sorrow. Slowly all the waiting people fall in behind them.

The funeral was of a twenty-one-year-old girl killed in a bus accident. She was on a bus returning from a dance in a nearby town. The bus was full of young people. It was night. Maybe drink had been taken. A row broke out. The girl opened the door and jumped out into the black. She died later in a Dublin Hospital. Was she pushed? Did she jump on purpose? Was it an accident?

The woman telling me all this said, 'It's going through a bad time, Clones. It's an unlucky town.'

'The wheel always comes full circle. Good times are ahead,' I say.

I meet up again with Stan Kelly. He's driving a car with an L-plate. In the pub he told me he wasn't allowed to drive long distances. 'I took a turn one time. Funny enough a friend was in Monaghan hospital. I drove the wife and his children to visit him. Holy God, there and then beside his bed I took this turn. I woke up in a bed beside your man. It was comical. It couldn't have happened in a better place. That was two years ago. It never happened since.'

'It was the smell of the hospital did it, Stan.'

'Aye. Or God was pointing at me. Then realized his mistake. So I drive only around the town nowadays.' Stan is a lovely, quiet, honest, neat, quick-witted man. His wife died some years ago. He brings up his sons alone.

Back in the Tower Bar they are shooting the scene at last. Matt and Vicki are saying the words well, but they look too old to my eyes. The lines I had imagined coming from the mouths of innocents are falling from older, more experienced lips. But they are good, Matt and Vicki. And if they're good enough, they'll be young enough for the audience. That's all that matters.

God knows how it's all going to turn out .

Finishing off the scene in the Tower, doing Matt's close-up. Like all American actors he knows how to exploit the camera. In close-up you can see he has his brain in gear. The last line he has to say to the girl is, 'Your ears are sea shells, your eyes dancing stars.' The girls on the crew love it. They ask each other when was the last time a man spoke poetry to them and meant it. 'I did recently to my lady,' Ken, the sound man, says. 'I said, "Hello, darling. Your eyes are piss-holes in the snow." And she didn't appreciate it.'

Someone knocks over a pint. 'Hate tha',' says Tony Devlin. 'Love kissin' but hate tha'.' Everything comes to a halt. The camera breaks down and has to be replaced.

In the town I meet a woman who told me that one day back in the fifties she met my English teacher. Fr. Morris was his name. 'Sugar', we called him. He loved Milton, Shakespeare and Patrick Kavanagh. He worshipped Kavanagh. He came from the same part of the country. 'Sugar' showed this woman an essay written by a young boy from Redhills. He said it showed considerable promise. Of course, the boy was me. I disputed the truth of this story, but backed down when I saw the alarm in the woman's eyes. Myths must never be challenged. I know it's a myth. My essays in school were painful. Last thing on a Sunday evening I had to drag out enough words to fill two pages. I'd hand it on the Monday morning and wait until the Friday for the result. The comments were always written in red biro. I can never remember receiving praise. And praise I would remember. A drop of praise – I'd live off it for a month.

The shooting finished in Clones, we move to the village of Scotshouse. Scotshouse is three miles from Redhills and in Co. Monaghan. The art department's headquarters are here. We're also using the community hall as a studio and this afternoon we're filming outside Connolly's pub. The village is an L-shaped street and smaller than Redhills. Part of the village is crumbling. I suppose the owner is hanging on for a bonanza. The rest of the place seems to be owned by the Connollys. Their buildings are done up spick and span. At the back of the village is Hilton Park owned by the Madden family. No Irish village is complete without landed gentry. Once upon a time, old Major Madden was the force behind the estate. Now it is run by his son and his son's wife. You drive into the place through beautiful trees, past a lake and lawns, before reaching a Georgian mansion. It is a spectacular setting. But like all the other places, money is the problem. Money and the weather. I think the Irish gentry are afflicted by not educating their children locally. They don't want to risk Irish accents coming into the house. If you have an Irish accent, you're Irish. You have a direct connection with the land. But if you're educated in England, your mind and heart are split. You can't put down proper roots. The hold on the estate weakens from generation to generation. You begin to sell off parcels of land to make ends meet. But the big house can be kept going only by the land . . . Then in desperation you turn to desperate measures – open a restaurant, try to attract tourists, breed sheep or horses, turn the place into a hotel . . . Local farmers do well with eighty acres. I can never understand why the gentry can't manage on hundreds. Maybe the struggle is too much for hearts to bear. Maybe the houses are just too big for modern man, with his oil and electricity bills. A man outside Connolly's says, 'Ah now, they're livin' in a time that hasn't lasted this long.'

We move outside the village and shoot a scene at a crossroads. Up from the cross, in the garden surrounded by trees and hills, is an abandoned house. Imprinted above the door is the date 1808. On the roof are decorated tiles, but the windows are broken and the tiles are coming apart. A long time ago someone turned the key in the door and walked away. The climate is slowly but surely caving in the place: crushing the stones, crumbling the brickwork, reaching into every nook and cranny with its damp, sticky fingers. Clouds gather above us and, with a sigh, rip open and deluge the entire countryside. I shelter under a tree. Drips hit the ground like stones.

When night falls we move outside the village and take over an elderly couple's bungalow. Electric cables run through their front room. Big lamps shine out behind the house and in front of it are massive towers hung with arc lights. These lights shine brighter than the moon. The narrow road is blocked with cars, vans and lorries. ADs and crew go in and out of the house and the elderly couple sit there, amazed with themselves that they've allowed such an invasion of their privacy. The art director sets about hanging up new curtains, except he hasn't anything with which to hang them.

'Have you got any drawing pins, dear?' he asks the woman of the house.

'No,' she replies, 'we only have them at Christmas.'

I remember the husband and wife from childhood. They were a young couple then. I sit with them chatting, laughing, trying to remove the curse from the invasion. A warm fire burns in the Jubilee cooker. People come and go all the time: 'Can I use your toilet?' 'Can I use your telephone? Only a local call.' The man of the house is Peter Herney. He came from Galway originally to work in McMahon's shop in Redhills. In 1945 he played in goal for the Annagh team that for the first time won the Cavan Championship. He has great memories and a great turn of phrase. Describing someone who was weak, with no strength, he said, 'He couldn't snap a mouse trap.' We sit and drink tea and talk about football and my parents. 'Your mother was a graceful lady. Your father was a fine man.' My eyes dim and I stare into the fire.

Peter Yates sticks his head round the door and looks at us as if we are three Martians. 'I want to talk to you about the swimming scene. It's getting cold now. Can you come up with an alternative? We'll talk later.' He goes out.

'When you got to compromise, you got to compromise.'

Peter Herney looks at me and smiles. 'There's more than

one way of killing a cat. If you don't bend with the wind, you'll end up with a sore back.'

Saturday 10 September

Day off. I meet up with Peter to discuss the script. What have we achieved so far? What have we not, as yet, accomplished? We plan, plot, change, move dialogue around. For instance, a cattle-driving scene has too much talk for such a complicated shot down a long, narrow country lane. We decide to move a chunk of it into a bedroom scene where it'll work better and with more point.

I have to rewrite the swimming scene. The water has become too cold for Matt and Vicki. It's all right for Anthony Brophy, who plays the part of their friend Prunty, but we can't risk Matt and Vicki getting flu. Only Anthony will get wet. He's a Dublin actor, after all. He'll chance anything. He's a real actor, Brophy. He's got a good background in Irish theatre where demands are made far in excess of the remuneration. A bit like this gig. We mustn't risk our stars in the lake. The comic relief, though, will be required to go in head first.

We talk around the end of the film. Like rivers flowing to the ocean, the story, characters, plot and intentions must all meet there. *Finito*. The scheduling has become complicated. Albert Finney's mother has died in England and he's gone home for the funeral. We have to rearrange his scenes. It's tough on Albert.

For the next week the plan is to work around him, do other things. In the evening Ann and I take Peter and his wife Virginia, Nigel Wooll, Phil Sidall (the camera operator), Tara, Kay Phelan (a friend of mine who every year helps to organize a great arts festival in the nearby town of Cootehill) and Deborah Harwood (my agent from London), to an extraordinary restaurant run by a German called Fred and his Scottish wife, Helen, who is a vet in her spare time. The restaurant is the front room of their house overlooking Lough Oughter. You can't find the place without the help of an Ordnance Survey map. It's miles off the beaten track in the heart of stunning country. Fred caters only for parties. You agree the menu in advance. It's either local game, meat or fish. You bring your own wine.

Peter and Nigel turned up laden with wine, champagne and brandy. By chance a famous Venezuelan harpist, a friend of Fred's, was staying in the house. On his wonderful old harp he entertained us royally after dinner. Mario was his name. He travels the world singing for his supper. We are quite a collection of international oddballs, all welded together by Mario's music. In the tradition of great harpers, especially Irish ones, he had a taste for wine, women and song. We stumbled out into the pitch-black Cavan night at four in the morning. We were so plastered I don't think one of us knew our own names. Ann drove home. Mercifully the roads were empty.

Day 25: Sunday 11 September

This morning I meet Michael Reilly in the village. He tells me that the parish council want to see the rushes of the pig-blessing sequence in the chapel porch. All sorts of rumours are spreading. Certain people are swearing that the pig was in the chapel itself – up at the altar rails, no less. I tell Michael that I doubt the film company will let anyone see anything until the film is complete and ready for viewing. It takes only a few fanatics to railroad others on to their rickety wagon. In a small community people are vulnerable. There are also complaints that the village hall has been out of bounds as we have been using it to store props and sets. We are paying for the hall. If we weren't there, the place would be lying idle. No matter how big or small the community, someone wants to jockey for position. The film company is the same. There are power battles going on all the time.

I thought the pig business had died down. It seems not. I'm worried. The last thing I want is to upset anyone. I don't care who they are or what they stand for, we're supposed to be having a good time. I'm sorry for Michael. He has to try to keep all sides sweet. He's someone who, after his day's work, runs the football team, the parish council, employment schemes, serves on various committees and gets an earbashing for his pains. He and the few like him make life worth living.

I speak to Nigel Wooll about letting the parish council see the stuff we've shot with the damn pig. 'What? Certainly not. We're not even showing anything to Castle Rock. Not until the whole picture's in the can.' I go to sulk in my car. I feel a twinge in my back. I get out of the car and can barely stand up. I've put my back out. Last time it happened, Shamie Connolly and John Collins took me to Tempo in Fermanagh to a woman who had the cure for bad backs. When you're desperate you'll try anything. I decide to drive to Tempo to see the woman again. Her name is Minie Geary. Going across the Border a British soldier waves me through. He's not wearing a helmet. Since the Ceasefire they've taken to berets. Near Tempo I turn off the main road and up a very steep embankment to where Miss Geary lives. She's a Catholic who looks after an elderly Protestant man. The cure was given to her by this man's sister as she lay dying.

The house has a great view of the Fermanagh hills looking towards Brookeborough. The kitchen is a big, clear and clean space. The floor is tiled – bright, creamy tiles. The old man says, 'Them there tiles come from Dublin.' He said it in such a way that you know they were brought from Dublin when Dublin was part of Britain. I remark how nice and peaceful it is around Tempo. 'Aye. Nawthin' to disturb us save the stricken of the clock.' For a solid Protestant, I'm amazed how he can tolerate the cure business.

Minie Geary takes me into the front room. With the Queen looking on, she ties a piece of cotton around my back with a knot in it. The cotton is tied next to my flesh. She tells me not to take the cotton off for three days and three nights and when I take it off I must burn it and not let it touch the ground before I burn it. Then she goes out of the room, I think to say a prayer. After a few seconds she comes back in. I give her a fiver for her pains – rather, my pains. She looks amazed and doesn't want to accept the money.

It's a quaint set-up, this Catholic lady and the elderly Protestant. They come to the door and wave me off. 'If this weather howls up it'll do us a power of good,' the man says as I start the car. He looks at the car, looks it up and down, and says, 'How's she for juice?'

I say to Minie, 'The cure . . . It must be all in the mind.'

'No,' she replies, 'It'll cure a bullock with a bad back just the same.'

Driving back through the checkpoint a soldier stops me. When he asks me where I'm coming from I tell him I was visiting a friend in Lisnaskea. I ask him where he's from.

'Leeds.'

'How would you feel if the Irish Army stopped you going freely about Yorkshire?'

'I'm only obeying orders.'

'Historically, that has proved to be a weak excuse.'

He notices an old Arsenal programme on the back seat.

'You an Arsenal fan? I might have ruddy guessed. Go on.'

My back is killing me. It's the bloody pig business.

Day 26: Monday 12 September

Filming at John Rudden's farm. The country up here is incredibly rough and raw. Scrubby, scabby hills of hedge, trees, bramble, whin, rush, fern, rock. The farm is on a hill looking down on a valley, yet surrounded by higher distant hills. It is rough, but beautiful. It is totally unspoilt. Looking around, you know that this is the way it's looked for hundreds of years. You can only get into the place up a long narrow, rutted, muddy lane. I walked up this morning, picking black-berries for breakfast.

We're filming the cattle-driving scene. Conor, the clapper loader, holds up the clapper: Roll 139. Inside a hedge, tracks are down for the camera. All the crew – make-up, hair-dressers, grips, electricians, drivers – are in the field sitting around on boxes, chairs, lens cases. The sun sneaks out from behind the low clouds and the dark-green grass lightens. People take their coats off.

This land is at the heart of the film and the novel. There is no place else like it in Ireland. In Europe. It is so harsh it chills you. Yet it's spectacular. It must be hard to wring a living from these small rocky fields. You can't till the land. John Rudden grazes cattle. His sister sells hen, duck and turkey eggs. A few months ago, thugs from across the Border ar-rived, tied up Babs with electric wire and made off with £400.

I sit on a box, cow dung at my feet. Fresh green grass shoots up through the dung. Down in the valley is an abandoned cottage. You can make out faint traces of human activity – thirty years ago. The remains of a garden beside the house is just visible; likewise, a path up to the door. But the people who lived there emigrated to Birmingham . . .

John Rudden comes along. He looks at one of the women, an elderly lady. 'Oh now, but. She'd still snap a trap.'

Later I get a lift out to the main road to where our vehicles are parked. On the wardrobe bus I meet Marie Conmee, an act-ress from Dublin, who is playing the part of Prunty's mother. Marie I know well. Years ago I acted with her. She's a big woman with a quick tongue. I notice Rosemary, the costume designer, is fitting her costumes as Marie sits. She's probably tired, having just travelled down from Dublin. She sounds tired as she speaks. She tells me the story of Godfrey Quig-ley's funeral. He was a well-loved Dublin actor.

'There was a great turn-out. The world and his wife turned up in Glasnevin. And do you know who was there? Jim Fitzgerald. Lookin' great. Three bottles of vodka a day before breakfast all his life and there he was lookin' better than the rest of us. I think he turned up for vengeance. He was the best director ever in this country. Could have been. He turned up to laugh at the rest of us who spent all our lives telling him he was killing himself. And there he is lookin' splendid. Jesus, any of us could pop off any moment. Godfrey was only seventy-one. Jim wanted to make a speech over the coffin, but we all sat on him. We didn't want the corpse falling out on the floor.' She gives a great sweeping laugh, then yawns.

Marie's a real trouper. She'll be great as Mrs Prunty. This is one bit of casting that's spot on, thank God. I wonder what age she must be now . . . Seventy, I'd say. At least. And still tumbling.

Day 27: Tuesday 13 September

John and Babs Rudden, brother and sister, live in the old family cottage surrounded by goats, pigs, geese, ducks, hens, peacocks, guinea fowl, dogs, cats, pigeons and cattle. The fields beside the house are surreal lawns covered in abandoned cars, vans, ploughs, harrows, mowing machines, hay rakes and grubbers. The old cars – Volkswagens, Mazdas and Fords – house the fowl. Foxes can't get into the cars. The amazing thing is that even though the bird shit is higher than the car seats, the fowl are spotlessly clean. This morning I watched as Babs opened a Mazda door and out hopped a flock of geese, their white feathers shining in the sun. Babs moves about taking little quick steps as she covers the ground, rather like a duck. She walks this way so as not to slip on the sticky ground. All the fowl eat out of her hand. She and John have an amazing affinity with birds and animals. You can hear them talk to them, and the birds and animals chat back. They have five old dogs. These dogs lie in a row, side by side. Whenever John or Babs pass by, you see five heads and tails wagging in unison.

The chimney on the back kitchen of the house is extraordinary. It is a big creamery can with the bottom cut out. To see the smoke coming out of this can is extremely funny. In the orchard, John has made a pond for the ducks. The water looks green, but the ducks don't seem to mind. Tied between two apple trees are hundreds of empty plastic oil containers. The oil is used in John's tractor. When empty, he hangs up each container with all the others on a line. It is a bizarre sight. On a tree in the lane leading up to the house he has nailed a goat's skull, complete with horns and painted red. Underneath he has written 'Buck Canal', by way of an address. If it wasn't for real, you'd think the art department had gone bonkers. Mike Southon says that this is the way the hippies tried to live and failed. 'It's a work of art, mate. I've never seen a place like it. And look at those hills and the valley!'

John Rudden is a ripe character with ripe language. We have a young man who is a midget, playing a 'small' part. When John sees him he says, 'Yon wee boy, he must have been made in the frost and fell out when the thaw come.' He is as singular in his descriptions of everyone else.

John Phelan, the location manager, comes along the lane and tells me that the DIY Brigade are still going on about the pig. They are determined to make an issue of it. John Rudden overhears us: 'They could be lookin' for to sue me oul sow. I'll put her in the dock. It wouldn't be the first time a pig appeared in court. Normally you'll see them sitting on the bench. I'd say they're after money, hah? Money or jealousy – what else drives us?'

John Phelan adds that some of the villagers want their houses painted back to the original colours – the colours they were before filming started. We don't finish for another three or four weeks. Why can't they wait a little longer? More pressure. I feel the length of knotted cotton sticking around my back. The pain is no worse, anyway.

I say to John Rudden, 'It was your sow. You were there. Please tell them she was only in the chapel porch.'

'When the devil's on horseback the truth's way behind in the field. They wouldn't believe me. Do you think I could get money out of them but? They're saying me sow isn't good enough to go inside the chapel. Could I sue on her behalf, hah?'

I sit in the sun and watch the filming. We're shooting a scene where Danny is having his hair combed by Prunty. Danny is going on his first date. They play the scene on the 'street' in front of the house. Then Marie Conmee as Mrs Prunty comes out and gives Danny money. Marie looks great. She's wearing cut-down wellingtons, thick stockings, a long brown dress, an old cardigan and a green beret on her head. She chuckles while she speaks and has a great knowing tone in her voice. She's perfect, except for the fact she doesn't seem to be able to remember her lines. She looks ill. Very pale. Her first line is to Danny, whose hair is wet and slick: 'They've greased you up like a gamecock.' When Marie says the line it comes out, 'You're greased up like a haycock.' On the second take she says, 'They've greased you up like a gamemonkey.' I go to her and give her the proper line and ask her if she's all right. She assures me she is. We do another take. This time she says, 'They've done you up like a prize hen.' Jesus. By now my back is killing me and my shirt button is doing a quickstep all over my chest.

I see Peter and Nigel Wooll whispering to each other. I think they are talking about Marie. Ruth Boswell joins them. Meanwhile poor Marie is sitting down inside the house. There is definitely something wrong. She looks more green than pale. Something has happened to her since the read-through in Dublin, only a few weeks ago. That day I remember distinctly how well she was and how strong and marvellous her reading was. I remember talking to her and

David Kelly, who plays the priest. She and David know each other from working together over the years. She asked David how he was doing workwise. Like all actors, David put a poor mouth on it. 'Oh you know, just pulling the divil by the tail.' She winked at me and looked at him. 'Did you ever hear such ballsology in all your life? You never stop, Kelly. Theatre, radio, television, films, the lot. Your oul mug is as well-known as Eason's clock.' Afterwards David and myself remarked on how great Marie was and never looking better. Yet here she is today, only a shadow of herself. I hear people mentioning the dreaded word 'recast'. A car drives up the lane and Marie gets into it. I want to go to her, but I can't. I haven't got the guts. I'm also too upset. Acting is a tough profession, especially when you are old and struggling. The car drives away down 'Buck Canal'.

The mobile phones are out and buzzing.

Maybe she'll be all right in the morning. She's got to be. If she can just hold it together for two or three weeks . . . The first time I met her was in Dublin when we staged Christy Brown's *Down All the Days*. Peter Sheridan adapted it and his brother Jim directed it. Marie and I were in the cast along with Vincent Smith, Garret Keogh, Hugh O'Connor, Geraldine Plunkett and a load more great performers. Christy Brown himself used come to watch us. On stage Marie swept all before her. She was larger than life. She didn't look actressy; she looked real. In the pub afterwards she'd be twice the size of life. A howl . . . I rarely met her after that. She stuck in my mind. I love people with passion.

Yet I let her get into that car and go down the lane alone . . . I'm going to pray tonight that she's going to be all right in the morning. Babs Rudden says, 'That poor woman's not right. She's hardly fit for to lift a cup a tay.'

The days are rushing past and the rushes are piling up. We watch them each evening. Albert never watches them. He's too experienced for that. The younger actors watch them.

They sit around laughing at in-jokes. It's like being back at drama school.

Day 28: Wednesday 14 September

I stood in front of my mirror this morning and looked at the string of cotton around my waist. I'm supposed to be a mature person, yet here I stand putting my faith in medieval superstition. Is there any hope for me at all? But I leave the cotton on. The production office rang to tell me that Marie Conmee has been sent home and we are looking for a replacement. We are insured, so we'll be able to reshoot the scene when we find a new actress. Marie has been driven home to Dublin. Maybe she'll never work again . . .? Sick, I sit looking out of the window at the sheep, the pheasants, the light striking the edge of the lake.

I go back up to John and Babs's. We're filming on the hills above their house. Clouds hang on the hedges and trees. The fields are full of bright-yellow ragwort on stalks of poison-green. From the hills we look right down into the farmyard. I can see Babs moving around, feeding her flocks of fowl. She goes from abandoned car to abandoned car, flinging food from a bucket into the windows. One car has droppings up to the steering wheel. The birds heads touch the roof. Pigeons flop down and crows swoop into the cars cadging food. The guinea hens chase the crows. They make a terrible screeching racket to scare them off. The guineas have lovely lines of white dots on their grey feathers. Red wattles hang down on either side of their beaks.

Matt, playing Danny, roars out in agony and sinks to his knees. He's been sitting in a jeep keeping warm and working himself up for the moment. Dusk is coming down and it's turning cold. By the third take he is emoting nicely and false tears are dripping down his cheeks. The chief make-up artist has squeezed drops into his eyes. Rosemary, the wardrobe lady, is emoting nicely too. She stands out of shot with a big blanket ready to wrap up Matt in it in between takes. You can tell she thinks Matt is awfully good and can't wait to fuss over him and tell him he's wonderful.

No one fusses over the writer. We're regarded as stoics who can take it all on the chin. 'Eh up, here comes the bloody writer. Everyone watch out.' When I was an actor I loved the wardrobe lady fussing over me. It's a perk of the job. 'You were marvellous, darling. So moving.' I notice the younger actors hardly ever speak to any of the locals. They are into fantasy and themselves, not reality. That's the great thing about Albert. He's interested in everyone. He's been around long enough to know it's important.

I see various members of the crew going to Peter Yates from time to time to suggest actresses to take over Marie's part. I sit around thinking up names myself, feeling a traitor. But if she is not well enough to do the business, why feel guilty? The show must go on.

We have a number of extras working with us. One of them tells me that Nellie Cassidy has died in hospital. I'm so glad I went to see her. She died of cancer – the 'bad lad'. I hear some of the men discussing who will get her land. Apart from a relation in Scotland, she was the last of her line. Another man tells me, proudly, he has been asked to dig her grave. When I enquire how long it will take him, he replies, 'Two hours.' I look surprised. 'Her family plot is mostly rock. Her brother Jimmy went down only two feet.' I overhear another man saying, 'I mind the time the uncle was buried. It was an ojus cold day. A thin skite of snow lay over the country.' The language here sticks up through the ordinary like the rocks in the fields.

As dark falls deeper, Babs continues to move around through the cars. Babs is about seventy. Her hair is short blonde curls. Her face is round and sweet-natured. She still looks an attractive woman. The harsh life has made little impression on her. On the outside, anyway. I don't know why

John is known as 'The Scud'. There's an expression round here: 'I'll hit you a scud.' Maybe it's something to do with that. I prefer to think that it alludes to the clouds scudding across the hills, or a ship scudding before the wind. John remains light on his feet and light in spirit and, with that twinkle in his eyes, scuds delightfully through his days.

I drive past Nellie Cassidy's house. Once the centre of so much talk, debate and action, it now stands empty in the night. The life has gone from it. I never saw a lonelier sight.

I turn into the demesne drive and crumble up to the house. The badger is caught once more in my headlights. As before, he runs before me bobbling up and down like a clockwork toy. This time I notice that as he bobs, his eyes light up into a yellow gleam as they are struck from the rear by the car beams.

There's a skite of frost on the grass.

Lying in bed I think back on the day. The most vivid image was that of David Kelly who, when he had finished his part as the priest, changed into his mufti – green corduroys, white shirt and a big, flowing cravat. I saw him step lightly from the wardrobe bus into the country road. A dainty sight, exotic as a leprechaun.

Before I left the set I spoke to the driver who took Marie Conmee to Dublin. 'Once she got into her room, I think she was relieved. You could see it. She was upset, but once she got home . . . you know.'

Day 29: Thursday 15 September

This morning I took the cotton from my back, balled it up carefully without letting it touch the ground, then burnt it. Result: I'm like a new man – if it weren't for the pain in my back. No, it feels a bit better. I'm sure it would have got better anyway. If there's something ailing you and it doesn't clear up after a few days, book the undertaker.

I called on Seamus Kelly in his shop. Seamus is old enough to have been a friend of my father's and young enough to be a friend of mine. He told me he was one of the executors of Nellie's will. Republican friends of hers had asked him if would it be all right to drape her coffin in the tricolour. 'Go ahead. Do whatever you want. It's nothing to do with me.'

Nellie was arrested on one occasion. Someone had left a revolver in her house. Though she believed passionately in a united Ireland, she understood her enemies' position and sympathized with anyone intelligent enough to give her a good argument and principled enough to believe in what they said. She could be waspish about her enemies: people she believed had no beliefs. She would neither forgive them nor even shake hands with them at a funeral. She came home from Glasgow during the war to look after her brother. Never went back. Never married. She lived right on the Border – the only artery that counts in the Irish body politic. She spent her nights reading novels. She said to me once, 'It is my fate to live my days in a spot where books are not at the top of anyone's shopping list.'

A friend who visited Nellie in hospital just before she died told me she pushed his hand away when he offered her a sip of water. 'You know the one tooth she had in her head? Her tongue was that swollen that she couldn't get it out over the tooth.' All her life she loved talking.

Today we filmed in a turf bog, shooting the scene where Prunty gets killed in a bog hole. It was an amazing scene in the bog. Normally it is a strange and private place: so ancient, barren, pure, almost sacred. But there we were with the full-frontal attack – trucks, vans, lights, special effects. We threw down sixty tons of stones on the old bog road so we could get into the place. The bog is known as Derrybeg, or the Back Island. It is right on the Border. The land of Fermanagh juts into Monaghan at such an angle that when you face south, you are looking into the North. The bog is a wilderness of heather, turf and hill. The actors had to get down into a bog hole. They were up to their necks in black, malevolent mud. Anthony Brophy had to go right under. The camera was suspended on an elasticated rope over the bog hole and fitted with a prism so that it could be lowered right down to the mud, yet film just above. There were scaffolding poles, tractors, trailers, a stand-by ambulance crew and a heated water tank and shower unit so that the actors could wash down in between takes. Rosemary was in her element running to Matt with blankets. The most marvellous sight of all was just a hundred yards from where we were, an old man and his son footing turf. They barely glanced at us. They are a tight people along the Border. They can keep emotions banked down if they want to; they can keep their curiosity in a bag. There we were with our incredible gear and action, and there was the old man bent over, his arse to the wind, arranging the turf at his feet. Looking at that unremitting image I realized there was a lot to be said for living in Camden Town.

In the middle of the madness an Ulster TV crew arrived to do an item for the evening news. The interviewer asked me how it felt to have my life filmed. I found myself eager to please and answer with the usual easy bull. I put on an agonized artistic expression then humbly hid my pain to show the great man I was and told whoever might be watching that yes, indeed, it was a strange experience. But as I looked round the turf bog with all the paraphernalia and craziness, the truth of the matter hit me right between the eyes. I couldn't recognize any of this, I was a stranger in my own country.

Later I saw a car come down the road, driving slowly, carefully. It was David Aukin from Channel Four. Only a few days before he had been in hospital for a gall-bladder operation. This visit was beyond the call of duty. The two of us walked up the hill and looked down on the British Army checkpoint on the Wattlebridge road. It's a mass of concrete and corrugated iron and state-of-the-art technology sunk deep into the land. The large observation tower has a cage of wire around the top. 'I know it's the latest thing,' David said, 'but doesn't it look as crude as a Roman fort?'

Day 30: Friday 16 September

This morning I went up to the chapel to attend Nellie's funeral. There were around a hundred people there. Fr. Browne spoke about her from the pulpit. He never once mentioned her surname – just 'Nellie'. Such is the warm intimacy of a small community. Sean MacElgunn, an old friend of Nellie's, read from the gospel and spoke the homily. Sean is an ex-priest who subsequently married. The night before the funeral he asked Fr. Browne's permission to read and speak. Thirty years before, Nellie had attended his ordination. Jimmy Cassidy had driven his parents and Nellie to the ceremony in the west of Ireland. When he eventually left the priesthood out of a crisis of conscience, he went to see Nellie and told her about his decision. The regrets, the guilt, all came spilling out. To leave the priesthood is a difficult thing to do in rural Ireland. Sean didn't do so lightly. Nellie wasn't pleased, but she accepted his decision because she knew it had been honestly taken. They remained good friends. It was a very charitable act of Fr. Browne's to let him play his part in the obsequies. Sean spoke in simple, moved terms about his old friend.

When they took the coffin out of the chapel it was draped in the green, white and orange flag. A Guard of Honour was formed by dozens of cockfighters. There was a number of Sinn Fein members among them. We followed the coffin up the path to the old cemetery and crowded around the open grave. They lowered the coffin in. When it hit the bottom we could still see the lid. It only went down three feet. Away in the distance a cold sun hit the Cavan mountains. We were all friends there. There were no relations. When the tricolour was removed by Gerry McMahon, the undertaker, it was handed to a local man who had served a prison sentence for 'an offence against the State'. An old man, thinking he was whispering, said aloud to a woman standing beside him, 'Let me grab you round the waist, Lily, for a bit of heat.' We pretended we hadn't heard. Fr. Browne carried on reading the prayers for the dead: 'We would all die. We would all rise again.' Everyone standing around that grave believed those words. The simple faith of the people is a collective phenomenon. It is indestructible. Round here, belief hasn't changed much in hundreds of years.

It is a humbling thing to stand beside a person who insists that yes, we will die, but yes, we will rise from the dead on the day of General Judgement . . . There is powerful succour in the embrace of the parish. They will help you when you're ill. They'll bury you with your friends. They will pray for you when you're gone. They'll drink to your memory in the pub. The parish is a great oak. Each parishioner is a leaf. The winter comes, but the tree is always there.

The funeral took place in the same cemetery where a few days ago we had been filming. I kept looking around for Albert and the camera. Albert is still in England burying his mother. Coming away from the graveyard a man said to me, 'I was working in Basingstoke one time. For an English ganger. His brother died. He took the half-day off for the funeral.'

'Maybe his brother was a pillock.'

'I didn't get that impression now. It was the lack of feeling struck home.'

A detective comes out of the cemetery and drives off in an unmarked police car. I hadn't noticed him in the crowd.

A woman whispered, 'Who do you think'll get Nellie's land?'

In the afternoon I was back in the turf bog where we finished off the death scene. We have been extremely lucky with the weather. Every day rain is forecast, but so far we haven't had a drop – this week, that is. The bog is a truly frightening place – black, old, alive. Yet at first glance it looks dead. I lay on a bank of heather and could feel the bank moving, feel the feet thudding into it twenty yards away. The wind whooshing above my head made a noise like tin rattling. Bog martins flew in and out of holes in the bank and about thirty yards from me a fox stood, watching, listening, sniffing the wind. It stood there for a full twenty minutes. Then it turned and ambled up the hill. The mud in the hole is Guinness black. It looks solid, but is liquid enough to drown you and hold you down for a thousand years.

I drove into Clones and met Catherine McGuigan. She helps out in a hairdressing salon. We sat in a room at the back and drank coffee, and she read me a poem she is writing in memory of her brother. One of the girls working in the salon is a first cousin of the young girl killed when she leapt off a bus. Death stalks the land . . . Catherine told me that, after her brother's death, young town thugs got a pitchfork and used it to break in the double-glazed windows of the place where he lived. They stole his video, computer . . . How deep the lack of love that can lead children to such crime.

I walked down Fermanagh Street and saw a girl I recognized from around the town. She has twin babies, but she doesn't look after them. She doesn't want to. Her mother in Armagh looks after them. This girl spends a lot of time in pubs and discos, enjoying herself. She's only twenty. She is small-built and stout. She hasn't got a good figure, but her eyes are big, brown and lovely. Something beautiful looks out at you. Her eyes are hard to resist. They ask men for help, for love and fun. But men abuse her. She abuses herself. She fights in pubs. Recently she grabbed a woman around the neck and bit her. Over a man, of course. Today when I saw her she was up an alley with a young fellow who wore jeans and a black leather jacket. She was shouting at him. He had his arms outstretched as if appealing to her, but she was turning him down. The young fellow seemed to be in her power.

As I walked quickly by them I noticed her pale face, her tubby tummy, the bright-red dress clinging to her stout bum and thighs. She's a walking disaster, but she wants to live, love and enjoy life. She has very little money. She doesn't care about her babies. She's only a baby herself. She wants to be where people are enjoying themselves. She has a thirst beyond her control. At first glance she looks as pale and quiet as a big fat mouse, but she's quick to show that she can fight like an alley cat and her beautiful brown eyes are always there behind the tears – living, hoping, trying to suck in love; trying to get warm arms around her ... She's a girl with passion.

Saturday 17 September

Day off. Last night I went to McMahon's pub. Billy Hayden and his band supplied the music – keyboard, sax, trombone, guitar, drums and a girl singer. All rock'n'roll and jazz. Billy plays sax. He is a son of Clarrie Hayden who, with his family, toured the Border villages in the forties and fifties, bringing theatre to the people. They set up a tent on the village green every summer in Redhills and brought magic into our lives. And glamour. I remember Billy's sisters. I fell in love with them every year and when they went for walks along the country roads during the day, my friend Liam McElhinney and I would walk behind them at a safe distance smelling their perfume, wishing we were linking their arms.

My film *The Playboys*, which I wrote with Kerry Crabbe, was based on such a travelling theatre group as the Hayden family. Like Winston Churchill sitting in the front row watching Richard Burton playing Hamlet, our local priest at the time, Fr. Traynor, sat in the front row of the tent each evening, reading his breviary and casting a cold eye on the stage – not for Art, but for smut and sex. TV put the travelling players off the road. Most of the actors went to Dublin or London.

Billy Hayden stayed local, married, had children, formed a band. His daughter had been singing with him last night. The pubs of Fermanagh, Cavan, Monaghan are his theatres now. In this whole region there is not one permanent professional company. You have to go to Dublin or Belfast to see a play. At odd times a tour comes to Enniskillen or Cavan town. That's it. The pub is the place you go to for live entertainment. The music roars, the chat is mighty, the pints fly down . . .

In the pub was a group of English fishermen. They come to Redhills every year and stay in a local b. & b. It was interesting seeing them in McMahon's: they looked so different and their Staffordshire accents sounded so strange. They all had moustaches. One of them, a young blond-haired chap, was as drunk as a monkey. He sat at a table, his head in his hands. He couldn't drink or talk. Eventually he lay down on a long bar seat. His mates had a video camera and recorded his abject state with great glee. I could see this one running and running in Hanley. Suddenly he jumped up, ran outside and just made it to the door before puking his guts up. He leaned against the wall, his hands up against it like he was being searched. He was a truly painful sight. I asked him if was he all right. 'I dunna want go whome tomorrow,' he answered.

It was nearly two o'clock in the morning as I got into my car. Someone rapped on my window as I was about to drive away. It was a young woman who had been drinking in the pub. She asked me if it was true that we had filmed a pig in the chapel and were we going to film a sex scene underneath the statue of the Blessed Virgin on the village green. At first I thought she was joking. She wasn't. We had put a statue of the Blessed Virgin on the green to give the picture depth, to fill the shot background. There is a pump on the green, but the art department wanted something extra. They thought of having a bench, a floral display, an old car . . . I suggested the statue. It is the symbol of purity. This is a love story and love is pure when it's true. We will not be going anywhere near the statue. It is there only for decoration. Yet the rumours are flying. Mind you, people spread rumours just to get others going. 'I have my faith and I love it and I wouldn't want anyone to make it a skit,' the girl said through the car window. Neither would I. That would be too easy. I assured her we weren't filming a sex scene under the statue – the mind boggles – and the pig hadn't been inside the chapel. She returned to the pub, satisfied.

I went home and lay in my bed, looking out at the moon skidding off the galvanized cattle sheds in the old orchard. I thought of the Miss Whyte-Venables, their ancestors, the roots they had put down in Redhills – yet they had never become part of the people. They were aloof and politically hostile to Dublin. Partition had left them stranded on the wrong side of the Border. Were they loved? Isn't that the only test? Maybe not. The lonely person, the stoic – there's a lot to be said for them. They're not continually swamping around in pulpy emotions.

I got up this morning and spent all day doing rewrites. It's akin to time in Purgatory: not as bad as Hell and a hope of Heaven to come, but bloody painful while it lasts.

In the evening I went to Shamie Connolly's. Cissie was out at bingo. The two of us sat drinking potheen. Looking into the open fire, we fought old football battles, old history.

'Pub republicans who send young ones out to die but won't go themselves sicken my craw. Is a country worth the spillin' of one drop of blood? Answer me that.'

'We kill foxes, badgers. Why not ourselves?'

'Now don't be talkin' arse-nonsense.'

Later, in silence, we watched the dying flames.

'Man dear,' Shamie said, 'time is getting short.'

'Watching Nellie's coffin going into the ground, I thought of my own end.'

'Were you afraid?'

'I wasn't. I was.'

'Why would you be? Buried with your own people in the clay and rock that grew you.'

We are an amazing people. Contrary, argumentative, witty, generous, mean, simple, profound. On the one hand, that girl in the pub asks me about the pig and the statue – no change there, you'd think. On the other, Fr. Browne lets a married ex-priest preach the gospel. This is real Christian charity: the act of a man with an understanding heart. We have a ceasefire. We are supposed to use it to inch forward from entrenched positions. It is satisfyingly ironic that at a Republican funeral Fr. Browne took the first step. I heard a man say he should never have taken such a step.

'Do you want us to stay bogged down in medieval mud for ever?' I asked him.

'No, I suppose you're right there.'

Day 31: Sunday 18 September

We're out at Lough Oughter shooting a complicated scene involving soldiers, actors and a helicopter. The lough is on the Erne River and is quite stunning. It is surrounded by low hills and trees, with not a single house overlooking. We are on the bank of a narrow passageway of swiftly flowing water connecting two great expanses of lake. About fifty yards from the shore is a crannog – a man-made island from the eleventh century. On this crannog is a stone tower with a chunk missing. It is all that remains of what was the stronghold of the O'Reilly Chieftains. It fell to the Cromwellians in 1653.

Swallows skim the surface, fish jump and plop. The clouds are low and just as we are about to send the helicopter up, down comes the rain. The helicopter costs £400 per hour when in flight. It was flown over from England and is piloted by an American who flew in Vietnam. The rain is a thick grey knit of misery. The helicopter cannot go up. We have to abandon the shots. The crew sit round under big green umbrellas. Some sit under bushes. Everyone peeps out at the gloomy scene. The lake water, as the rain hits into it, looks as if it's being plucked.

I sit in the catering bus. Mary Lou and Anne, who cook the food cheerfully, get on with it as usual. Their faces are always flushed and smeared in perspiration. Brendan Croasdell, a jockey-sized Dubliner, helps them. He makes the tea, keeps the bus clean. Rain whacks into the bus windows. 'What can you do?' Brendan says. 'Two things it's not worth wasting your breath on – politicians and the weather.'

Tony Devlin comes on to the bus and grabs a hunk of bread and cheese. He looks out at the rain. 'Hate tha'. I don't mind kissin', but hate tha'. It's the curse of McCracken, that's what it is.' He goes off into the rain, the rain weeping from his oilskins. Some of the crew complain that no one has organized a television set. The All Ireland Football Final is on today: Down versus Dublin.

I drive into Cavan town to buy a newspaper. The man in the shop tells me he has read my novel, *A Border Station*.

'What was your father like to live with?' he asks me.

'Why do you want to know?'

'Well, my oul fellah sometimes would go for three weeks and not speak one word to a soul. Living then was like being in solitary confinement. How did we cope? Don't ask me.'

'I won't.'

'Go on. What sort of man was he, yours?'

'He went to America in 1980 to visit my sister and his own sisters. On the Sunday they went to mass. The plate came round and my father put a note on it. My sister saw that the note was $100. She knew this must have been a mistake. He wasn't renowned for flashing money above the average. She drew his attention to the plate and his $100 bill. It *was* a mistake. He thought he'd put down $10. Too late. The plate had gone along another pew. Now for you, me and most others, that would have been the end. Not my father. After mass he went round to the sacristy and asked the surprised priest for his money back. The priest looked into those steely blue eyes and, like many's the one before him, wilted. The priest looked through the collection and, sure enough, there was the $100 bill. My father put it back into his wallet and left $10 on the plate. That was the kind of man he was. Just because he was in New York, he wouldn't give in to embarrassment or sham etiquette. He thanked the priest for a lovely mass and went on his way. At that moment he was the happiest man in America.'

'Ah now that's a good one. A real Cavan man, hah?'

'He was Galway, actually.'

'Do you know how copper wire was invented?'

'No.'

'Two Cavan men fighting over a penny.'

'Forgive me if I don't laugh. I heard it before. In truth, Cavan people are too generous for their own good. They're letting the world and his wife buy up the county – lock, stock and barrel.'

'You're exaggerating'.

'I know. But it's an exaggerated kind of a day.'

I went home and watched the match on television. Over the demesne the rain still pelted down. Crows flew into a diseased elm. It's spooky, bare branches look like something out of a fairy story. The spot where the witch lives. The crows swoop up and down and then land in the field. They peck at the ground and eventually fly deeper into the wood.

Driving back to the film set I could smell the slurry spread on the land. Every so often the pig breeders have to get rid of thousands of gallons of pig slurry. Certain farmers allow them to spread it on their land. It's supposed to be good for it. I always think that as well as the grass the weeds grow thicker on slurried fields. And the smell is sickening for days after it's been sprayed on. Some of it also seeps into the rivers and lakes. It kills off the plankton, fish die – no fish, no tourists. It's a golden county, Cavan. But somehow we always try our best to kill the golden goose.

At Lough Oughter when Peter sees me coming he booms out, 'And where have you been?'

'I've been depressed. This bloody rain,' I reply.

He looks at me, concerned, then smiles. 'Depressed? Why? We've got something in the can. We don't come to these parts expecting day after boring day of ninety degrees Centigrade. This isn't California, thank God. Cheer up. After the rushes this evening let's crack open a nice bottle of vino.'

'Yeah?' I say. 'I was just thinking ... All the talent we've got – the actors, the great crew, the equipment, the bloody helicopter, the scenery, the money – and it's all no guarantee of success. Isn't that a bitch?'

Peter laughs. 'Oh dear, we are in the dumps. Not knowing is what makes life exciting. And by the way, I've offered Mrs Prunty's part to that actress you met.'

The last day we were in the turf bog an actress came over from England to be interviewed by Peter. Later he told me she was in his caravan and asked if I would go and see what I thought. Her name is Carol Nimmons. She's much younger than Marie Conmee and has a very posh South Kensington accent. She sat in the caravan looking warily at the dismal scene but, like all actors, eager to please. She told me she came originally from Co. Down and that she had a good ear for accents. I suppose when she went to England she had to decide whether she was going to be an Irish actress, or adapt and pretend to be English. She certainly didn't strike me as ideal for a Cavan farm woman, a Babs Rudden character. I listened to her reading the dialogue. She had a good go at it and a naughty chuckle in her voice. Her eyes were full of hope, as in: 'I hope I'm going to get the part.' It amazed me that we couldn't find someone in Belfast or Dublin. But that's actors: always out of work until you go looking for them. I told Peter I liked her. Now she's hired. At least that emergency is over.

Someone shouts, 'It's a wrap.'

'What's this film costing, Peter?'

'Five and a half million. Dollars. Peanuts, dear boy.'

I think of my father and his $100. I wonder if the Americans will ask for any of it back.

On my way to view the rushes I go into the Leggykelly Inn. Some of the local boys are watching the football highlights on television. One of them is Brian Traynor. He wears a baseball cap and has a voice like a fog horn. He works for various farmers. 'I work hard. Therefore I drink hard.' He told me that he had to be up next morning at 6 a.m. to go to Navan for a load of oaten straw. The big farms in Meath grow the stuff. No cereal is grown in Cavan. 'All day you sweat and ache. I love a drink. A bet. I'll lay odds on who'll win the All Ireland. Any takers? Come on. Come on.' His voice full of hope and humour roars around the bar.

I say, 'But we know who won the final. It was played today, Brian.'

'I'm talkin' about next year, yah bollix.'

Day 32: Monday 19 September

The helicopter swoops down over Lough Oughter, beating the surface, slapping the trees to bits. It hovers above the shore, minces the water, turns it into smokey circles. Then away with it buzzing down the lough, curving out over the hills. At least the rain has held off, though the sky is as dull as pewter.

On the catering bus I sit with Anthony Brophy, who is hanging around waiting to do a scene. 'In the bar the other night,' he says, 'one of the English guys ordered drinks. Says to me, "You're Irish, Anthony, you'll have a whiskey." Jesus, man! I could have said, "You're English, you'll have a cup of tea and a cucumber sandwich."'

'You should have said, "Sure, I'll have a triple, thanks."' I reply. 'He wouldn't say it again.'

'When you did *The Playboys*, did it make money?' Anthony asks.

'I don't think it lost any.'

'Tell us.'

'Bit early in the morning for this, isn't it?'

'Go on. We got time to kill.'

'It'll kill anyway. OK. The headline in *Variety* when it opened in America was "Crits Flip for Goldwyn Pix." We got nineteen great reviews out of twenty-one. Myself and Kerry were in Santa Monica for the opening. Afterwards they drove us in limousines to a big bash. Drove us fifty yards. "Why the hell didn't we walk?" I asked them. "This isn't London, man. You could walk in London and maybe arrive without your clothes. Here if you walked at night, your clothes might arrive, but your body would be missing." Anyway, then the LA riots break out. America shuts down and tunes into CNN twenty-four hours a day. The first major day of the riots I had a meeting with the producer, Laura Shuler Donner, at Warner Bros. Studios, about writing a script based on Emiliano Zapata. When I got to her office the staff were going crazy with fear. They were all running around watching the riots on the TV monitors. "Shit, man, they're coming up Fairfax. I got to go and protect my property." Another one of them would run out. Gary Ross, the writer who wrote *Big*, kept shouting, "Don't get on the box car!" This had something to do with Auschwitz. Get out of town, quick. He did. Soon I was the only one left sitting with Laura. "My staff come first," she said. Fair enough. Then her girl brought us in lunch. Laura sits there eating chips and a salad. She's a thin lady. There's more meat on a butcher's apron. The door opens and in comes Dick "Lethal Weapon" Donner, her husband. LA is burning, but all he can see is his wife eating chips. "Honey," he said horrified, "you promised you would not eat any more french fries." In the heel of the hunt Kerry and I were curfewed in our hotel. Made it to Hollywood and weren't allowed out. It was kinda like a Belfast with swimming pools.'

'What happened to Zapata?'

'He was trapped by government forces in the end and shot.'

'No. The film they wanted you to write.'

'Did a few drafts. Never heard another word.'

'Jesus, man. How do you think this'll go?'

'If there're no riots, earthquakes, fires, floods, war, plague, monetary collapse, we're in with a chance.'

'Jesus, man. It's slightly easier in fringe theatre.'

Anthony is great value as a person, as an actor. He's fresh, and works and worries in a relaxed kind of way all the time. And he's always game for a laugh.

'Is there anything I'm doing you're not happy with? Tell me, man, is there?'

'No, it's great what you're doing. Besides, I'm afraid of saying anything. I'm in enough trouble giving line readings as it is.'

I walk up a steep hill. Everywhere you look is water – lakes, rivers. In the distance the mountains appear blue, nearby Bruce Hill dark. Then it begins to drizzle. Everywhere disappears in the grey knitting. There isn't a puff of wind. The drizzle dances straight down. It hops and jigs on to your face and clothes, soaks you without you noticing. On the drive back to Redhills on the back of every signpost are Sinn Fein posters: 'Seize the opportunity for peace.' I come to a halt beside one of these signposts. A farmer comes towards me with a herd of cows. Just for the hell of it I let my window down and say hello.

'Well,' I say to him, 'are you seizing the opportunity for peace?'

He looks very cross. 'They blow the place to bits for twenty-five years and now they're talking peace? Don't make me laugh.'

'I hope you don't mind me asking . . . Are you Catholic or Protestant?'

He looked even crosser. Very gruffly he said, 'You've got a cheek asking.'

'I'm a cheeky kind of fellow. Sometimes.'

''Bout time you learnt manners. Learn manners.'

He walked away angrily from my car and with a thwack planted his stick on the back of a bullock. Probably not the first political beating the poor animal received.

I met Michael Reilly in the village. He told me that someone in Birmingham had phoned home to say they heard something about a pig running around in the chapel. The DIYs are spreading the rumours themselves, trying to whip up rancour. I really am amazed. They are insisting I ask Mark Huffam, the production manager, to allow them to see a video of the pig scene. They don't need to see the actual film, a video will satisfy them. Mark worked on *The Playboys* and is very popular locally. He's from an utterly Protestant, Unionist background in Antrim. That he is being asked to become arbiter in this peculiar Catholic madness is enough to make a cat laugh. The DIYs are determined to give us a good bite. Someone wants to take a chunk out of me, anyway. In fact it's not about religion at all. It's about humour and a lack of humour. You grab an incident, turn it into an issue, work and worry people about it, make a name for yourself. What can they do? Just weather the storm for a few more weeks and then . . . I don't even want to know their names. I've deliberately never asked Michael who they are.

Later I meet Mark. He sweeps into the village in his Range Rover.

'If we showed them a video, do you think that would satisfy them?'

'No.' I reply.

'There's your answer. The vast majority of the people are on our side. I can tell you're worried. Forget it.'

The DIYs are in full cry, but it's a drag hunt. There'll be no prey at the end of it. It's the fact that it was a pig. If it had been a dog or a cat, a horse even, no one would have said 'Boo'. A pig is a funny animal. Or not. Unloved, except when served crispy between two slices of bread. It's a funny business, the blessing of animals and things. Aer Lingus have their planes blessed. Ships are still blessed. I once saw a woman having a clutch of hens' eggs blessed. She was hoping for chickens.

Day 33: Tuesday 20 September

At a road junction just outside the town of Belturbet, the art department have erected a British Army checkpoint: green corrugated sheets, watchtower, 'sleeping policemen', road signs, warning lights, army and police jeeps – the lot. Very impressive. All the traffic on the busy road is fooled by it. Drivers look out and wonder whether they have gone astray or if the British have moved South. Our ADs and a local Garda wave them on or stop them when we are filming.

In a field off the road the helicopter is on stand-by, waiting for a break in the clouds. We need a panoramic view of the countryside as the film's final image. We tried to get it this morning, but the pilot was forced down by the low, dark clouds. Suddenly the clouds clear and the sun comes out. Peter, Mike Southon and Phil the camera operator drop what they're doing and run for the helicopter. In seconds they are soaring up into the shiny air. Later they return very pleased. They got what they needed – an endless tapestry of fields and hills, the wet grass gleaming.

We break for lunch. Mary Lou and Anne in their mobile kitchen have organized a four-course lunch for 100 people. Their wagon is parked along the Belturbet–Enniskillen road. No fuss from these women. Job done. Enjoy.

Using our checkpoint we shoot the scene where the boy meets the girl after she has told him she is pregnant. Matt as Danny watches her coming through the checkpoint on her bicycle. He stands waiting for her to get to him, his hands in his pockets. Not the most dynamic picture. I mention it to Peter. At a politic moment I see him whisper to Matt. Matt takes his hands from his pockets and looks a bit livelier. Another minor triumph. Maybe actors are deliberately recalcitrant in creating mood, which gives the real moment, when it comes, an edge. Maybe his hands were cold . . .

We are beside a place called Stag Hall, near the Catholic church. A local woman tells us that the church was built in 1846. The parishioners are going to celebrate the 150th anniversary in 1996. How, I wonder, did the Catholic Church build a big stone edifice in the middle of the Great Famine? Who paid for it? Was it a relief scheme?

Under the road runs the remains of the narrow-gauge railway from Leitrim to Belturbet. Leaning on the parapet of the bridge I look down on the narrow track. In the twenties and thirties my father journeyed along here on his way to Dublin from Drumshambo, Carrick-on-Shannon and Ballaghaderreen. He was stationed in those places when he first joined the Garda Siochana after the Civil War. I remember him talking about the narrow gauge. He gave it a romantic ring. 'Aha, me boyo, we'd be tucked up under a blanket on the hard seats and outside, the snow thick on the windows. The narrow gauge – it was like a big toy.' Looking down on the entrance arch of the bridge I could believe it. So narrow you couldn't imagine anything other than a toy getting through.

When he journeyed along here, just under where I stand, he was much younger then than I am now. I imagine him looking out of the window, looking up at me – tall, thin, dark-haired, blue-eyed, strong, glowing with handsome hope. Cattle walk the track now. I can see my face/his face reflected in a puddle. Even my perspiration smells the same . . . In my mind I hear the whistle of the train, the rattle of the wheels, the smoke billowing along the carriages as they go under the bridge and my father looking out at the snowy land, hoping in his heart for love and maybe even fame. Love he found eventually when he found Lizzie Moylett, my mother. O lucky man.

At our checkpoint lots of people sit around waiting for

action. Ruth sits on a chair chatting to various people. She calls me over. Someone asks me if I have read the article in the *Guardian* about Protestant families South of the Border having to flee North because of the IRA murdering them and seizing their land. For some reason I explode.

'Yes, I believe every word of it. The IRA and the Catholics are the cause of the whole trouble. We are to blame for the last thousand years of history. You British are so good and civilized that butter wouldn't melt in your mouths. It has nothing whatever to do with you lot. You wouldn't know anything about seizing land. The only thing you lovely darlings have ever done is gone about the world bringing cricket, tea and cucumber sandwiches. Give me a fucking break.'

I stalk off and sit panting in a hedge. I hear various English voices say, 'What's up with old Shane?' Why didn't I keep my big mouth shut? It's bad manners to insult guests in one's own country. Oh hell. I feel all weedy now and apologetic.

Rain. 'It's a wrap.' We've lost half a day.

Night. I watch the rushes. The swimming scene. Brophy gets into the freezing lake bollock-naked. Vicki and Matt appear as if they've just emerged. They haven't. They are wrapped in towels pretending to dry themselves. Then Matt removes his towel. He looks like Tarzan. Like he's just spent the morning pumping iron. Probably has. I mention Matt's mature physique to Peter. 'Great,' he says. 'It'll look marvellous on the poster.'

In the turf-bog scene I notice Matt and Vicki are wearing gloves. How did I miss this when we were shooting? There they are up on the screen in gloves. I have never in all my life seen anyone in a turf bog in gloves. The turf, when you are cutting it, is soft, sensuous. You love to feel it. Someone tells me they decided on gloves because in the following scene the two of them are making love. The audience might be put off by seeing dirt under their fingernails as they maul each other. Couldn't they have washed their hands? I sing dumb on this one. It's too late now, anyway. I can't go round all day with steam coming out of my ears.

As I'm leaving, Peter tells me that in the final scene between father and son, Albert wants to embrace the boy only once. The way I've written it is that the father embraces him, but the boy rejects this easy attempt at indulgence. The father is hurt. But later, when the boy understands more, the two of them embrace, completing their emotional journey. I think this is right dramatically and far stronger. We are to meet in Albert's caravan at lunch tomorrow to discuss it. Albert has returned from burying his mother.

On the way home go into McMahon's for a drink. Gerry serves me. He tells me he's just seen a Protestant man whose wife has died. The man came to Gerry and tearfully told him that fellow Protestants wouldn't allow him to have Gerry as the undertaker. The job had to go to a Protestant firm in Lisnaskea. Gerry and his father before him had always buried the deceased members of the man's family. This was why he was upset. 'I'm sorry, Gerry,' he said, 'they wouldn't allow me.'

'Is this gospel, Gerry?' I ask.

'That I may drop dead. They're not all like that. I buried Johnny Roberts and he was the local Orange leader, as you well know. Johnny was a friend of my father's. I think what's happened is that the Ceasefire has put everyone back in their trenches for a while. People are going to go back into themselves until they see the way the wind's blowing.'

'On the surface, politics has changed. Underneath, though, things have gotten harder.'

'That's right. On all sides people have been shot, murdered. Now that it's stopped, your first reaction is going to be bitter. We're in for a bitter time. But things will change. Eventually.'

'Folk love being bitter. It's all they've got to live on.'

'What are you having? To drink.'

'Think I'll have a pint of bitter, Gerry.'

'The British planted the North. Rooted out the natives, took

139

the land, and called it democracy. It stunk like South Africa.'

'London planted land. Rome planted minds. I don't know how we're sane at all. Assuming we are.'

'How do you find the bitter?'

'It's . . . bitter. *Slainte*.'

'Good health. Where are you tomorrow?'

'Back up at John and Babs Rudden's. Can't wait.'

Day 34: Wednesday 21 September

The geese, the ducks, the hens, the guineas, the mewing peacocks, the doves, the cats, the cows, the goats, the blessed pig, the dogs, and John and Babs are waiting for us first thing in the morning. And above us all is a clear blue sky and a rising sun.

Carol, the actress who has taken over from Marie Conmee, is doing her bit as Mrs Prunty. A whole day's work has to be reshot. The insurance company is paying for it all. The first thing Carol has to do is feed the ducks. She's in her Mrs Prunty clobber and carries a bucket of feed. She's standing in a net-wire pen beside an old car. She has to open the car door and entice the ducks out with the feed. The ducks won't come out for her.

'How do you talk to ducks?' she asks.

'Chuck-chuck-chuck' for hens. 'Beep-beep-beep' for turkeys. But I can't remember what you say to ducks. I go over to Babs. She comes across to the pen, taking her rapid short steps over the sticky ground.

'Weet-weet-weet-weet-weet-weet-weet. That's how you call ducks. I call that one Darlin'.' When Babs walks away the ducks look after her and complain. 'Quack-quack come back, Babs. Only like you, don't like this one, quack-quack.'

Carol tries again, but instead of hopping out of the car the ducks go further into it. It's too nerve-wracking. For me anyway.

140

One of the extras today is Ollie McKiernan. He's a big, smiling, gentle man, in a cap, donkey jacket and wellingtons. He was one of the men who dug Nellie's grave. 'We dug in the wrong place first. We dug over the part where Jimmy's buried. We come down on top of him. Nellie said the left of the plot as you face the headstone. But she forgot. We dug on the right and got three foot. Don graveyard is pure rock. One time I mind a grave and the top of the coffin was level with the ground. They had to build the earth in a big mound over it.' I ask him about the political situation and the chances for permanent peace. He's very easy-going about it all. 'Oh, it'll happen. When you're sick of something you'll vomit it out eventually.'

The girls in the film crew are talking about last night's rushes. They argue whether Matt looks great or ridiculous.

I say, 'Far from looking a shy innocent, he looks like he could bull six women agin a hill.'

'And can I be one of them?' Dee, the hairdresser, chips in. We all have a laugh. She's probably right. Audiences will love him. And he is very good.

After lunch I have the meeting with Peter and Albert. Albert looks tired after the emotional strain of the funeral and all the travelling, but he's raring to go. I state my case.

'The father hands him the £100 he took from him previously. Right? He thinks money can buy an emotional response. He embraces the boy, right? But the boy won't lift his arms to embrace him back. Then another character interrupts the moment. Briefly, right? The father is hurt. But right at the end the boy does embrace his father. This has more emotional power for the audience. I'm convinced of it.'

'I disagree. Two is too many. It needs only the one. From where I'm standing. What do you think, Peter?'

Peter says he'll try it both ways. He says my way will be hard to shoot.

'I don't know what you've got in your mind, Peter, but I don't see it. Why should it be hard to shoot?'

'When we get to it we'll see. We'll decide then.'

It wasn't too painful in the circumstances. Maybe Albert's right. If he can't feel it, what's the point him doing it my way?

After lunch we shoot the scene where Prunty does the boy's hair – the scene that poor Marie couldn't fully cope with. Someone told me at lunch that she is in hospital in Dublin, but no one seems to know what's the matter. Nigel Wooll has sent her flowers on behalf of us all. From my point of view this is a nice gesture, but an easy one. I should get into my car and go to see her. But I'm not going to do it. All the time we've been here I haven't budged from Redhills and the surrounding area. I'm too caught up in it to move further afield. In front of the back door to Babs' house Matt sits while Anthony wets and combs his hair. Carol comes out to them with the money. The place is awash with crew, lights, wires, trucks . . . Completely unphased by it all, three white turkeys sit down behind the actors. A white goat stands a few yards away watching. Seven dogs lie sleeping. A cat, with dainty steps, picks her way across the 'street'. White doves perch on the guttering just above the actors' heads. Smoke comes out of the big creamery can on the chimney stack. The turkeys are a hoot. They spread their wings, leave them sloping out and down, then sit tentatively on the ground. Ruffling their feathers they cover their legs as much as possible, then close in their wings a little. They sit there in the sun, their wings still spread open.

We move to the hill overlooking John and Babs. Albert and I sit in a hedge chatting about theatre. We have a grand old time expatiating on the uselessness of academics when it comes to getting the great plays off the page and on to the stage. He tells me about the time he was performing Hamlet at the National for Peter Hall. A friend of Albert's had suggested that when Hamlet hears someone behind the arras in Act III, Scene iv, instead of one stab through the cloth he should slash and stab at it like mad. If he was in a saloon bar in the Wild West and he was having trouble with an enemy, and he heard someone behind a curtain, he'd empty his six-gun into it. Hamlet should act the same way. Albert thought it was a great idea. Peter Hall turned to his resident academic and asked his opinion. 'No,' spoke this august personage, 'I don't think so. Hamlet is trying to get his camel through the eye of a needle. He is on a one-track voyage. He would stab the arras only once.' 'His camel through the eye of a needle? Bloody hell, I never knew that that was what the play's about.' There are ideas men and actors men. You're lucky when you meet a director with brains and the ability to draw on actors' instincts.

Tonight the moon is yellow and full and rising slowly up the sky like an old drunk climbing a hill. A wisp of hanging cloud gives it a beardy look. I walked home out the long laneway from John and Babs's. In the mercury moonlight I picked blackberries – plainly visible, ripe, cold and lovely. Over the boggy fields the mist balanced on reeds, rushes, ragwort and hedge. I wouldn't swap that lane for paradise. Last night, anyway.

Day 35: Thursday 22 September

This morning the mist was still there. Driving out on the Cootehill road to the Protestant church, the cobweb-covered hedge was full of it. For a mile along the road the hedge was strung thorn-to-thorn with gossamer trampolines and circus shapes. It dazzled the eyes. The morning light was trapped like diamonds in a window. The secret world must be full of spiders.

We filmed in an old shed and farmyard. The special-effects boys blew up the shed and produced a great fire. We had the Cavan Fire Brigade, the Army, the Ambulance Service, loads of extras, taking part in the fun. And all day the sun shone high and hot. I played the part of the doctor. No lines – £40 for the day. Had great gas with Albert ad-libbing. Every time he saw me coming he'd say to the extras, 'Watch out, here comes Dr Death. One touch of his stethoscope and you end up in the morgue.' Two of the extras had to play SAS men. I had to pronounce them dead. 'Definitely dead before my arrival. Pity. They could have been part of my statistics had I gotten to them first.' All of this out of earshot, of course. I love it when acting goes anarchic. The laughter is a great release.

One of the soldiers asked me about writing. 'I wish I was a dreamer like you,' he said. I was well-pleased at this remark. Sums it up.

Vicki Smurfit came to me at one point, very bright and cheery, and asked me if her performance was all right and to tell her when it wasn't ... Surprised me, this. Never came before. Anyway, it is Peter's job, not mine, to gauge their performances. But I tell Vicki, sure, it's great what she's doing. What else could I say? Mind you, she is getting better all the time, gaining in confidence and energy. I think she's going to be good. Today Matt seems to be in a mood. Glum. He's probably fed up and homesick.

Near by is the Protestant church. It is a small rural gem kept spick and span, and lit at night with a floodlight. It has a beautiful stained-glass window by Evie Hone depicting the sower going out to sow some seed. This was paid for by the Whyte-Venables family. So too was the pulpit. On the walls are various memorial plaques to the last males of the Whytes and the Venables, and the two combined. One plaque commemorates 'Two lamented sons', a John Boyle White and a James Whyte, 'Erected in 1831 by Eliza, wife of Francis Whyte. Sole representative of those two most ancient families. Whyte of Tuddington. White of De Albaville.'

Robert Sturgeon, a church elder, owns the old rectory. It stands at the end of a drive in lovely grounds, surrounded by mature trees. Flowers grow around the front and the house itself is painted white. It looks in fine order. Standing under a chestnut tree, Robert and I discuss the Ceasefire. We approach it from oblique angles. He knows I'm Catholic. I know he's Protestant. We ask careful questions of each other. What was it all for – the Troubles? In a strange, brutal way for justice? To end a corrupt system of government? To kill Protestants? Was it worth it? Did it really have to happen? Are people mad, or are they driven mad by intolerant politics? Will things change? We knew we didn't have the answers but, standing in the shade of the tree, it was good asking the questions. Maybe we have the answers, deep down, but won't face them yet.

I sat with Shamie Connolly by his open fire when night came. He had me in stitches with his stories and language. 'Oh, now, she gave me some tellavatin'.' 'The big-bellied fecker tried to kick me up the immaculars. Go way out a that before I bate you with the flat of me cap. At the wind up I hit him a cementer and the last I saw of him was sailing into the middle of the following week.' Connolly could raise a row among a bunch of Trappist monks. He does it for sheer divilment. And to pass the time. He has a rare ability to walk into a crowd of complete strangers and have steam coming out of their ears within seconds. He has no fear whatsoever of saying what is in his head. And to shout it aloud. It's very hard to get the better of him.

One year Connolly and I went to the Ulster Football Finals to see Cavan play in the Minor match. Cavan were one of the great teams, but since 1969 they haven't won a thing. Yet the support is still fanatical. So when the under-eighteens managed to get to the provincial final, the legions of the damned turned up in their thousands – me and Connolly among them. In our seats we were surrounded by supporters of the two teams appearing in the Senior final. Within minutes Cavan were getting a severe drubbing. There was one young chap playing for them who had red hair. Shamie decided that he was responsible for the débâcle. 'Holy God, where did they find him? Marshmallow fingers. He couldn't catch the bus, never mind the ball.

There's more football in me oul Grannie. And she's been dead a century. Take him off to hell outa that before we're disgraced entirely.' Soon he had everyone around laughing and amazed at his full-frontal attack. Half-time came and went and when the teams came back out on to the field the lad with red hair was still there. Connolly exploded in exasperation. 'Ah, sweet Mother of Moses, no. Surely to God there must be someone better on the subs' bench? If this is all we have in the county, Cavan football will never rise again. Who, in the name of Jazus, is he anyway? Does anyone know?' Sitting right in front of us was a dark-haired man with a young boy beside him. All through Connolly's tirade this man had kept a dignified silence, but now he turned round and said, very quietly, 'I know who he is. He happens to be my eldest son.'

An absolute silence fell over us all. But Connolly wasn't beaten to shame. Immediately and utterly deadpan he replied, 'Well you ought to be proud of him. He's playing a blinder.' All the Ulster fans surrounding us gave him a round of applause and even the father of the lad on the pitch had the good grace to laugh. For the rest of the game Shamie, at strategic moments, praised the player. 'He's not a bad gauson at all now, give him a chance.' Afterwards he told me he felt bad because the young boy in front of us must have been the player's brother. 'Can you imagine what that wee boy must have felt listening to an eejit like me attacking his big brother, who must be a hero to him? Ah now, I could have bitten me tongue off.'

Staring into the open fire, the turfy flames prancing, a shot of potheen in hand, Shamie in full spate, I weep inside that one day that fire will go out for ever.

But not today, not today.

Day 36: Friday 23 September

Back at Stag Hall and our checkpoint. The actors are getting ready to be 'shot'. Matt, the American, is walking up and down the road in a mood, not talking to anyone, in a complete strop. He's working himself up for the scene. It's interesting watching the different approaches. Anthony Brophy gets into character full of good cheer for the world. He's concerned, but determined to enjoy himself. He has to 'feel' the part and if the feeling is right, the part will look after itself. Vicki skips on to the set, does the scene and skips out again. Matt growls about or sits alone. Albert has the experience, feeling and technique to make any moment work. You see him mapping the ground out before he puts a foot forward. Then when he does, he knows he's on solid ground and can pull any emotion or thought out of the air. Yesterday I mentioned Laurence Olivier to him and how he had inherited the mantle of greatness first worn by Burbage. We talked about Olivier's strange, almost affected tone – the last remnant of the old days when actors, according to Albert, sang Shakespeare.

'It's all rubbish now. The modern world doesn't need all that handing-on-the-sword stuff.'

'You were supposed to pick up the sword from Larry. Why didn't you, Albert?'

He looked around at the fields, the cows, the hedges, the ragwort drumlins, the mud. 'Because people ask me to do films in strange places like this.'

There's a Garda with us today directing the traffic. From Kerry he told me he had been stationed along the Border for the last twenty years. 'Ten years of that I was in Clones. Strange place, that. The people are different. That's my opinion. Yours is different. You'd go into a pub for a drink and they'd know you were a policeman. And they'd bang their glasses on the bar until you left. Politics, you see.' Along the Border, feelings are hidden only when they have to be.

In the afternoon we moved back to Redhills and up to the chapel. At the bottom of the brae is the house where Mrs Fay and her husband Bill lived. Mrs Smith and her family live there now. We have rented her front room for the afternoon to do a scene with Albert and a woman dancing. While waiting for everything to be set up, we sat in the garden in the brilliant sunshine. Albert discussed with me an up-coming scene where the father waltzes with his son. In a cruel, lonely, desperate gesture, the father grabs the boy and forces him to dance. To demonstrate what he intended to do, Albert grabbed me and, in his pinioning embrace, forced me to do a crude dance over the garden lawn. In this brutal embrace I was helpless. His eyes tore into me as he demonstrated his intentions for the scene. It was like being gripped by a force of nature. The scene I based on a moment when my father showed me how to do the old-time waltz. He did it out of the usual rag-bag of mixed emotions between fathers and sons. Albert, in his hunt for the truth of that moment, came up with a real whiff of the past. Very uncomfortable. For me. For him, the utter honesty of an artist seeking his path. Just a little way off I saw my daughter Tara watching us and laughing at my discomfort. She knew what was going on in my head. An odd moment. And right outside my old school. In my old teacher's garden.

When Albert released me I retreated to a safe distance. I saw the present-day teacher, Fiacra Moore, coming out of the school and over to where I sat. He asked me if I would come in and talk to the children. He knew I had been unhappy as a school kid and this was his way of wiping the past out, the slate clean. I agreed to go in, but first of all went off to my car to comb my hair and spruce myself up. Then I entered St Brigid's feeling very nervous walking over the old red tiles. Once in the classroom the children calmed me down. There they sat in rows, all dressed up in neat blue uniforms and all smiling. They stood up and in one voice greeted me in Gaelic. Boys and girls all dazzled me with smiles and giggled at me like we were old friends. Like I was one of them. Which I hope I am.

They asked me questions about making films and an eleven-year-old girl asked me about placing the camera. I saw on Fiacra's desk a brief history of film-making and a reference to *Battleship Potemkin* ... *Citizen Kane* ... What a massive change from my suffering days. Days caked with fear and loathing. One boy was completely taken up with bungee-jumping and how we filmed it. He had hilarious theories about it. 'If you were doing a bungee-jump and you had a big meal of food on you that could make your head so heavy, you could crash into the ground and that would give you some headache, I'm telling you. Isn't that true? Can't that happen?' I agreed it could. 'What would happen if you jumped out of a helicopter and the propellers cut your parachute string, but you crashed into a tree, but underneath was a load of turkey feathers, but not that many. You'd still hurt your head, wouldn't you?' 'It's best not to get up in a helicopter unless you can keep one foot on the ground,' I answered. He seemed happy with this.

At the end of my visit one of the children stood up and, in a formal manner, said, 'In honour of your visit, could you please ask Master Moore could we not be given homework this weekend?'

'It would displease me greatly if Master Moore gave you anything even resembling homework this weekend.'

At this they all cheered. I was with them, the years fallen away, my heart beating with theirs, my face as innocent, my voice ringing round the room. Then one of the children said, 'Do you know Master Moore got married in the summer?' At this they all cheered. Coming away I knew things had changed. And for the better.

Back on the film set John Phelan handed me a mobile phone and I found myself speaking to the BBC in Belfast. They wanted me to appear on a chat show that night and were sending a limo to pick me up. At five o'clock I was in the limo and on my way. The car was black and the chauffeur wore a dark suit. All along the way people looked at us with a wary eye. They thought we were undertakers. I convinced myself that the chauffeur was a Protestant. He had an aloof, cold manner even when he was chatting freely. Definitely a Prod. As it turned out, I was wrong. He was simply skilled at hiding his origins. Like people of all persuasions, he had to box clever to live during the Troubles. He told me he'd had a drink with the Shankill Butchers. They thought his name was Johnston. I was ashamed of my wrong diagnosis. But that's what the damn Ulster situation does to you. Makes you look at people as objects, not as flesh and blood.

I don't know why I went all that way to appear on TV. I always end up making glib remarks which make me sweat with embarrassment. The presenter is the pimp. You're the whore. The audience are the punters. I did five minutes on the show, made a dick of myself and five minutes later was driving back to Redhills. Mist lay all over like the country was on fire. At times the driver had to slow to a crawl. The mist was so low, so dense, sometimes I had the sensation we were up in the clouds. But we made it back by midnight.

I hit straight for the Olde Post Inn where the film crew were having a party. I walked from the misty night into a wall of traditional music, singing and drink. As well as us lot there were local people. I fell in with two men who used to work on the Great Northern Railway. Though Beeching closed it down in 1956, they were still full of it. They loved talking about it: the men, the trains, the passengers from all over Ulster. 'I mind working all nights at Ballyhaise Junction. Seven trains a night would come in on the narrow gauge from Leitrim. All cattle and pigs. One night an oul cow lay there and wouldn't get off. She was fast asleep. Then we found out she'd been dead for three days.'

They threw us all out at three in the morning. But such is the desperate dare-devilry of man, two of the lads begged to stay on and offered £25 each for two pints of Guinness. The management unwillingly obliged.

Tara and I drove home. The mist was now even thicker. I'd drunk only lemonade so we made it into the demesne with no bother. The trees in the mist looked as if they were at the bottom of a lake.

I lay in bed thinking of a remark the Belfast chauffeur had made. 'I practise me religion right enough, OK? But no one I know ever come back from the dead and said to me, "Yes, Peter, it's true. God is a fact. I met him several times." But in every society, not just the UK, we do each other in. On no basis of certain fact whatever.' With utter assurance we kill each other, suspect each other, ruin each other's lives – all in the name of religion and bent politics. The Queen is the Defender of the Faith ... The Pope knows all the answers ... Ordinary people die.

Saturday 24 September

Day off. Gave the world a break. Lay in bed till it was time to go to bed.

Day 37: Sunday 25 September

In Scotshouse Community Centre. On Roll 195. Lots of extras from Redhills and around about. One of them is Eugene Leddy, a legendary musician from Butlersbridge. For longer than anyone can remember, he ran a ceilidh band playing at dances and carnivals throughout Cavan and further afield. In 1942 he did his first recording in Dublin for Radio Éireann. 'We weren't allowed to stamp our heels to keep time. One of the lads couldn't play without stamping both heels. We had to make him take his shoes off. The smell was so bad we could hardly get a note out.' He's eighty-one now and still a massive man. He arrived on the set carrying his fiddle and on the catering bus after breakfast he couldn't resist getting it out of its old black case and playing a few tunes. His hands are huge and now stiff with age, but he could still gently tease out lovely music. 'Music has been my life. She'll give me up before I ever desert her.'

On the bus were some of the Protestant boys from Belfast. They listened to the music with interest, but it was obvious that they were a little embarrassed in front of each other. Irish music is ghetto music, a symbol of Nationalism. Even music has been fouled up by the twisted situation. The boys beat the tables keeping time with their fists, Lambeg-drum style. One of them shouted encouragement to the old man, but you sensed he was almost sending him up. At first. Then the power of the music took over and everyone went quiet and listened. The fiddle had bridged gaps.

We filmed the wake scene. Albert went among the extras, who were playing the mourners, receiving their sorrow. 'Very sorry for your troubles, Sergeant.' With a bow of his head and a huskiness of voice he epitomized grief. One of the extras was Cissie Connolly. She was also given a few lines to say. Nigel Wooll arranged a car to pick her up and gave her a caravan of her own. He wanted to repay the hospitality she and Shamie had given to all the members of the crew who drop into them for tea and apple pie.

Cissie said her lines with brilliant understated simplicity. In her youth she acted locally and once rehearsed the part of Juno in the O'Casey play. But our local priest, Fr. Traynor, stopped them putting it on. He considered O'Casey an evil influence. I remember him sitting in our house one morning and explaining to my parents that 'O'Casey was like a dirty crow flying over the pleasant green countryside and landed only to wallow in filth whenever he could find it.' It was hard to resist such certain language. Then. Albert was amazed by Cissie's acting. 'An Irish crowd are like an Italian crowd. They know what to do from their own lives.' Though Cissie had her own caravan all day long, it was full of people. By the force of her personality she had turned it into her home. Each time you passed by it, you could hear excited voices and laughter.

Peter told me that we were going to be visited by Army Archerd and his wife. He writes a column in the *Daily Variety* which is read by all in Hollywood. It's the *Farmers' Journal* of the film world. He has a fearsome reputation, apparently. Stories began circulating round the crew. He booked into the Dorchester Hotel on one occasion and changed his room six times . . . He can make or break careers . . . He can force cows to produce more milk. No, that's someone in the *Farmers' Journal* . . .

When he duly arrived in Scotshouse he turned out to be slightly built, elderly and wearing a bomber jacket bearing the logo 'Planet of the Apes Hong Kong'. His wife had a similar jacket. Old age in America is considered a disease. It is everywhere now.

He's staying in the Slieve Russell Hotel where Peter and Albert and other key people are staying. Apart from complaining about 'low wattage' in his rooms, he and his wife are being as good as gold. Talking to him you realize that behind all the hype and supposed power he has his cross to carry – write a few thousand words every night of his life and fax them to Los Angeles by deadline time . . . and the words, for the most part, must massage the heavy egos of the industry.

Day 38: Monday 26 September

The Scotshouse Community Centre is beside the creamery. Before the EEC, farmers delivered milk on horse-drawn carts. Ireland was dotted with these creameries. In Redhills we had one opposite our house. My mother often sent me over for a jug of cream, fresh and on your doorstep. Each morning the farmers of the area met, gasbagged, poured their milk into the receiver, chatted, went home. Going to the creamery was a social event. Now the creamery building is shut. A big tanker pulls up in front of it. The farmers come on tractors towing shiny aluminum vats. The tanker sucks the milk from the vats. The tanker has a computer. It records the temperature of the milk. It can tell instantly if the milk is sour. The computer records how many gallons have been delivered and issues a chit with the printed figure. The operation takes seconds. In less than a minute the farmer has come and gone. All social significance has been wiped out. No talk, no tangle of horses, carts and men.

This morning I saw a tractor drive up to the tanker and in seconds pull away. But then it stopped and the driver shouted to me, 'Do you mind the times we twisted hay ropes?' At first I didn't recognize him. But soon, in memory, we were back in Richard McManus's fields overlooking Redhills village. 'Do you mind me and you would go under the ash tree in the corner of the field for shelter from the sun and we'd twist the ropes? Do you mind Richard's oul mother and her with the leg et of her with ulcers? Scissors, we called her. No one could live with her. She'd see off a saint.'

We twisted ropes with a piece of stiff wire shaped like a starting handle. It was encased in wood and was hooked at one end. We hooked a twist of hay on and, as he twisted, I fed the hay to him from a warm pile at my feet, taking care not to let the developing rope part from the pile. By the time the rope was long enough he'd have backed out of the shade into the burning sun. On good days.

'Do you mind the name of the oul mare Richard had?'
'I do.'
'What was it?'
'Kitty.'
'Aye.'

'Do you remember Mary McKiernan brought her into the kitchen for a laugh one day? And couldn't get her out. She was so big she wouldn't lower her head to go out the back door. Do you know the only way she was got out?'

'Tell me.'

'Richard turned her round and backed her out.'

'Don was one clever man. Mind how he could play the organ? "Way down upon the Swannee River", hah? Aye, man, surely. God rest his soul.'

A car drove up and out got Army Archerd and his wife Selma. My friend drove away on his tractor. Army and Selma are shown on to the set. When they see Albert enter the acting area they react like teenage fans. They strain on tiptoe to get a glimpse of him through the false walls of the set. Later I take them to see the Maddens in Hilton Park. We drive in through the lined-up regiment of trees, past the lake and up the crunchy avenue to the gorgeous Georgian house. I thought maybe they might be interested in staying there – if not now, at another time. Lucy Madden meets us with customary charm and shows them round the house.

'It was built in 1735. It was burnt out twice,' Lucy tells them.

'Were you insured?' enquires Selma, worried.

Lucy glances at me. We know the fires were political.

'God, can you imagine the money it costs to keep a place like this going?' Selma says aloud, putting her finger on the Anglo-Irish dilemma.

'We're getting an EEC grant to develop the gardens and the grounds,' Lucy tells them.

'They do that, do they? Wow! Beef mountains, wine lakes and mansion piles. Gee.'

'What a lovely house. May I take a photo?' Army asks.

When we drive away, near the lake we see Johnny Madden talking to a labourer.

'So he strides around the estate while she's inside doing the cooking and cleaning?'

'It's called division of labour between consenting parties,' I say.

'Not in America it isn't.'

'What's it called there?'

'Bullshit.'

'They're trying. They deserve great credit. They have inherited a great weight of history. How much can humans bear?'

'Sure. Don't get me wrong. It's a beautiful house. But . . .'

When I got back to the house in the evening it was to greet my sister Flo, who lives in New Jersey, and my brother Brian and Mary, his wife. My agent had given me a bottle of Dom Perignon to celebrate the start of the filming. This was a more appropriate occasion to down it. As a police sergeant our old man had protected the Whyte-Venables and the demesne. Now here were his children *in* the place, sitting back in the grand rooms, lording it, quaffing champagne. Brian did a superb imitation of the old man and in a voice laden with mock emotion shouted to the heavens, 'We did it for you, Daddy!' We fell about, but underneath was the real pain of the past.

I had to leave to have dinner with Army and Selma. Peter and Virginia hosted it in the Slieve Russell Hotel. Matt and Vicki were there, as well as Nigel, Ruth and Mike Southon. Selma is the only person I've ever heard chastise a waiter because she *likes* what she's eating. 'Take this away from me – NOW! It's too nice.' Old age, fat, smoking, drinking, sex . . . all diseases.

Albert wouldn't come to the dinner. He hates publicity gigs. He's done it all so many times before. He knows what sells films is word of mouth.

We film the scene where the father grabs the boy and forces him to dance. The way Albert grabs Matt is brutal. His face is raw with emotion. The dance could turn to murder. It is truly shocking.

During lunch I show Flo and Brian around the set. Brian goes and sits at the desk where Albert, as the father, sits filling in forms, writing letters. Brian picks up the pen, straightens his back, and somehow lengthens his upper lip and tightens it exactly as our father did. He glances up at us, sideways, just as the old man did if you went in to see him while he was coiled and tense, filling in police reports. The way Brian does the imitation is so spot on it is uncanny. Exactly as it *was*. Flo and myself simply roar with laughter. Albert can't compete with Brian's recall. Yet acting has little to do with the past reality of the case in question. Reality cannot be repeated. It can only be recreated. What you get is the actor's version. My brother was brilliantly accurate. He was there as a kid; Albert wasn't. Brian can skate on the surface, but Albert has to show what is underneath.

The father in the story is my father and yet has nothing to do with him. I've tried to recreate the man's energy, impact and power over the lives of children – a power he didn't know he had. He knew he was strong, of course, but he didn't know his effect on the imagination, the black and white shadows with which he could fill a room. This energy he handed on. Trying to deal with this energy is like trying to grapple with consubstantiation. The past is bread and wine . . . How do you make it dance?

My sister Flo came with me to see the rushes. We watched the scene where the boy's aunt takes the ring off his dead mother's finger, 'In case the undertaker gets it.' It's a vicious scene of greed and common sense. The ring is hard to get off. The aunt licks a bar of soap and rubs the dead woman's finger with it. Afterwards Flo tells me that she removed the ring from our mother's finger when she died. Then she showed me the actual ring. She was wearing it. I touched it. My mother's golden wedding ring . . .

Back in the fifties a woman we knew left her husband because she could not stand the terrible situation in which she found herself. In those days it was a hell of a brave thing to do. When she met my mother, they discussed her decision. To this day the woman remembers what my mother said to her: 'Marriage is like that wedding ring on your finger. It goes round and round and can never be broken.' It was amazing then how certain we were in our beliefs. There was no such thing as doubt. Doubt was outlawed.

Day 40: Wednesday 28 September

I drove into Fermanagh this morning, heading for Enniskillen. Got out of the car and sat on the shore of a lake. All around me grew bulrushes and reeds. Out on the water two swans floated. I heard running about fifty yards to the right of where I sat. I thought it was a bullock coming down to drink. It was a man. I could see him through the rushes. He wore pyjamas tucked into wellingtons and a jacket. He ran straight out into the lake. He went on in waist-high. Then he stopped. Then slowly he went out further. He was out past the rushes and reeds now and I could see him clearly. The wind stirred up his hair. It lifted the one hank of hair he had on his white skull straight up, as if blown by a hair-dryer. He went right out, very slowly, until the water was up to his neck. He stopped. He was bobbing in the water. The water was lifting him, but the water in his wellingtons was weighing him down. He managed to anchor himself and didn't move for a full minute. I knew if he took one more step forward he would drown. I didn't know what to do. Should I shout to him? Maybe he did this as some kind of ritual every morning . . . Out on the water the swans floated and stared across at him. His head was still. His lone hank of grey hair lifted and fell and stuck out at the side of his head. He twisted his head from side to side. I could hear him groaning. Then he stepped back and very slowly turned round. He began walking, lumbering through the water, towards the shore. He stumbled but, with flailing arms, managed to prevent himself from going under. The wind whipped through the reeds and rushes, crackling them together, making the sound of fire ripping through autumn leaves. When he gained the shore he walked straight up the field. I stood and caught a glimpse of his face. An ordinary face in agony. He had, I think, failed to drown himself. I waited for some time. I didn't want to come upon him in his sorrow. After an hour I went back to my car parked up along the road. No sign of the man. I saw a cottage in the distance. Smoke came out of the chimney. I thought I heard a child crying. I didn't go on to Enniskillen. I headed back to Redhills and Scotshouse.

The crew are in the community centre working fast, getting the lights ready, the furniture, the props . . . Mike, the director of photography, is chasing shadows away and creating them somewhere else. He and Peter discuss the position of the camera in all the set-ups. At one point Mike's gaffer shouts from up a ladder, 'Kill the juice in the bouncer!'

Outside at the creamery the farmers drive up to the bulk tanker. The tanker driver rejects someone's milk. The computer decides the milk hadn't been cooled enough.

Peter and Nigel stride out from the community centre and stand talking. They discuss how it is we are over schedule yet under budget. Someone at Castle Rock isn't pleased. Ruth and I chat about the rushes we've seen. She's very pleased and thinks all the performances are good. Up the road is a farmyard. There's a big black plastic-covered silage pit. Downwind of it the seepage stinks.

We all move back into the community centre. The actors come on to the set. From time to time I whisper in Peter's ear. I hate doing it, but watching the rushes is too late to intervene. Good comes from it. The other day I said something to Peter when I saw the way the aunt was taking the ring from the dead woman's finger. Peter suggested she lick the bar of soap. It was a Dickensian brainwave.

When it comes to the crunch the actors are on their own. It's like watching an athlete do the pole vault. You can show him the jump, hand him the pole, advise him, but in the end he has to take a running jump at it himself and do it in his own way . . . I watch them doing it their own way and doing it well.

The hairdresser and the make-up people and Jonathan, the stills photographer, dress Tara up, do her up and take her photo. She's going back to university in a few days time. They're just having fun and because they like one another. When I see the result I pour cold water on all their efforts. I hate fashion and the whole rotten scene . . . girls starving themselves to sell clothes for the fat wallets. There's more morality among the whores at King's Cross. Tara is a good girl who worked hard, eagerly and smilingly. She's up at 5.30 a.m. and not in bed until near midnight. Peter's wife, Virginia, remarked to me how well the family members have done. So far. Simon Finney works like the clappers and stays cheery all day long. Today I saw Toby Yates coming back with the second unit having spent from dawn filming the rising sun, lakes, rats, cattle, the setting sun. He glowed with boyish enthusiasm. Like his father . . .

Everyone works hard. And I think they get on well together. I haven't seen any blood on the floor. With the possible exception of my own. Of course, it's better for all concerned than working down a coalmine. Not that there's any of those left.

Driving on the Redhills–Scotshouse road today you couldn't help but notice the sheep droppings. The road was covered with them. Coming home tonight was the same: flocks of sheep were being driven along to somewhere or other. Their glassy eyes shone in the headlights. I asked the girls who were shepherding them what was up. 'We're all day at the sheep dipping.' In the middle of the flock I could smell the dip. An acrid smell of Jeyes fluid and dung. I drove on, the car full of it, even when I closed the window.

Earlier in the day I had nipped home and was no sooner in the door than the phone rang. Peter wanted to see me. I had to shoot back to Scotshouse. He was rehearsing the scene with Albert and Matt where the boy tells the father he wants money for an abortion. They wrestle with the words and actions. Like a man chopping wood, Albert splits everything open to find the sense of it. In the tiny, cramped space of the set, I got a whiff of what it must be like acting with Albert. Like going a few rounds with the champion – energy, swift punches, craft, boing-boing! Peter, when he directs, tries to guide the actors. He never forces things on them. He encourages them to find out for themselves what he knows is there.

A few minutes of watching Albert and Matt and I can see the metaphorical blood flowing, the snot flying across the ring, the grunts and groans. Acting is a punch-up.

Day 41: Thursday 29 September

I spent the morning driving round the Border roads. Lecky Bridge outside Clones had been opened for the forty-second time by the locals on Sunday and closed by the British on Monday. Many of the roads are narrow and run through marshy hills, across rivers and come back out on to a main road only a short distance after leaving it. You wonder why these roads are closed. Often there isn't one Protestant house along the way but, like trying to get rid of rabbits, you close off all bolt-holes except one. These roads are political bolt-holes. They exist as much in the mind as in reality. One laneway across a river had been blown up by the Army. Locals spanned the river with railway sleepers. Someone set the sleepers alight without seriously damaging them. This 'bridge' was passable. The Army hadn't interfered with it. It was a bit hairy driving across on the sleepers. One false move and you could plunge into the water. All around this part of Fermanagh, Cavan and Monaghan was great fruit-growing country. But I saw only one orchard. It was full of old, scabby trees. But bright-red apples hung in the damp morning light. At a checkpoint a British soldier stopped me. He wore a beret, not a helmet, and in his arms cradled his deadly baby. He was from Telford. 'Things are quiet. But the Sinn Fein is opening the roads. And what if they starts tearing down the checkpoints?'

I gave lifts to various thumbing people. On the road between Clones and Cavan I lifted a middle-aged man with a rough, lilting Mayo accent. I knew he was a tinker, a traveller. He thought I was English and spun me a yarn about being from Donegal and that his Bentley had broken down. 'She died on me comin' up a hill. Coughed and spluttered and conked, sir.' His fingers were stained with nicotine. His left hand was brown up to the wrist. He reeked from cigarette smoke. It clung to his clothes and hair. It seemed to come from his boots. He stunk of smoke like a pub at closing. 'Do you take a smoke, sir?' he asked, offering me one. When I dropped him he walked into the distance, smoke billowing back over his head.

A young man was walking from Redhills to Clones. He wore a woolly hat, a Man. Utd scarf and a Barry McGuigan moustache. He told me he had come out to Redhills from Clones to drink. 'Drank all mornin' there in McCaffrey's. Good pub, that. You get fed up drinkin' in your own town.' I asked him what his hobbies were. He was unemployed. 'I hunt the hare.'

'Do you kill many?'

'Never try to. Kill the hare today, you won't be able to hunt him tomorrow.'

'Any chance of getting work?'

'None. The meat factory is just killing now. No boning done at all. I used work in the boning room. It's a seasonal trade as well. Work is wantin' badly in the town.'

'You're a Man. Utd fan?'

'No. I found this on the chapel wall one mornin'. Keeps the cowl off me neck.'

I got the sense of a young man who wanted to keep moving, keep out of the house. He talked quickly and guardedly, as if he was speaking to you over the rim of a pint.

Back in Scotshouse John Rudden had arrived with his sow for second-unit pick-up shots. The art department had rigged up a space that looked just like the chapel porch. One of the crew wore wellies, trousers and a brown coat that Declan had worn when we shot the scene originally. They wanted close-ups of the pig. A vet was in attendance. I watched as this elderly man went into the wagon and gave the sow an injection. His hands shook badly. He looked drunk. I was wrong. His hands shook from an injury he had sustained to his nervous system. He was now retired. He had thick silver hair, was tall, with a longish, reddish face. He looked sad and spoke quietly. Everything he said or did was done in a gentle way. He sat on a window-sill at the side of the old creamery as we talked.

'I was one time stitching a gash in a horse's leg. It was night. He was in a small stable and vicious. A woman outside the half-door held a tilley lamp. I inserted the first stitch and, well, the horse lunged. The woman outside took fright and fled with the lights. So I found myself in a small stable with a mad horse in the pitch black. I squeezed myself back into the corner. Just in the nick. The horse kicked back at me. I felt the hooves graze me ears as they clanged back into the walls at either side of my head. I cursed the woman from a height.'

'How did you finish the job?'

'I put a touch on the nose and a firm hand on his neck to calm him.'

He had a great memory for horses and people. 'There was a

Protestant man in Gowna who had the cure for farcy. What he did was stand the animal in a river, facing east. From the book he said three prayers. Farmers swore by him.'

'What's farcy?' I asked.

'It's glanders – a massive swelling on the leg. I was called one time to a house. A steep lane led up from the house to the Gowna road. The horse couldn't be got up this steep hill. She had farcy. I injected her. Or whatever I did, I can't recall to mind what, now. Two days later I called back. The stable was empty. I was full sure the mare had died. No, the wife told me. She was fine and gone to Gowna. Even though I had fixed her, they still took her into Gowna to the man with the cure. When I got back and told my boss he said I should never have gone near the family. They owed him a fortune for treatment over the years. But I bet they paid the fellah with the cure.'

Later I sat near him as he ate his dinner on the bus. Because of his shaky hands he had great trouble getting the food into his mouth. Milk spilt from a cup on to his trousers. I pretended I hadn't seen it happen and he pretended as well, but all the time I could see the damp patch on his thigh. When he spoke he had a twinkle in his eyes and an amused tone in his voice. Man and his follies with animals was a never-ending wonder. 'A firm hand on the neck. That'll calm anything. A woman. Even a man. Who or what likes a cold, nervy hand?' I could have listened to him for hours. He had precise knowledge.

The old sow behaved just as badly with the second unit, but they managed her in the end. I asked John Rudden if he had a name for her.

'I have now. I call her Madonna.'

At the end of the day I gave a lift to a man heading for Ballyconnell. He was about twenty-eight and was coming from the cattle mart in Clones. He had bought five bullocks there and was selling them to an exporter at Dublin docks. His father was still in Clones with the car. He had to get home and pick up the cattle lorry, drive back to Clones, load the bullocks and take them to the boat. He would sell them to Dillon the exporter and would make a profit on the transaction. He wouldn't even have to feed them. Someone at the mart would give them a bail or two of hay. He had the whiff of his trade – cow, dung and piss. 'Meat is money,' he said simply. He pronounced meat as 'mate' and beast, 'baste'.

Before I went to bed I walked down to the lake. It was pitch black. I couldn't see even a glimmer on the water, but I heard the plop of a fish jumping.

Day 42: Friday 30 September

Back at Lough Oughter today for the love scene. Driving through Belturbet I saw old Frank Rice, a local character, standing outside the post office. He was wedged in the corner of the main wall and porch. Frank is elderly, unshaven, dishevelled and poor. He exists in a caravan, but he wears his cap at a jaunty angle and the white plimsolls on his feet give him a rakish touch. He has no teeth. He smokes and does a trick with the cigarette in his lips. He sucks the lighted fag into his mouth, hides it there and then brings it back out. Another trick he performs is to place his cap on the pavement, carefully step away from it, and then execute a bully-head along the ground so that his head ends up slap into his cap. After this performance he stands and sucks his cheeks into his toothless mouth and grins. His grin is boyish, even though he is in his seventies. He still looks like what he once was – a circus clown. He toured Ireland with Duffy's circus, first as a ring labourer, then a clown. He's not forgotten his tricks. Each time I meet him I see canvas over his head.

This morning I gave him a few quid. Frank loves a pint. He sucks it down swift and efficient, like a snipe feeding. When I gave him the money, he looked at it as if amazed.

'I never asked you for this, did I?'

'No.'

'I'm a good man.'

'The best, Frank.'

He sucked the fag in his lips into his gummy mouth and I waited until he brought it back out again. Then he took off his cap.

'You don't have to do that, Frank.'

He wanted to do something for the money. He had not begged. The pride of the Cavan people is astounding. You see an old man outside the post office. You think he's nothing, ordinary . . . He's bloody amazing.

I heard Peter say to Army Archerd, 'I've never felt better on a film – the fresh air, the people. Do you know we have not had one single robbery on this film? Not one piece of equipment stolen. You know what film sets are like for thieving.' The people in Redhills leave their front doors open. Children and neighbours spill in and out all day. Small communities are best. Even allowing for the fact that you can't keep much secret. Redhills restores faith in humanity.

Down at the lake Vicki and Matt lie naked on the forest floor. The camera is above them on a high platform. The earth, in the end, swallows all. In every field you drive past can be seen abandoned ploughs, mowing machines, wheel-rakes, cars. All are being eaten by grass, dock, nettle. The very clay seems to grow up around them. Iron is easy meat; flesh, no contest at all. There is a boat moored by the shore. It is full of water. The wood is rotting. Nests of water insects scuttle and slide in and out of the cracks. The blue nylon rope mooring the boat is green with slime and mossy rot.

All over the land are the abandoned houses slowly tumbling to the ground. Today I saw an ancient cottage with grass growing up the walls. Approaching, I thought it had been painted green. The roof beams were caving in. The door hung on one hinge. The thatch sprouted great tufts of grass. It looked like Famine or bailiffs had tumbled the life out of it.

Yet all over the place are the new houses. Big brick structures with pillars and new slates for the doctors, solicitors, vets, accountants; white bungalows for everyone else.

Tonight Ruth threw a great party in McCaffrey's pub. The place packed, drink flying, the traditional music belting out, a girl's voice singing on her own. Even the musicians were pissed. What am I talking about? The musicians were pissed arriving.

Saturday 1 October

Day off. Albert took the entire crew to the races at Fairyhouse. Hired coaches, laid on food, drink, booked the Arkle Room for the day. Horses, people – Albert was in his element. And so were we all. Most of the gang had never been to a race meeting before. The greener they were, the more money they seemed to win. Albert is a generous man. OK, he can afford to be, but he doesn't have to be. He just is. Day off – day out. A beano. Hadn't been on one since I worked in a furniture factory in Bromley-by-Bow. Albert is utterly down to earth and modern. Yet his generous act was that of a world gone by. At the end of the day he stood in the middle of the Arkle Room and we cheered him to the echo. He has brought the actor–manager traditions of the theatre into the world of film.

'No. No, it was nothing. Thank you. Just a bit of fun. Coming near the end of the film and you've all worked so hard! We need a day out. Just a bit of fun, that's all.'

That's everything. He's been handed the sword, all right, and is using it well.

Day 43: Sunday 2 October

Rain this morning – thick, grey and deadly. We are in the barracks garden. The Chief of Police came to the village the other day. As a new man in the division he was touring the stations, getting to know the men. He arranged to meet Sean Doris at one o'clock. Sean is our local Garda. Utterly honest, hard-working, dependable; without his help we couldn't survive. He lives with his wife and three children in the barracks and is the only policeman in the place. The Chief arrived at one o'clock precisely, knocked on the barracks door, but got no reply. He decided to go to the pub and have a coffee and sandwiches. At half-past one he went to the barracks door again, but still no sign of Sean. Then it dawned on him. He was trying to gain entrance to the film barracks – the one built by Mark Geraghty and his design team. The real barracks is just outside the village. Our fantasy must be pretty real to cod the Chief of Police.

In the Leggykelly pub I had a drink with Jimmy Brady. He is famous throughout the Border counties. Retired now, he was once the best-known importer–exporter in Ulster. Whatever you wanted, from lengths of steel to apples or artificial manure, he'd get it for you. He drove a Ford V8. The Customs only had Anglias. You never met him but he was laughing. He's still the same. He was a friend of my father's. My mother was in hospital in Dublin having a baby. My father asked Jimmy for a lift there so he could visit my mother. Jimmy, when he was on business, drove a pick-up truck. It had a box seat for the passenger. My father sat on the box the whole way to Dublin, not knowing he was sitting on razor-blades. Blades were cheaper in the North than the South. The cargo had legal protection the whole way to the city. When the baby was born my father ordered a new pram. Brady got it for him across the Border. He wheeled it past the Customs and delivered it to the old man in the Leggykelly. But first he removed the load of butter he had hidden under the panels of the false-bottom. The Customs or my father never knew.

He was once summoned to appear at the District Court in Belturbet. He drove up to the court-house in the old pick-up. 'The Garda lads were outside when I drove up, having a smoke. The judge, oul Lavery, hadn't arrived yet. When they saw me coming they started laughing. But, Lord, they got a surprise when they saw Lavery step down from the passenger seat. Hadn't I come across him and his transport broken down. I give him a lift. Lord, you should have seen their faces. They straightened up right quick and had to salute the Justice. First time ever I was saluted going to court. Lord, them were the days.'

'What happened when you appeared before the Justice?' I asked. 'After all, you had done him a good turn.'

'Ah, oul Lavery wasn't bad at all. That day, anyway. He was lenient. Natural enough. "I seem to recognize you," he says. "That's right, your honour. We met recently." "Case dismissed." Lord, the times we had. Do you know what I'm going to tell you and this is God's truth? That I may drop dead if I tell a word of a lie. We had the best fun ever. Them days will never come again. Do you mind I used to be umpire for Redhills at football matches? One day we were playing in Kilafana. Do you remember the way the goal-posts would be loose in the ground from cattle rubbing up against them? Anyway, I was on one post with this other fellah from the opposing club on the other post. Wasn't he in Sinn Fein at the time and he was trying to sell tickets for a dance. He asked me would I buy a ticket. "How much?" "2/6." "No bother," I says. Anyway, didn't his team kick the ball and she was sailing over the bar for a point. But at the last second didn't I lean against the post and shifted it a good two feet so the ball sailed wide. Your man couldn't say a thing. Cos he knew if he did I wouldn't buy a ticket for the dance. Ah, now, there used to be ructions.'

He has the biggest twinkle I've ever seen in a man's eye and the happiest laugh I have ever heard. He has spent his life on the high-wire of the Border and enjoyed every minute of it. Customs and Excise are no more. In Europe we are all one.

'Ah, now, I wouldn't bank on it. Where there's a Border there'll always be an edge.'

The trees when I looked out this morning were autumnal gold. The season has snuck up on us. The grass had a lick of frost and the car roof was covered in a variety of leaves. Tara having gone, I'm now on my own. Up until now I've never lived in an otherwise empty house. I lie in bed listening to every little noise: the water gurgling round the copper arteries, the pump kicking in like a weary heart, the dripping tank in the attic a defective bladder. Sometimes I hear mysterious dunts against the outside walls. Probably animals beating each other up. This morning I was woken by a bluebottle walloping against the window-pane. In the moonlight I see sheeps' eyes glistening like marbles. Cock pheasants go 'gonk-gonk' and rip through the trees. Just as dusk comes down the woodcock flit out from the trees to feed on the ground. You can barely see them ghost past.

The ghosts of Dorothy and Gladys appear all the time now. Walking along the avenues they flit out, and I see them walking quickly past and hear their rounded English vowels . . .

'Who are you?'

'I'm the sergeant's son, Miss Whyte-Venables.'

'Oh, are you? Well don't walk on the daffodil, there's a good boy. You're hurting it.'

They walked through the woods every day, covering as much of it as they could, keeping an eye on it all, looking for possible thieves. During the war, when iron was very scarce, they found one of their own tribe cutting the iron railings along the avenue and loading the lengths into a cart. The lengths have never been replaced. I sometimes walk on the croquet lawn in front of the house and I imagine I can hear the click of mallet on wood and then silence as the players pause to listen to children shouting in the woods – my own voice among them. We played in the shadows of trees all day long. We swung on the huge bough of a Lebanon Cedar which curved down towards the ground and dangled from it by our ankles. The tree is still there, but the bough has snapped . . . Voices, play, thick brogues and tweeds, and my mother pushing a pram on a Sunday walk – all gone. Why? What's it all about? I don't know.

I met an old woman on the road today carrying plastic shopping bags. We stood and chatted. She told me a little about her life. 'I used sit on a stone wall with me good coat and hat on and me crying. Trying to pluck up courage to leave. But I never. He beat me regular. He was a giant of a man. The drink put a century of ruin on him. Poisoned all that was right good in him. Sent him to the rats.'

When I got to where we were filming, people were talking about last night's rushes. Everyone thought they looked great and that Matt was excellent. 'He cried real tears in that scene.' Peter is convinced he's going to be a big star. Everyone is pleased with Vicki's performance, too. She brewed up a storm of emotion in the miscarriage moment. She awakens to find a rat in the bed and goes crazy. You can't get rid of rats. They can survive famine. They invade our dreams. They can gnaw through iron. We're using an empty garage in Castletara to film some of the internal Prunty scenes. The place is full of rats. Round the back of the buildings I saw one snouting over the ground, using its tail as a lever when it wanted to get off the ground to climb a piece of plywood leaning against a wall. It stood on its hind legs with curled tail stiff against the ground and prised itself up like a squirrel. With rare purpose it sniffed and gripped its way up the plywood. When it came to the wall – rough concrete blocks – it paused, head flicking, then deciding not to go on landed on the ground with a slovenly plop.

They shot the close-ups of the love-making scene in this garage. The art department had turned part of it into a wood by a lake. No one was allowed in as they shot the scene. Instead of a multitude of eyes watching the nude grapplings, only ten people were allowed to watch. I tried to get in, but the AD wouldn't let me.

'Sorry, the set is closed.'

'But I wrote the damn stuff.'

'Sorry.'

'Peter's in there.'

'He's the fucking director, Shane.'

'Matt and Vicki are in there.'

'What? They're doing the scene.'

'Only jesting.'

'Oh.'

It's a weird morality that I can write a love scene but I'm not allowed to watch it being shot. I peeped in, though, round the side. As the couple lay on the ground, kitless, everyone turned chastely away. You could do a really funny scene with them all wearing blindfolds. Including the lovers. Not to mention the audience ... Lisa Mulcahy, the first assistant director, with her beady eye spotted my beady eye peeping and I had to scarper before I was caught and excommunicated.

I met a man whose fields I used to work, winter and summer. Sowing spuds on steep hills, with a ripped hessian sack on my head like a cowl to protect me from the driving rain. Thinning turnips following a horse-drawn slipe, mud and muck up to your knees ... It never worried me. I knew I could go home to my mother and have some love and tea. This friend told me that his son was going to turn the farm into a golf course. Sacrilege. There's generations of blood, sweat and tears in those fields, but the EEC is forcing farmers out of farming. Food will be grown in France and Germany only. Ireland will be one big golf course. With a hole in each county. Is the land worth fighting for any more? Maybe EEC set-aside policy is a subtle solution to our political problems ... I'd be willing to die for land you could sow and reap. But who would be prepared to spill blood over a damn golf course?

I drove back to Redhills and out to Drumlaney lake. Shamie Connolly and I rowed round the lake in my fibreglass boat.

Going out to the boat we had to tramp and slurp through marshy ground.

'What could you do with this land?' I asked him.

'Sell it. Be the gallon.'

Shamie is still immensely strong. His chest is still as stout as a tar barrel, and every time he pulled on the oars the boat lifted and skipped over the water. His face is beaten hard by the weather, but the boyish look of devilry has never left him. A life of hard labour hasn't diminished by one whit his youthful spirit. He attacks everything he does with gusto. Especially words.

'Man, dear, I seen meself and Tommy Rennicks goin' up to Hillsborough to work for a big Protestant farmer. They always were last puttin' the crops in. Then the two of us arrived. Man oh man, we put in thirty-seven acres of corn and thirty-seven acres of spuds. You should have seen Rennicks walking down a field with a fiddle broadcasting the seed. He had a high step like a horse. Powerful. The tractor and harrow couldn't keep in along with him. That season there was only one other farm done before us. Us two and a whole mehil of men worked there. Rennicks and meself could cope any of them. One of them tried it on one day. "Go way to fuck before I make a spring-well out of you," I says. He come on no more.' 'Mehil' is from the Gaelic *meitheal* and means a work party.

Walking home we come across a quill from a swan's wing. 'The fox. You see the way it's bit across? That's the way they do it. I put me hand in a den one time to grab a fox be the hind leg. She barked and squirted piss at me. Man dear, it was a sight.' Like the old houses the old people are going, but the young will turn out just as colourful. The village is full of children. You see them playing or standing around tanting one another, or running through the fields. The land teaches them. The lakes. One swan's quill lying on the ground is a mystery; two, and there has to be an explanation.

Driving down the demesne avenue the pheasants flock

after you. Hundreds of them. Their grey plumage, like the trees, is beginning to turn colourful. On 1 November they'll all be shot.

Day 45: Tuesday 4 October

Back at Lough Oughter to finish off the swimming scene. The whole countryside is covered with a hard frost. A grey-bearded coldness lies on every field, though the sun rises up a brilliant blue sky. Out on the lake the water quivers with light. I get into a boat and row way out. The loch is an immense stretch of water. It doesn't look big until you get out on to it. It curves its way round corners and is almost cut in two by wooded land jutting out from scabby hills. There is only one house visible – an old two-storied stone house painted white, standing on a hill away up the other end of the view. It has to be a peach of a spot to live. This stretch of lake and the Erne River must have looked exactly the same a thousand years ago. The way the sun shines it makes a golden path all the way up the centre of the lake. Up this heavenly stairs I row, the droplets falling from the oars and hitting the water in a long chain of rings like a Celtic collar. A heron staggers on to a rock, seems about to topple in, but rights itself with an awkward flap. From where I am I cannot see one human being. Throughout history this lake and land has been fought over. I can see why.

When I get back to the shore I sit with Peter and natter. The sun is quickly de-icing the land. 'On a film,' Peter says, 'you must eat well, keep warm and sleep well – if you can.' He has had a theatre background, which is why writers mean something to him. It was he who insisted I should be on the set every day. Not wanting to write himself, he is dispassionate about the material. He can look at it clearly, without wanting to destroy it. Finished at the lake, we head back to Redhills. In the garden at the back of our barracks the actors rehearse the scene. The embrace business crops up immediately. They do the scene with one embrace only. Then they try it with two embraces. I'm a nervous wreck watching them, listening to them. In the end they agree that my way is best. Albert gives it full throttle. It works well. For me another panic over. The acting problems solved, Peter sets about the camera angles, refining until he gets a position for the camera that puts space between the men – emotional space represented by the onion bed the two of them are working at; the onion bed on which the mother/wife died in the film's opening. Looks good.

The sun is high above us. It dazzles the tree-tops in the demesne. Crows swoop up and down. The film crew work flat out – set-up after set-up. I hear them discussing the end of the whole shoot – the scheduled end. It keeps stretching by a day or two. Alan Boyle, the chief make-up artist, and Rosemary, the costume designer, talk quietly together about when they'll be able to set off for England.

'It'll take me a day I suppose to get all the frocks sorted.'

'Hm. I must call the travel agent.'

'I've got a new puppy. Adorable. Can't wait.'

Alan is very easygoing. He's been around a long time.

'I worked in wigs at the RSC. I did the *Marat/Sade*. If I was doing Shakespeare I'd say, why does Pistol have to have that coloured wig? Nothing in the text about it. OK, I know Bardolph has to have a peculiar nose. Because it's mentioned.' He gives 'peculiar' a soft, camp emphasis which is very funny. You can see the nose in question – and very snotty, big and red it is too.

From 5.30 until 5.55 we sit and wait for the sun to come out from behind thin bands of passing clouds. When it does come out, it is low down casting long shadows. Phil, the camera operator, and his camera are dark stains across the actors. Peter and Mike Southon sit discussing what they should do if the light goes completely; if it gets so low down that it won't shine into the garden.

Peter takes a final puff at his cigar. 'We've had a bloody

good day.' He tosses the end of his old cigar behind him into the weeds.

'It's a wrap,' Lisa shouts.

The village is packed with our trucks, vans and cars. I meet Sean McCaffrey outside his pub. The crew are already inside quaffing pints, thirsty as if they'd spent all day in the desert. Sean and I talk about the blessing of the pig. 'It's all a load of hogwash,' he says. 'Over and done with. Should have seen your face at the height of it! You got to cry. Otherwise we'd all be going round laughing.'

The village green, as we talk, is full of kids. They are skipping about, running and chasing. Small girls sit on the grass facing one another in a circle. Each has a doll. They are putting on funny voices, pretending the dolls are talking. There is much nodding of dolls' heads and squeaky cries of interest and excitement: 'Illo, Mees Molly. 'Ave you coming from din-din?'

Looking around I know I'll drive away in two weeks' time. I won't be happy. The village is at the heart of a way of life that is possible and good. OK, you're not going to find many people chatting over the plays of Ibsen or the latest Tom Stoppard, but the capacity for enjoyment and the interest in people and happenings and politics is immense. And when the chips are down, they help one another. No old person will be found dead in a room weeks after the event. There is loneliness, but there is also a hive of folk keeping it at bay. Looking at the kids on the green, I suppose half of them will end up in England or America. There aren't many economic miracles round here. The only miracles are the people themselves.

When I was a kid, a man came home from Australia. He'd retired. It was 1956 – An Tostal year. An Tostal was a government gimmick to attract tourists to the country. It means 'the gathering'. The towns and villages were supposed to put on music and events to entice the dollar-wavers to our shores, but it never caught on. An Tostal died out, but this man who came home that year we called Tom Tostal. We kids would crowd round him, asking him about Sydney. 'There's a railway station in Sydney, it's got so many lines and trains and signals and engines you couldn't imagine it possible. Huge.'

In all innocence I asked him a question: 'Is it bigger than Ballyhaise Junction?'

He took one look at me and you could see all hope draining from his eyes. He had spent his entire life working in Australia and dreaming about one day coming home. When he did, he found the life so puny, the minds so small. He upped and left and was never heard tell of again. Every time I come home I think of him. Like he's a warning. At the time, though, Ballyhaise Junction was bigger in my mind than Sydney was in his.

When we were in Scotshouse filming in the community centre we used Connolly's pub quite a bit. Aiden and his wife did sandwiches, dinners – whatever anyone wanted. It's got a Star of David illumination on the gable end and slap-bang in front of the entrance, an ancient tree. Tonight, while watching the rushes, John Phelan whispered to me that Aidan's son had died. He was only twenty-six and the family pride and joy. Eventually he would have taken over the farm and pub. The son died from 'the bad lad'. All the time the father was serving us in the pub, his son was upstairs in bed, dying slowly. The father never mentioned his sorrow. It was too much for him to give it tongue. People are as brave as lions. Though breaking inside, they can still pull a pint and say, 'Ah, good man, how's it going?'

John Phelan says the son got a kick on the head and developed a tumour, 'But that might be a rumour.' There are always plenty of kicks to the head flying about. The local newspaper, the *Anglo-Celt*, catalogues most of them: 'He insulted me girlfriend, your Honour,' or 'He spilt drink on me fiancée's dress and wouldn't apologize, your Honour.' The more banal, the more lethal. Sitting in the dark watching the rushes becomes a dream, a nightmare. Is any of this real at all? The stuff on the screen and the stuff in the fields and streets ... Everything underneath you cannot see – the heart-break.

Day 46: Wednesday 5 October

This morning we had to shoot a scene we'd already completed, owing to defective stock. We're insured. The scene is Albert as the father shaving by the window, in reminiscent mood, thinking aloud: 'One good murder, that's all I ask. And me the only one able to solve it.' It's difficult for him having to do this all over again. Previously he had acted the scene well, wiped it from his mind and moved on. Now I saw him psyching himself up, limbering up physically, then moving into the acting area. Entering the ring. He does it better this time. He always brings something new to the argument. For instance, the business of breaking down the door into his wife's room. He was very reluctant to do this. He didn't want to appear a brute. But when it came to doing the take, he didn't ram the door with his shoulder first; he thrust at it with his hips. It was desperately sexual, born of frustration. He seemed to be fucking the door. Then he charged at it with his shoulder and broke it in. It is an amazing image and speaks volumes about the deep, animal lust at the root of relationships.

While they were setting up the shots I came across an old Garda Siochana Correspondence Register. This is a big book in which every letter received at the barracks is recorded. The date of receipt, the sender and a synopsis of the contents are entered. It is a highly detailed collection of information about the goings-on in the area. 'Alleged assault on Referee.' 'Alleged altering of Blue Card.' 'Speed meter detections.' 'Dangerous driving.' 'Larceny of Morris 1000.' 'Description of suck calf lost by Seamus Maguire.' 'Re. General Election.' 'Unexpected warrants.' There are hundreds of entries in the register. There is another book which has the name and date of birth of every man, woman and child in the district. I bet the local Garda in any Irish village would know how a person votes. They'd certainly know who was a member of Sinn Fein.

I drove into Monaghan and went into a Catholic Church. I entered the confession box and sat where the priest usually sits. I listened to the silence and imagined what it was like to hear confessions. I heard steps and saw a woman enter the empty chapel. She saw my hand pull at the velvet curtains. She entered the box. I heard her kneeling down. I slid the shutter back and we stared at each other through the grille. I could just make her out in the gloom.

'I saw you coming in. I keep an eye on the chapel,' she said.

'Hope you don't mind. Never sat where the priest sits before.'

'There's thieves about, you see.'

'Yes, well, I better go.'

'No, you're all right where you are. I saw your car pull up and I knew you were a gentleman.'

'It's only a second-hand Volvo.'

'Doesn't matter. I can tell be your voice. And the rings on your fingers.' She lit a cigarette. 'I do often come in here for a fag. My family are dead against it. Smoking. I like the peace.'

'Have you anything to confess now that I'm here? A murder, maybe? Lust, anger, gluttony, envy, sloth?'

She laughed. Already the box was full of smoke. 'I'm a divil for the Lotto. The priest sits, the penitent kneels.'

'That's as it should be.'

'I often sat in there meself.'

'What's it like living round here?'

'Ah now, don't you know, quiet as the grave. Oh sorry, I never asked you.' She held a cigarette up to the grille and poked it through.

'No thanks, I don't. Your penance is bingo seven nights a week, a nip of whiskey before you go to bed and a toy boy waiting on you when you get in. Goodbye.'

She gave a great rattle of a chuckle as I clattered out of the box and away. Rings on my fingers? I haven't any. Never have.

When I arrived back in Redhills I saw John Phelan and P. J. McMahon standing together talking and laughing, all rancour forgotten. At the time it seemed such a big issue – the money. We'll be gone in two weeks. It'll all be a dream.

In the vegetable garden at the back of the barracks Peter is with Matt and Albert, finishing off from yesterday. They discuss a move. Albert suggests a certain move and Peter agrees.

'The move is in the script, Peter,' Albert says.

'Gosh, is it? I must read it sometime.'

They laugh.

'Yes, to actually read the script is quite a wise thing to do,' I say.

They look at me and all go, 'Ooh. Ooh. Ooh.'

We went to lunch and so did the sun. We eventually came back, but the sun didn't. We had to move location back up to the disused garage at Castletara. A local man told me they sold tractors from there at the height of the EEC farming boom in the seventies. 'Twenty new tractors a week drove out of there. Some money, boy.'

I was about to drive off from Redhills when I met Tom Conlon who runs Clogher Market. I enquired about McCracken. He told me that on the previous Saturday McCracken had blocked the entrance to the market by placing a lorry in the gateway. He did this to divert the customers into his own market across the road – the area where our vehicles had been chained in. No one would go into that place so hundreds of cars backed up all the way out on to the Clones road. Result: traffic chaos. Tom Conlon didn't try to force the lorry out of the entrance. That would have been taking the law into his own hands. What he did do was call the RUC. Normally the RUC would not have come within an ass's roar of the place. But with the Ceasefire, the whole situation had changed. Out they came from Newtownbutler and by the time they made it to Clogher they were very angry. They had been forced to walk the whole way in from the main road. The lorry was removed, McCracken was charged with various offences. He had become a 'victim' of the IRA Ceasefire. All the time Tom Conlon was telling me this, he had the bewildered look of a man who cannot understand the weirdness of human behaviour. Certainly there is nothing worse than a bad neighbour.

Tom was on his way back from the funeral in Scotshouse – Aidan Connolly's son's funeral. Many people from Redhills went to it. I saw them driving out the road wearing dark suits. Mark Geraghty, the production designer, paid his respects to the family. Someone told him that Aidan had been seen at the family grave days before the son died, trying to come to terms in advance with the coming doom. Trying to steel himself against the on-rushing disaster. We hang on to this planet by our fingertips.

Out at the tractor shed it takes us until 5 p.m. to get the first shot in the can. I duck and dive around the set chatting with the actors, trying to tell them what was in my mind, trying to help make things better – without Peter seeing me, of course. I told Peter that I thought Carol, playing Mrs Prunty, should do such-and-such. He grabbed me by the lapels in mock anger and shook me: 'We're on her back at the moment.' But I notice that he did speak to her and the next take was better.

Anthony Brophy sits on the catering bus waiting to be used. 'Did you ever notice,' he says, 'how old men's ears are so big? The ears and nose don't stop growing.'

'Neither does hair or nails. When you're dead, I mean,' I reply.

I walk into the hairdresser's and ask Dee to cut my hair.

'Cut it all off. Please. Sounds hair-brained, I know.'

'Yes? Are you sure? A Number One?'

'Yes. Skinhead.'

She cuts the lot off. I come out looking like I'd just been released from a Siberian prison. Albert is the first person who sees me.

'What have they done to you, son? I'll bloody kill them.'

Later, in the pub, people look at me and laugh. 'Holy God, you look a dose.' Sometimes to get a grip, to get out of a rut, you need to shock yourself. I wanted to look harder. Maybe Death will dodge around me and pick on someone softer. No, we're all softer.

Day 47: Thursday 6 October

Roll 235. The massive corrugated doors on the tractor shed are wide open. A wind cold enough to shiver the goolies on a brass monkey cuts through the vast space, rattling the lamps and brooming up the dust on the concrete floor. Two hot-air blowers stand idle, not even plugged in. Someone is saving electricity, I suppose. The doors are open while the crew get everything set up.

Peter comes over and immediately grabs me by the lapels again. In a sing-song, mischievous, but none the less serious voice he says, 'You've been directing the actors again, haven't you?'

'Who?'

'Carol.'

'What?'

'You told Carol to do a look at Prunty's reaction to the letter from the taxman, didn't you?'

'I confess.'

'She was doing a big-eyes-to-heaven number. I asked her, "What's all that?" "Shane told me to do that."'

I try to wriggle out of it but can't. I'm furious with Carol, of course. She's landed me right in it. All I was trying to do was help. She went over the top . . . then brought me with her. If I'd been in her situation, would I have bitten my tongue? Don't know, can't say. Oh, to hell with it. I'm still glad that I spoke to her. I've got to put my oar in where I think it's needed, so that one day in the future, when I'm sitting in some cinema watching the film, I won't kick myself for not saying something at the time to the director. The director can't see everything. Contrary to actors' opinions, they are not God. They need help too.

Half the crew seem to have the flu. Mike Southon has it bad. He sits in his canvas chair wrapped up in padded jackets and misery. A doctor is on the way. Loads of people go round sniffing. 'Have you got the lurgy as well, love?'

Tony Devlin says to me, 'You know why, don't you?'

'Why?'

'The curse of McCracken.' He goes away laughing when I tell him about the RUC arriving down at Clogher.

It's odd being the writer, but only when you are at home writing. Seeing it filmed and being there, I've got to admit, is a gas. Painful at times, but what luck to see the whole thing coming together! At home – silence. Except for the noises in your head. On the set – noise and bodies tumbling all around you. In your head – silence. As an actor I did rep., tours, seaside summer seasons, Fringe, the Abbey, the NT . . . Great fun with your friends, but then I found myself going off on my own with blank paper and a biro. My public living gave way to a private kind of existence. Continual reflection. What's it all about, Alfie? Facing the blank sheet of paper is like sitting down to a never-ending exam. You are in the room doing the exam on your own. You are also the invigilator and there is no way you can cheat. You'll know eventually if you've passed by the audience's applause . . . The writer is pimp, whore and punter all combined. I've never met a satisfied whore and the pimp is pleased only by the day. The worst thing about writing is that it's in your head all the time, especially when you are not writing. It's a bit like sex mania. Even on Christmas Day when the family are murdering one another over Trivial Pursuits, you're itching to sneak up the stairs to sit at the typewriter. The Arts Council should take over the running of lighthouses. Stick a writer in each one. Ring the coast with the maniacs. That wouldn't keep us happy, though. We need people so we can subject them to our scribblings. 'Darling, what do you think of this?'

Outside the tractor shed, the ground is strewn with rough stone. OK for tractors. We all have to walk carefully as we crunch about. I sit in my car as it's warmer. It's a laugh watching the goings-on. The crew jump up and down from the back of trucks, fetching and carrying lamps, poles, lengths of wood. A painter has a huge flat lying on the ground and is painting it with a roller on a long handle. As he paints he sings, 'I belong to Glasgow, dear old Glasgow town . . .' He thumps the roller against the flat as he sings, keeping time with himself. A man steps out of a van with a tray-load of chickens and carries them over to the kitchen truck. He stumbles on the rough stones. A chicken falls from the tray. He picks it up quickly, slaps it down on the others and flicks the neck up so it isn't dangling over the edge of the tray.

David Kelly, in his priest's costume, is talking to Suzanne Nicell, the second assistant director. David is tall, thin, with grey hair and a pronounced nose. He looks like the kind of actor you see in a Fellini film. I can't hear what he is saying to Suzanne but he pantomimes his words with actions. He has his back to me. I see him pointing to the sky and wagging his long finger. Then with two hands he makes round movements as if describing a football. Then he bends down and holds his right palm about two feet above the ground. Then he elaborately points to the sky again, this time standing on tiptoe. He turns his head and I can see he's wearing dark glasses. He claps his hands once, the right hand shooting up from the left. His right hand held aloft, he stands stock still. For a moment. Then he flaps his elbows like he's flying . . . All the time Suzanne looks at him, mesmerized. His mime over he turns and carefully, daintily, walks across the stones and into the 'studio'. I like David especially for the way he looked after Marie Conmee for the short time she was with us. He told me she'd lose her way in the hotel corridors and he'd have to find her and direct her to her room. He also visited her in hospital in Dublin recently.

'I don't think Marie is long for this world.'

'Yes? No?'

''Fraid so.'

From my car I see Albert, in his uniform, step down from his trailer. He sniffs at the cold air and prowls over the stones and into the shed. I get out of the car and sit in the back of a truck. A make-up girl talks to Rosemary, the 'frocks' lady.

'I hate travelling on the catamaran.'

Nikki Clapp, the script supervisor – dripping as usual with pens, pencils, biros, stop-watches, clip-board and script – says, 'I had to miss the girls' night out in the Olde Post Inn last night.'

'Why?' asks Ken, the sound man.

'I had the lurgy, didn't I?'

Brendan Croasdell, one of the caterers, walks by, three electrical connections in his hands. In his Dublin accent, fag in the corner of his lips, he says, 'If youse want fucken tea yiz'll have to give me electricity.'

Malcolm, the Cockney grip, calls after him, 'Either way it'll be shocking.'

Peter calls over to me and we sit in his caravan cutting dialogue.

'Good. That means I can do it in three shots now. We must get out of here today.'

Ken shows me a machine he has that can select the best sound take. The actor says a line. It is recorded from different directions. The receiver can select the strongest level.

Lisa Mulcahy – 'Quiet please. PLEASE!' – sticks her head out into the fresh air and closes her eyes. She stands in an 'I'm very relaxed' position. Back straight, her hands held out a little from her body, index fingers and thumbs making circles. She stands so for half a minute. Then, incredibly, three oranges appear in her hands. These she juggles expertly in the air. They blur around her, plop back into her hands. She disappears back into the shed.

Tony Devlin trips over a cable. He shouts out 'Agh!' as if he's dying. People rush to his aid. Penny, the nurse, her pale face flushing, runs over to where he lies. Tony has hurt his knee. His face winces. 'Hate tha'. Don't mind kissin', hate tha'.'

I shout over to him, 'The curse of McCracken strikes again!'

A doctor goes into the shed to minister to Mike Southon. Mike has been as grumpy as a bear with a sore head . . . Anne O'Neill, a caterer, goes down with the lurgy and has to go home. Now the kitchen is under-staffed and, to make matters worse, the oven keeps going out. The crew are already assembling for lunch. The Belfast boys are always first in the queue, always obstreperous and witty. Tommy Hamilton is first of the first always. He is well-built and very Belfast. Yet he is forever going round putting on a Noël Coward voice. He preens and prances, flicks his head. 'Terribly nice to see you, dahling. Let us run away, hand in hand, to a more pleasant beach than this.' This morning I heard him as he sat over bacon, egg and sausage. 'I'm too young, too talented, too rich, too much too soon.' He's a hoot. Obviously a frustrated actor.

I drive back to the house. The pheasants gather round, as silly as domesticated hens. Why bother shooting the daft buggers? You can catch them easily, two at a time.

I walked down to the lake. When they were renovating the old house they dumped bricks, plaster and other rubbish at the edge of the water. This debris they covered up with earth to make a landing stage and parking area. But some of it still sticks up and I noticed a notebook wedged between two bricks. I pulled it out and saw that the notebook had belonged to a girl. A Protestant girl. It contained accounts and lists of names. One page was headed 'Ordermarks 1924–1925'. On one side of the page was written 'Christmas Term' and underneath, various dates. Opposite the dates were entries such as 'From Miss Boyle for not having time to do my German

Exercise', 'From Miss Boyle for not opening the windows in the morning in Junior A', 'From Miss Boyle for not bringing down my umbrella before church (and it did not rain)', 'From Miss Boyle for making a noise going to bed', 'From Miss Smith for not understanding properly'. Another page was headed 'Presents Received . . . Dorothy Craig gave me a Calendar. Maud Reid gave me a painted box. Elizabeth Hinds gave me coat-hangers. Jean Anderson gave me an Autograph . . .' Yet another page was headed 'Fortune'. Written underneath in nib and ink was 'Lucky Day – Wednesday. Lucky Colour – Cerise. Lucky Number – Eight. Lucky Flower – Poppy. Motto: A little cheerfulness goes a very long way. Character – August girls get a move on wherever they go. Industrious and full of ideas, there seems no end to their energy. They are never satisfied until they reach the top of the tree and, sometimes, not even then . . . August girls attract people who are out of the ordinary. August maids like company and bright cheery surroundings. They are not fond of being left to themselves for very long . . .

> Wear a Sardonyx, and for thee
> Life will hold felicity.
> The August-born without this stone
> May live secluded and unknown . . .'

Like the contents the hand was big, plain and cheerful. Gushing. A life written down and lying preserved under debris at the edge of a lake – a lake she must have looked on many times . . . I loved the entry about being punished for not understanding properly. And as for Elizabeth Hinds giving coat-hangers as a present, well, how mean can you get? I don't know whose the notebook was – there was no name or clue. But whoever she was, I liked her. Her world seemed narrow and petty, but she was determined to give it a go. With the help of a sardonyx. I bound the notebook in a bit of silage wrapping and placed it back between the bricks. The girl's spirit lies in the words and the words lie by the water.

I drove to the Slieve Russell Hotel in Ballyconnell. Peter, Mike and the important members of the gang stay there. Down in a basement room the editors have made an editing suite and in a big room have fitted up screen and projector for showing the rushes. A local man operates the projector. He worked in cinemas in the West End and Soho all his life until he retired and came back to Cavan.

The Slieve Russell stands in the middle of nowhere. Driving up to West Cavan, a most desolate and beautiful part of the country, you come round a bend on the Enniskillen road and there it is, rising out of the fields. It is, to look at, a delicate mixture of Las Vegas and a convent. It has restaurants, a gym, a swimming pool and a magnificent golf course. And miracle of miracles, it gives employment to hundreds of people who would otherwise be on the dole or living in Sheffield. It was built by Sean Quinn, a Fermanaghman. He left school when he was twelve. On the morning he was due to take the eleven-plus he hid in a hedge because he knew if he sat the exam he'd end up having to go to college. He stayed at home with his father and worked the small stony farm. There were more stones than clay. He started a quarry. From that, a cement works . . . With the money piling up he built the hotel.

Sean Quinn owns hotels and pubs all over Ireland. In today's *Irish Times* it is announced he has purchased the Cambridge Hilton in England for £12 million. West Cavan is an area devastated by famine, emigration. He gives work to over five hundred people. He is also the only man in Ireland actually to shift the Border. His main quarry is right on it, so when they have a rock blast, the Border is shifted northwards by a few feet. Like all men who have made money he is quiet, solid and unassuming. I spent an evening drinking with him. By midnight I was plastered. He hadn't even sat down. I remember saying to him how amazed I was that there could be such riches in bloody stones. 'You can sell anything,' he said.

'I mean look at you – you sell words. And everyone's got thousands of them.'

I sit in the foyer of the hotel and wait for the crew to return from location. A man sits beside me and asks me about the film. 'I saw *The Playboys*,' he says. 'What's it like coming back for a second bite at the cherry?' I tell him it has been harder. We seem to have had more trouble, more people grumbling, folk wanting more money. 'Ah, that's always the case,' he says. 'First time a virgin, second time a whore.'

As he gets up and moves off, Vicki Smurfit joins me. She has been in the gym and wears a tracksuit and has a towel around her neck. We sit and yap and worry if the whole thing is a pile of poop. Peter's wife Virginia joins us and we chat away and start bitching about Kenneth Branagh and Emma Thompson. That's how out of touch we are. Then Sean Quinn himself comes over and buys us a drink. I congratulate him on purchasing the Cambridge Hilton.

'I had to do it with money,' he says. 'Your daughter got there with brains.'

'Yeah, and when she's got her Classics degree will you give her a job as a waitress?' I ask.

'No bother. I've got a couple of people in this place with Classics degrees. My waitresses are the best-educated girls in Europe.'

When the crew get back they are in foul mood – cold and lurgyfied. Then it is announced the projector has broken down.

When I return to the house the central heating breaks down. The place is cold enough for a regiment of ghosts. I sit and wait, but none turn up, so I go to the pub for warmth. I sit beside a teenage boy and girl out from Cavan town. The girl is pregnant, but they are not married and are not getting married.

'Why didn't you use condoms?' I asked rudely and bluntly.

'We don't believe in them,' the boy said. 'If you use them

you are not in true love. The world's gone terrible artificial. You know, food in tins and packets. Cartons of milk and them with chemicals.'

'Is this what you think?' I asked the girl.

'For now I do, anyways. What do you think of pure love?'

'It's a concept lodged deep in the imagination.'

'That's the only nation I'd die for – imagination,' the boy said.

'Only Puritans use condoms,' said the girl.

'Are you religious, the two of you?'

'We are,' said the girl. 'We are daily communicants. With nature.'

'Are you working?'

'Yes. We make bread, cakes, sandwiches. We sell at fairs, marts, football matches.'

'And my father died,' said the boy, 'and left me a bit of a legacy.'

'You sound like a pair of hippy aristocrats.'

'We're trying to live flesh to flesh. Spirit to spirit. That's all,' said the girl.

The band started up and we couldn't talk any more.

The girl had blonde hair, clear features, blue eyes, a small pretty nose. In between drinks she rested her joined hands on her unborn baby. The boy, about eighteen, had tar-black curly hair. He wore a shirt with no collar and tartan trousers. He rolled his own cigarettes. In view of the way he spoke, it surprised me he smoked. The girl drank pints of Guinness. He drank bottles.

In between numbers I asked them about the Ceasefire.

'One thing about the Troubles,' said the girl, 'it kept drugs out of Belfast. Dublin is full of heroin. Belfast will go the same way now.'

'Mark my words,' said the boy.

Day 48: Friday 7 October

A mist today, as grey as the corrugated sheets of the tractor shed. Mike Southon at least is feeling better and is better humoured. The crew move around with cables, lights and props. They talk excitedly of the end being in sight.

'Another week, me hearties.'

'Don't sound so bleedin' cheerful, mate. I'll have to go home to the wife.'

We lost so much time yesterday it'll be Thursday at the earliest before we finish. Today we're shooting Prunty's wake. Anthony Brophy is laid out in a coffin covered with the tricolour. A black beret and gloves rest on the flag. Two extras dressed all in black, faces masked, stand at the head of the coffin. The scene is about Matt as the boy discovering that all the time his best friend was in the IRA. He learns at the death, the second-last secret of the country. Prunty's run is over and without him his run is ending . . . but life out of death. Life out of death eternally. The set-dressing is excellent: bare and black, with the shock of the green, white and orange flag. That potent symbol summoning up our hopes and fears. The white is for peace – peace between the Orange and the Green.

One of the extras is a middle-aged woman with a great husky voice. She sounds a bit like the woman I met in the confessional. We bump into each other on the stones, our feet crunching as we stand talking. Straight out she says she had been an alcoholic since she was twenty-five. 'Up to then I hadn't a drink ever. Till one night I went to a pub with friends. And I took the plunge and had a port wine. Me mother, if she knew, would have killed me. Jesus. But from that port wine on till three year ago I had the drink. Me husband, me children, I'm telling you, they suffered. I ended up in the psychiatric. But thank God, now I've been great in recent times. But the urge is still there. I don't go into pubs at all. But round here where else can you go to socialize?' That

191

urge. That pain . . . One way or another we've all got them. I love the honesty of the woman, her bravery. The country is full of hooks: drink, cigarettes, heroin, horses, dogs. And religion. Because if you're on one hook you need another to get you off. 'I prayed, I prayed, I prayed to kill the urge.'

The sun comes out and the place takes on a different feeling.

'Heh, the sun!'

We discuss whether we should move immediately to Redhills and finish in the garden.

'It's too late,' Mike Southon says. 'We'd never get back, set up in time and get it all done. Anyway, look – it's gone in again.'

The forecast is good for tomorrow and for the next while. Tomorrow, though, is our day off so it'll make no difference if the sun is splitting the stones.

When they start shooting I go in and sit in a chair by the fire of what is Prunty's kitchen. Carol, as Mrs Prunty, is in the bedroom. The camera is on her. Albert, some extras and Matt are in the kitchen. I'm by the fire warming myself with imaginary flames. They do Carol's bit, then Peter tells Albert, Matt and the extras to run through their scene. There is a big pause. I feel eyes sticking in my back. I turn and look. It's Albert. 'We can't do the scene, love. There's a strange plain-clothes detective sitting by the bloody fire.' I slink off, muttering. But it's a good definition of a writer, all the same: a plain-clothes detective, mingling with people, smelling out crime, or clues. I stand at a distance and watch.

When Carol's scene is shot, as is traditional, the crew applaud her. Her role is over. She has done well at short notice. As an actor, saying goodbye has extra poignancy. You wonder whether you will ever get another part. I think of Marie Conmee. She's in hospital and I haven't yet written to her. For such a lack of grace I feel truly guilty. There's so much guilt about we must enjoy it. Marie was perfect – a great, shambling, eccentric, world-weary woman, yet strong. Except of course, as it turned out she wasn't. She has a great laugh, Marie. It is full of innuendo and smut, yet girlish – perfect for Mrs Prunty. But what's the use, it's all over now. Carol's luck was in. And she grabbed it with both hands.

Anthony Brophy lies in his coffin for another take. The extras look at him and at the flag. An extra moves the beret and gloves from the green part of the flag to the white. 'That's right.' Peter smiles and whispers, 'They're giving themselves away today.' He meant that they must be in the IRA. I tell him that isn't the case at all, they simply know the customs of the country.

Albert strolls out into the sunshine. 'When I did *The Dresser*, I had to lie dead for about twenty minutes, while Tom Courtenay went on and on with that speech. What gives you away when you're pretending to be dead is the pulse in your neck. Mike Southon's just told me that now they can move a piece of dead skin over the pulse by computer.'

'Not many people know that,' I say. He laughs.

'And you know something else? Lisa "Quiet please, PLEASE!" Mulcahy is the granddaughter of General Richard Mulcahy, a close colleague of Michael Collins. And Nigel's assistant, Kate Douglas, is a direct relation of Alfred Lord Douglas. I've been bursting to say all that. Thank you for giving me the opportunity.' He laughs.

Mention people or horses to Albert and he responds every time. He loves the quirks of living. The knotty parts. Individual himself, he's concerned about individuals. Especially when he's acting them. He's brilliant as the sergeant. He gives it such weight. Everything he says is studied. Deliberate. This is a man who doesn't waste emotion. Unless he's pushed. Outside the set I sit with some of the extras. Inside the 'studio' we can hear Albert's voice, strong and judged. We can't hear him all the time, but when we can the extras stop talking and listen. At the end of the scene he comes out and walks back to his trailer. Paddy Martin, an elderly man who was also an extra when we made *The Play-boys*, puffs on his pipe and, smiling, watches Albert walk the whole way across. Then he says, 'What a lovely man is Albert Finney. Yon's one of the finest gentlemen ever come about this country.'

'I wouldn't like to get on the wrong side of him for all that, Paddy.'

'I wouldn't like to get on the wrong side of you.'

Tonight is the wrap party. Nigel is organizing it. He's hired the Slieve Russell and admission is by ticket only. Though we have a week to go it's been decided that tonight's the night. Not everyone has been invited. So not everyone is pleased. People are phoning up and asking, 'Why am I not invited?'

'I can't cater for the world and his wife,' Nigel insists. People find out that John and Babs Rudden aren't on the guest list. They are furious at this omission.

'They can have my invitation,' I say.

'What'll you do?'

'Not let into my own party? That would require a sense of irony which I don't think the bouncers possess.'

I hand over my invitation and someone goes off to take it post-haste to John and Babs. I bet they don't come, anyway. They won't leave their animals, fowl and house. They should send the old sow.

I sit with Brigid McGrath, an extra. She was married to Max McGrath, in whose memory the local football ground is named.

'He lived for the football. When he was in the Army in Athlone, he'd cycle to Redhills of a Saturday night, play the game on Sunday, then cycle back to Athlone. Must be sixty miles that. Each way.'

'I think he's the only man I've ever seen play the game without committing a foul.'

'He was very fair. Do you mind he used always say, "It's not over 'til the final whistle"?'

'What sort of man was he to live with?'

'The best. He never once in his life hit the children. And we had eight of them. Now.'

'You can't say fairer than that, Brigid.'

I drive over the Border to buy a few bottles of wine. Coming back, I go down to Wattlebridge. From the bridge over the Finn River there is a fine view of Castle Saunderson. It is a big wedding-cake of a building with turrets, tall chimneys and mock battlements. Perched on a hill above a gracious bend in the river, it looks like something out of a dream. It was born out of political reality. In the seventeenth century the Saundersons arrived from Scotland and seized the land from the natives. Down through the years until 1922, they ruled the roost and returned MPs to Westminster. As rampant Orangemen, during the Home Rule debates they constantly declared that the native Irish weren't quite developed enough to rule themselves. After the Treaty they found themselves out of power – by the width of the Finn. The castle is in Co. Cavan. Despite being bigots, the Saundersons were a remarkable people. They rebuilt the castle after fires a number of times. They had a tennis court, sailing boats and their own racecourse. It is overgrown now, but you can still trace it under the briars, scrub and wild hedges. They had a stone-breaker and a Hornby oil engine for sawing timber. They fought for the Empire in numerous wars. Then the twentieth century caught up with them and passed them by. In more recent times they sold out to a Pakistani supermarket owner. He did some kind of a sale to a local man, who became the first Catholic to own the place. He, in turn, put it up for sale. Almost immediately it was badly damaged by fire. There is a court case pending with Lloyd's of London.

If you don't adapt to new circumstances you die. The Saundersons didn't adapt. They couldn't abide dealing with Dublin. They gave their hearts to London. Their bodies and ashes lie in the grounds of the private chapel attached to the castle. Their pet dogs are buried with them. But wouldn't it be better to have the Saundersons there now than to have it as

it is – half-burnt, dead? The lawns are overgrown, the beautiful brick-walled orchard tumbling, the trees are scabby with
moss and half-hidden by nettles, and the only noise is the cry
of sheep and the doomy caw of crows. Men dream, women
work, children play . . . but not any more along this stretch of
river.

As I drove up to the bridge I noticed a man leaning over,
looking down upon the water. He was a middle-aged man in
a green hacking jacket, tight trousers tucked into walking
boots. As I pulled up and got out I saw him glance at my
English number plate. He smiled as I joined him on the
bridge. When we began talking he assumed I was from
London. I didn't make him any the wiser. He was from Co.
Down.

'I walk the Province every two years. This is as far South as I
come in this direction.' He said it in such a way I knew he
meant he'd never set foot in the Republic. On principle.

'You should try Dublin some time. Booming. Booming.
Money. Energy. Confidence.' I said this to get him going.

'Yes. And for why? The EEC trying to destabilize Ulster.'

'What do you do for a living?'

'I farm. My son's taken over. Why don't you want us?' By
this he meant England.

'You're bad neighbours. Don't get on with the people living
next to you. You haven't set much of an example. You invented gerrymandering. You . . .'

'No we did not. That originated in Massachusetts in 1811.'

'Well, you took to it like a duck to water. Your future is the
island of Ireland, not Bristol, Guildford or Clapham Common.
Adapt or die. The years have caught up with you. Look at
that castle up there. They didn't adapt.'

'You're asking too much.'

We stared down at the flowing river.

'The English don't want you. They don't know who you
are. Though they invented you.'

'Why are you crowing about it?'

196

'I'm sorry. The Irish have had to crawl out from under a lot of big stones. But they're doing it. They're trying. The Finn flows into the Erne. The Erne flows into the sea. Lives have to merge. About time Ulster had a party. Have fun. Invite the neighbours. There's nothing worse than a bad one.'

'I hate the haters who hate us. So-called friends. I walked here from Enniskillen. I have relations buried in odd cemeteries all over the place. I visit the graves. Every two years.' He took out a hip flask, took a nip, offered the flask to me. Brandy. He leaned his back against the parapet and said, 'Take for instance a family row or a row with friends. You can keep the row going for years, no bother at all. Politics is the same. It's easy. No bother at all.'

'True. True. We can all be bigots. Blood is thicker than water. And bigotry is thicker than blood.'

'Hell, to my way of thinking, is confusion. Not knowing what to do. I mean, what's the solution when there's no solution?'

'The island is too small for murderous squabbles and political yelping to Westminster. They'll knife both traditions if it suits.'

'I just don't know. My father had a squabble with a man over a horse. After buying it the horse broke down pulling a plough. The families haven't spoken for sixty years. And that's only an animal, not a country.'

'So what you're saying is there's no hope?'

'I think so. Is there any hope when there's none?'

He was less glib than me, that's for certain. I'm removed from the pain. His hair was dark, grey at the edges. I think he dyed his hair. His face was strong, red. A long face with a long upper lip. He took off his spectacles and with a white handkerchief wiped the lenses. Then he put the spectacles back on and carefully adjusted them on the bridge of his nose.

'Ah well, nice talking to you,' he said.

'And you. Thanks for the brandy.'

I reversed the car and drove off, catching a glimpse of him walking away North.

I went to the wrap party. John and Babs weren't there. What can you do at a wrap party but make a dick of yourself? Most people did. I didn't take one drink. I think talking to the man at Wattlebridge brought out the Puritan in me. The fastidious nip he took at the flask was a warning of the dangers of excess. He was a lonely man and he made me lonely. I hate saying goodbye ... and a whole week of goodbyes are looming.

I met a journalist from the *Anglo-Celt*. He told me that people had written in to the newspaper complaining about the sow in the chapel.

'You know the kind of thing: "Pig desecrates graves" ... or was it "defecates on graves"? Can't remember.'

'Yeah?' I'm shocked all over again.

'Forget it. A few nettles don't ruin a field of hay.'

'Even one nettle stings. Maybe we were wrong to have the pig in the porch. Maybe I was making a skit of religion.'

'There's no institution above a bit of humour. Are you being serious? Relax. What are you having?'

'Just a tea.'

'Jesus. Are you ill or something?'

I sit up in bed half the night, the covers tucked under my chin – a picture of misery. No, there's no ghosts in this house. They've been scared away by the all-night long, battery-operated Bord Failte regulation lights in the hallway and kitchen. They'd send a lorry-load of poltergeists scurrying, never mind Dorothy and Gladys.

At the party I sat with Cissie. Looking at my skinhead haircut she said, 'I bet any money you get a cold. Sure, it's like taking the top off a hot-water bottle.'

Saturday 8 October

Day off. Any of the film crowd you meet have red faces and sore heads. But the third assistant director, the wonderful and hilarious Mary Gough, who was an expert horsewoman before she broke her back and came into the film business, is having a party at her house in Ballyhaise at noon. Then everyone is going back to Redhills to Sean McCaffrey's pub. There they will sup into the small hours from whence they will emerge and, I suppose, go home for a quiet drink.

My head is full of the man I met at Wattlebridge and what he said: 'What's the solution when there's no solution?' and 'Is there any hope when there's none?' That's what I feel about most things. We scurry about like wrens building nests. The wren flips and flits all day long carrying moss. In and out of the bush where she's building she goes, a tiny piece of moss in her beak going in, nothing coming out but worry. The moss might all be gone by the time she gets back to the tree or stone. No, still there. Moss, beak, fly, build . . . All day she frets and hops, driven by instinct. When the nest is built it is no bigger than a plum: big enough for the wren; no defence against a cat, if the cat could see it. The size of the nest is it's defence. Last night I looked out of my window at the stars and felt tiny. I hope the cat doesn't see me for a long time. The cat is God or Nature or Luck and I don't mind that. In the end. But imagine getting terminated by your fellow wren? Over land that's going to bury you eventually. Doesn't matter if the deeds are lodged in Belfast, London or Dublin. The Ceasefire isn't a solution, but it *is* hope. Or is it our fate simply to go on killing each other? We're in a Greek tragedy and maybe it's going to last for ever . . . The other night I saw two men fight outside a pub. One shouted to the other, 'Go way before I fill your boots with blood!' Is that what it is to be in this neck of the woods? For ever?

I nipped across the Border at Leggykelly and headed for

Drummully. When you cross into Fermanagh there is a sign welcoming you to the county. It has been placed there by Fermanagh County Council. The welcome is written in Gaelic. *'Cead Mile Failte'* it says at the top. Lord Brookeborough must be turning in his grave. Fermanagh is predominantly Catholic. Lord Brookeborough, a former Prime Minister of Ulster (I think he retired in 1963), when asked what he would do if a United Ireland somehow came about replied, 'I would lead my people to South Africa.' I wonder where he'd lead them now? England? I doubt it.

Driving along the narrow country roads, nine times out of ten any oncoming car will be driven by a local farmer. Hunched over the steering wheel they always raise one index finger in salutation. They don't let go of the steering wheel; they just flick up a finger. In at the back of Drummully Protestant Church I met such a farmer. From our respective vehicles we raise index fingers at each other, then as we squeeze past he lowers his window and stops when we are opposite. There we are, wedged down an overgrown lane, our side-view mirrors flicked askew, bang-on face to face. He's about sixty, I'd say, wearing an old suit jacket and striped shirt and a battered brown hat.

'Are ye lost?'

'No. Yes. I'm looking for the spot where "White" Peter Connolly lived.'

'He's dead. And his sister.'

'Thought he must be by now.'

'Aye. Mind that time the bomb was in Newtownbutler? He was in the pub and the police told everyone for to get out and go? "White" Peter went back into the pub. No one was going to tell him what to do.'

'Maybe he'd forgotten his wallet.'

'There wouldn't have been much in it.'

'Go on.'

'The bomb went off.'

'God.'

'He lost only the leg. It was afterwards he died.'

'I see. From the injury?'

'Not at all. He come in one night from drinkin'. He had the wooden peg he then. Or plastic, was it? He sat in front of the fire and threw paraffin on. They say the paraffin spilt on his wooden leg. He lit up. Burned to a stick. The wooden leg was gone and he was unable to escape. Aye, the drink.'

'Poor Peter.'

'Don man had the world at his mercy in his youth. Do you mind him?'

'I made hay with him. For Richard McManus.'

'Aye, in Clonooney.'

'No. In Redhills. After they left Clonooney. "White" Peter came up every year to help with the hay. He'd let himself into the house in the middle of the night and be asleep in the chair when Richard came down in the morning. He always arrived on July 1st. If we had our lunch in the field he'd lie on our rakes or forks. That meant no one could go back to work until he did. He liked a long snooze in the sun.'

'He had wine, women and song. And the horses. If you leave the horses alone, they'll leave you alone. The women aren't like that. He trained to be a priest one time in Maynooth. Aye, I know who you are now. Took me a while. Move on in there and you'll come to the house.'

'What a way to die.'

'That's the truth. Fell asleep in front of the fire. And he had the false leg stretched out to the flames. He wouldn't feel a thing till it was too late.'

'Is it true Nationalists are in the majority in Fermanagh now?'

'They're in the majority everywhere west of the Bann now. But that means nawthin'. People can be herded out.'

'Do you think it'll happen?'

'It's happened plenty times before. Sure it happened only twenty year ago. No, numbers don't mean a thing. What has to change is the way men think.' When he said this he rapped on the side of his car with his index finger. The rest of the time his arm simply dangled out the window. He stared into space and then, as if exhausted with the effort of tapping with his finger or exhausted at the topic, he quickly slipped the handbrake and moved off. All the time he'd kept the engine running.

I reversed into a field gate and drove back to Leggykelly, went into the service station there and washed the car. A man came up to me and watched me spray on the water with the high-powered hose. He was a young fellow and kept moving about – a live-wire kind of bloke.

'Yiz had the party last night in the Slieve.'

'That's right.'

'Yiz never invited many of the locals.'

'Didn't we?'

'Yiz fuckin' didn't. Not like the last time. *The Playactors. The Playboys.* Why?'

'Nothing to do with me, mate.'

'Fuckaff, sure you wrote it. Yiz fuckin' didn't play fair. You know?'

'Life just isn't fair.'

'You can fuckin' say that again. I got in anyways the last half hour.'

'So what are you complaining about?'

'Only I codded me way in I wouldn't have got in at all. I was to meet a girl there. But she wasn't fuckin' there. I was there. She fuckin' wasn't. I never seen you there.'

'I left very early.'

'Fuckaff. Yes?'

'True.'

'Yes? That's a fright. Fuck me.' He sat back into his van and when I looked I saw him yawning. When I'd finished washing the car he was leaning his head on the steering wheel.

'Heh! All yours,' I shouted.

He hopped out. 'Thanks. Fuckin' great. Good luck.'

When I woke up this morning I decided I was leaving the house. I went down to the sitting room and phoned the Slieve Russell and booked a room there. The central heating is still out of action and David Patton, the landlord, is on holiday. Besides, I want to leave before I have to – when the film's finished. I don't want to be in the house at the end. I want to break the happiness, get out, yet I'll still be around. There's an old sepia photograph hanging in the hallway. The house is as it was in the fifties and, in the fields along the avenue, the hay has been made into cocks. It looks so gentle and idyllic I can look at it only for a few seconds.

The sun always shines in the past. I walked down to the lake. The trees swished green and gold and leant out over the water. A mist hung low among the trees and rolled very slowly over the lake. When the Whyte-Venables were here there was a jetty and boat-house made from pine logs. Neglect and age tumbled them. David Patton was in the process of renewing it when the logs he had ready for the job were stolen. A brace of ducks came in above the trees, swooped down into the mist, skimmed the surface and, seeing me, flew quickly away down the other end and out through a gap in the trees.

I walked into the woods and, along an avenue, found the stump of a beech tree my father cut down. Miss Whyte-Venables gave him a wispy ash tree, but he pretended she had given him the big beech. By the time she discovered my father's 'mistake' it was too late. She called her trees her 'beauties'. Like her cats, they were her friends. When she saw her beautiful beech cut down, chopped up, she almost fainted with grief. We knew plainly he had acted deliberately. He liked Miss Whyte-Venables as an individual but he hated her whole class, what they stood for and what they had done to Ireland. I think he cut the tree down to get his own back. As a policeman he willingly protected her and her demesne. He carried out his duties assiduously. But there must have been, all the time, a part of him rebelling. It manifested itself in the cutting of the lovely copper beech. Perhaps greed played a part in his act. There was a whole winter's burning in the beech. The rotten ash would have lasted only a few weeks. No doubt like us all his motives were mixed. At the time I'd never heard of Chekhov but subsequently, when reading his plays, I always returned in my mind to my father and Miss Whyte-Venables and the copper beech. A whole era was ending in Ireland. My father, without realizing, had taken an axe to it.

I sat on the stump, walked through the shadows. The mist and the trees clung on to the night. On the hill near where the orchard used to be I heard the horses whinnying. That was the only sound. The sheep were quietly grazing, all of them in a line, all with their rumps to the breeze. I went back to the house, packed and left it all downstairs. I'll come back later.

We're in the vegetable garden for positively the last time. We need the sun so we can match up with the stuff we already have in the can. The mist is so heavy it looks as if cotton wool's been dumped over the entire village from a great height. Peter arrives and steps out of the Mercedes. With him is Nikki Clapp, an entire office hanging from her neck. The car driver heads for breakfast. Peter wears his blue anorak and cords tucked into white socks and brown boots. The cigar is already to hand.

He goes down the side of the barracks and into the garden. He stands on his own at the onion bed. Holding up two fingers he works out points of view. Then he makes a rectangle with thumb and index fingers and, peering into this imaginary lens observes the garden. He stands very still. He is utterly concentrated. He is being as quietly meticulous as my father sharpening a saw.

Nikki comes down to him. She stands beside him and opens the script. It is full of pencil lines and observations written out in great detail. No one says a word. Then Peter says, 'The stuff we've already shot . . . Albert is so good, why bother going on to Matt at all? At this point.'

'Yes, hm, yes, quite,' Nikki says.

Having satisfied himself as to what it is he is going to do, Peter relaxes, puffs his cigar, smiles. 'You know it was Tracy's wedding reception last night?' Tracy is a receptionist in the Slieve Russell. She is one of many, all of them twinkling spirits, who'll do anything to help. Well, nearly anything . 'It was held in one of the big conference rooms. It was so good. The band played lovely Irish music. We should have had them for the wrap party. I've been thinking . . . the thing I've been slowly realizing over the last few months . . . the Irish are a gentle people. I think it might well be that it is the English who are violent. There we were at Tracy's party – it was after ten when Virginia, Albert and myself arrived. They'd been partying since 1 p.m. Yet the great mix of men, women and children were enjoying themselves in the most wonderfully gentle manner. And they'd been at it for hours. Can you imagine the equivalent in England? Apt to be staid and dreary, or a punch-up over a pub.'

It is always a nice moment when English realists succumb to Irish romance. So I refrained from telling him of the times when I've been clobbered at Irish weddings, not to mention funerals and other such festive occasions.

Owen Conlon, brother of 'Clogher Market' Tom, arrives in the village in a pony and trap, clip-clop over the bridge, and the sun comes out. I climb aboard and we set off to visit Pat Smith and his sister Kate who live a few miles outside the village. Pat was, is and forever will be a horse-dealer. In the old days you'd see him going the roads alone with troops of horses. He'd let me hop up on one and I'd ride with him for miles. Only trouble was having to walk back. The Conlons are relations.

'I remember, Owen, when all you had was a bicycle.'

'Yes. I'm evolving backwards. What came before the pony

and trap?' He holds the reins, hands apart and flaps them at the pony to make it trot on. He and I were at school in Clones. We have hardly spoken in thirty years but, because we were book-boys together, we chat away like we had never been out of each other's company.

The black cob is remarkably placid, totally unafraid of traffic or dogs. Going down the braes he occasionally slips on the shiny tarmac, but nothing serious. I'd forgotten what a jogging the body takes in a trap. Every bit of me hops like pebbles in a riddle. Owen now and then clicks his tongue and at the wordless command the pony clips along effortlessly. A dog suddenly dashes out from a house and right under his belly barks furiously. Tommy trots on, his head turned away as if the dog isn't there.

'He isn't deaf and blind is he, Owen?'

'He was born with a grand temperament. Some of us weren't.'

People, when they see us going by, cheer up. Cars slow down and the occupants look back. It's a tidy journey to Pat's house. By the time we get there, the pony is sweating and my cornflakes are trying to get back out.

Pat and Kate Smith live in a bungalow built in front of the old family cottage. The cottage is newly whitewashed and looks habitable. Though they have moved into the new, they cannot break with the past. It's amazing how many brothers and sisters remain in the old homeplace, unmarried. Something to do with property rights, or parents living long, or lost opportunities ... Or maybe a baleful eye cast at the state of marriages around them.

Pat Smith is a tall, lean man with incredibly light blue eyes. There isn't a pick of surplus fat on him. Though he is over eighty-five years of age, he has only a slight stoop when he walks. His face is spare with few lines and those deep. He wears a cap and when he looks out from under the peak at a horse his look is hard, without any emotion whatsoever. He remembers in minute detail a vast amount of horses going back seventy years. I imagine he remembers more horses than people. When he recalls a particular animal he plunges straight into the telling without having to search through his memories with difficulty.

'He was apt to be horrid wicked. I had him haltered to the tail of the animal I was riding. Twenty-five pounds I bought him for and I was takin' him to Clones for to sell. Didn't he take fright at a goat in George Howe's hedge, reared back, snapped the rope and away? I found him in the Widdy Smith's garden. "You'll never ketch her," says the Widdy, for he was ploughin' round the garden a holy fret. I caught him and took him to Clones. I was selling him for twenty-eight pound to some Northern dalers when along come Joe Reilly who knew the animal and says he, "Yon's a quiet horse." The dalers heard him and moved on. I followed Reilly round the fair of Clones and says I to him, "If you're not buyin' kape your nose out of my business." I had to bring him home and put him in a shed. He kicked up a horrid pile. A holy tarra. I put a touch on his nose, took him outside and tied him to the wall. I gave him a lamentable batin'. I sold him eventually for thirty-three pounds.'

He talks about taking dozens of donkeys to the docks and getting a shilling for each one. He remembers every penny he earned, because every pound earned was hard got: 'I worked for men who got the profit and all I got was hardship.'

Talking about a blacksmith he said, 'He got ojus unfaithful. He hated shoeing a horse in the end. He was afeered of them. Once you lift a horse's hoof to shoe her, you must never put the hoof down till you're done. On three legs she can't kick. John James North, now, in Redhill – if you were in a line of men waitin' and it come six o'clock, you'd have to go home and come back the following day. He got that unfaithful.'

'If he'd been shoeing all day he was probably very tired by six o'clock,' I ventured.

'Aye, but to send a man away and have him to come back. Ojus altogether.'

His use of the word unfaithful is unique. From another world. The contract between men and horses and blacksmith was like a marriage. 'You have to be a butty man for to be a blacksmith. Tall men get ojus back trouble bending and lifting a hoof. And if the horse lunged you'd get a quare jolt on the spine.'

When Owen drove into the yard he looked at the cob and said he'd got the itch and was too fat. I helped take Tommy out of the shafts, trying desperately to remember the names of the different parts of the harness. Grass grew around the house and Pat told Owen to let the horse go. 'You needn't be one bit afeered of lettin' him ate don grass. It's not too rank for him.'

Owen and I went into the house and had tea and cake. I couldn't remember ever meeting Kate, Pat's sister. 'Well, I don't mind you. I mind your mother well but.' The kitchen is big and square with an old Aga cooker. Furniture is meaningless beyond function to people of Pat's generation. All that mattered was land and horses. They've never been aware how rich in language they were. Are still. 'He was a boy could throw out poetry like hay off a fork. He had words at will.' This about a man who made up songs about horses.

We went across the road and down into a field. Pat still tramps from horsefair to horsefair looking for a good buy. He had three horses in the field. They came up and stood still for him. He looked at them and walked round them all the time appraising them. The field was steep with a great view of the country.

'It's a grand view from here,' I say.

'You'd hardly notice it and you used to it. Hup there.' He caught hold of the horse's mane and pulled her head around. As he pulled his hand across her ears she nibbled at the lapels of his jacket. 'Any fool can ride a horse. Ketchin' them is a different story.'

When we got back to the house and it was time to put

Tommy back in the shafts the truth of his remark became apparent. Tommy ran round the house and when we blocked his path he turned back and ran the other way. But the garden was small and he couldn't escape.

'Howl up outa that, whoa, whoa there. Lave him, lave him. Whoa. Whoa. That's the good boy, whoa. Whoa now. Now.'

Owen and I sat snug in the trap as the cob trotted without fuss all the way back to the village. The harness jangling, the hooves clopping, stayed merrily in my head long after Owen and Tommy, in brilliant sunshine, went out over the humpy bridge and home. As a boy and now, I've never heard Owen raise his voice, lose his temper.

Back in the reality of the garden, Peter and the gang are hard at work. The clear blue sky above has put them in great humour. I sit on an upturned box and watch. When the scene is shot that will be the end of filming in the village. Today-week I'll be in Dublin or London. It'll all be over. The fuss about something. The pony and trap ride was a fantasy. And the filming is a fantasy. So where's the reality? It's confusing, but is it Hell? The man at Wattlebridge said Hell was confusion. At this moment I think it's Heaven. Well, maybe.

I walked across the green to the pump and drank the pure, cold water. An elderly lady and, presumably, her daughter walking along the road beckoned me to them. They were well-dressed. The old lady had a silk scarf around her neck and wore a beautiful overcoat – long, brown, with a fur collar. I could smell the perfume on both of them.

'Do you recognize me?' the old lady asked.

'No,' I replied, 'sorry.'

'There's nothing to be sorry about. I knew your family.'

'What's your name?'

'That's neither here nor there. Are you as good a man as your father was?'

'Well, I'm as good a man as my mother was.'

She ignored this. Her daughter never said a word.

'How many children did they have?'

'Eight.'

'Would you be able to cope with the like of that?'

What is this – a test of character or fertility? The whole parent nexus is boring. After you reach shaving age it's pointless blaming them or others for your own defects. Let them rot in peace. And get on with it.

'No.'

'You're as good as neither of them so.'

They walked away, got into their Datsun and drove out along the Scotshouse road. The old bitch. She must have come with the intention of getting a whack at me and succeeded. If her only test is the simple logic of numbers, may she never be disillusioned. Especially if she lives in the North. Never saw the pair of them before. Marvellous the way they can come up to you and get a dig in. I bet she'll enjoy her dinner today. Well, I hope she does.

I ate mine down by the football field on the catering bus. You soon get fed up with the stodge of film food, yet you can't get enough of it. They pile your plate with veg and meat and, after that, who can resist the great dollops of pie and custard? There's quite a few who can. They'll eat only salads and fresh fruit. This end of the twentieth century is going to produce some of the healthiest corpses that ever went into a cemetery – most of them from showbiz.

John, the driver who looks after Vicki, works his way through an impressive pile of chips, cabbage and half a cow, and explains his theory of war and film-making to another driver, who steadily reduces an Everest of cabbage, turnip, spuds and ham. It's a good job you can't be breathalysed for vegetables. These drivers would be banned for life.

'Well, there's a *film* crew . . . and there's a *tank* crew.'

'Yeah, yeah.'

'They shoot. We shoot. They have magazines for ammo. We have magazines for rolls of film.'

'Yeah, yeah. And film mags. Like what you read.'

'That's right. But that's not relevant. They wear uniforms and most of our lot go round in combat jackets and boots.'

'Yeah, yeah.'

'Course, there's dead bodies in war and dead bodies all over the cutting-room floor. See?'

'Yeah, yeah. That's very interesting, John. Are you going to have a pudding?'

Some of the Belfast boys sit together drinking tea. They tear strips off Clones. 'Fuck me,' says Victor, 'it's serious yon spot. See me – I had to fight the thieves away. They clattered each other in the pubs every night. Yon place is depressed, mate. Sick.' I didn't leap to the town's defence. I had a second helping of apple pie and custard instead. And clattered into that.

Later I went to see the Redhills versus Drung football match in Bunnoe, which is a crossroads with a church and hall and the football pitch. The pitch is on the level, but at the back of one of the goals is a big hill of stubble. This must be the only field in Cavan to produce corn. The hill is so steep I can't imagine how they can get a tractor to go up and down it without tipping over. At the end of the pitch and across the road is Foy's mill – the last water mill in the area to which farmers brought flax and, later, corn. Until recently the mill never ceased to turn for 170 years. The big water wheel is over thirteen feet in diameter. It'll probably never turn again. The centre of the parish now is the football field. The game of the year is always against Redhills. It is the Derby of Derbies. In feeling – Arsenal *v* Spurs, along a river, beneath a drumlin, surrounded by thick, high hedges, whin, ragwort, cattle and people standing right on the edge of play.

To avoid relegation Redhills have to win, but so do Drung. The players butt into each other so hard you can hear flesh and muscle slap and crunch. Not only do the players know each other, but so do both sets of supporters – men, women and children. There's a battle on the pitch and a sporadic, good-natured vocal war off. It's a ritual that has been carried on nearly as long as Foy's mill – in fact, since 1888. And all for parish glory. The ball keeps sailing over the Redhills bar. And into our net. But 'It's not over till the final whistle'. The fight back begins after half-time and Michael Reilly's pep-talk. I stood among the players in the middle of the field as he gave it. Blue and yellow jerseys soaked in perspiration stuck to the players' backs as they listened. Their faces and hair looked as if they'd been doused with water. Michael's own face, head and body is a lather of sweat as he speaks. 'Are youse going to take it lying down? For feck sake, get stuck in. We have the beatin' of them if you're first to the ball and don't give the bloody thing away. Come on now, we have to win this and that's all there is to it. It's not over till the final whistle.'

Redhills pile on the pressure, pile up the points, get a penalty . . . and miss it. Defeat. End of story.

On the way out a Drung man says to us, 'Youse didn't have the luck today.'

'We never needed luck to beat yiz,' someone says back to him.

By the time I got back to the village the scene had been shot in the garden and the unit had moved back to the tractor shed. I went into the avenue for the last time and loaded up the car. I forgot a pair of trousers, went upstairs to fetch them and, coming back down, tripped on the bottom step. That was Dorothy Alice and Gladys Caroline Whyte-Venables letting me know they were still there. And they would be long after I'd gone, in fact and fantasy – for ever!

I drove past the big copper beech, the oaks, ash, cedars, the old orchard . . . now a cattle-shed. Like a character in a glorious cliché, Gladys spent many of her evenings in the orchard dressed in wide-brimmed hat, veil and gloves, tending her bees . . . 'Now, now honies, now, now, no fuss, no fuss. Sleepy-bye-byes.'

Out of the gate and away.

In the tractor 'studio' they shoot, for the very last time, Matt as the boy trying to break down the door into the room where his girlfriend Annagh is asleep. The boy's actions mirror his father's. We're not like our parents, we *are* our parents – Frankenstein and monster, all in one. As he breaks the door down, Prunty and another man see him. The other man is played by an extra from Clones. Leo is his name. He is tall, well-built, with a big head of black curly hair. His face is pale and for the part he is unshaven. In between takes we talk about Clones.

'The PVC factory, the German meat factory and the other meat plant – that's all we've got. The meat plants are only two days a week. Sure, you know that. And the PVC will employ only men from the North.'

'Why?'

'They'll work for below the union rate. We won't. Would you?'

'If I had a wife and eight kids I might.'

'You haven't.'

'I wouldn't. I don't know, I might. It's a hard situation.'

'Aye. If you have principles, you get a bad name.'

'If the Ceasefire is permanent the town might pick up.'

'There won't be a permanent ceasefire. The Brits won't leave. That's the bottom line. It'll all burst out again. The soldiers have changed their helmets for berets, but they're still turning cars over at the checkpoints.'

'I read in today's *Sunday Times* the Loyalists are going to call a ceasefire and London is going to accept the Ceasefire as permanent.'

'I'll believe it when I see it for myself. Anyway, the Loyalists won't give one inch.'

'Yes, but reason it out, Leo. They won't give an inch. So the killing and dying goes on for another twenty-five years? Men can see. It's better to give an inch than get six-foot-by-two.'

'I think people like fighting and dying. Look what's going on all over the world. I'm gloomy.'

'Well cheer up, here comes tea and gorgeous cakes.'

We drink our tea, eat our cakes and talk about another great Clones passion – handball. It's like Eton Fives, or, more accurately, squash without racquets. Clones produced one great player who was an All Ireland Champion – a man called Shamie McCabe.

'I played with him loads of times. Do you remember his brother Philly? He was some handballer. He'd stand in the middle of the alley and dominate. And he'd never take off his shirt and tie when he played. We'd be stripped, but Philly would be in his suit trousers and the shirt and the tie knotted nicely. He'd take the jacket off, all right. Fold it neatly, lay it down and then pull his shirt sleeves up a little. He'd give each sleeve a little tug. Then he'd get the ball, bounce it beside him and cuff it hard up against the wall. He'd take it off the back wall without lettin' her bounce and whack! Then he'd be ready for a game. A pound a corner and he'd be pleased as hell when he won. Some handballer. Shamie was champion, I know. You know where he lives, don't you? In at the back of the court-house. He has his wee garden full of jam jars with paper flowers, white and blue. Shamie was some handballer. The heart of his hand was hard as the toe of your boot.'

From the 'studio' comes Lisa's voice: 'Quiet please. PLEASE! We're shooting a film here.'

'It must be grand coming back to do a film, hah?'

'It is. But I try my best to make it sound miserable. In case the gods punish me for gloating and having a good time. You know that Irish thing.'

'It's better than working in a meat factory, anyway. If you could get it.'

'Some people would say the film business is a meat factory, Leo.'

'They've never worked in one.'

I slept in the hotel last night. Can't beat a bit of luxury. There's more ghosts in hotel rooms than there are in old houses. Hundreds have slept in your bed. Hundreds of arms have reached out and turned the bedside light off in just the same way as you've done. You lie in the same dark, churn through more or less the same thoughts, try to drift off, knowing that a few hours ago, a totally invisible stranger was doing just the same, in exactly the same position in the bed you now lie in ... Spooky. But only when you're on your own.

I came down to breakfast this morning, bought a newspaper, skimmed through and came to a piece with the heading 'Actress Marie Conmee dies'. Under the headline was a photo of Marie when she was much younger. I wouldn't recognize her from the photo even as I remember her when we first met thirteen years ago. 'The Sligo-born actress, Marie Conmee (61), died in St Vincent's Hospital, Dublin, yesterday after a short illness ...' I'm shocked to think she was only sixty-one. When she walked away from the film set that day she looked eighty-one. I'm shocked and guilty. Never sent her a card ... Will I go to her funeral? Bet I don't. When is it? Doesn't say. Marie Conmee ... a horse of a woman. Wild at times, but you couldn't ignore her. And a great, great laugh.

I drive out to the location to tell Peter and the crew. They already know. Nigel is organizing a wreath. He's tried to find out where to send the wreath, but apparently Marie hasn't got a family. Perhaps that was why she was such a free spirit. Her friends were her family.

This morning we are at Lough Oughter again – the other end of it, this time. We're at Senator Dolan's house overlooking the lake. This is the white house I saw the morning I rowed up the lough in the brilliant, icy sun. In this morning's hot sun it looks just as good. The countryside here is absolutely stunning. You look down on lush, buttery fields, trees and the vast stretch of water trembling in the light. Every bush is full of singing birds. Cows lie down in deep grass; sheep sit chewing the cud under the shade of an oak.

In front of the house are lawns divided by a gravel path running up to the front door. On one side is an orchard. On the other side of the house are stone outhouses and a curious enclosed yard with a cement wall. In this yard are bits of agricultural machinery from a previous age. Right behind the house is a hill that sticks up like a breast and nipple. On top are two abandoned tractors. The decaying wheels are deep in the ground and the big headlights stick out at the sides like the eyes of starving children. The tractors look like surreal sculpture.

The film crew have gone to town on the house. The doors are open, with cables snaking in and out. Lamps are everywhere. The narrow road in front is gorged with vehicles. Because the day is so warm and beautiful everyone is smiling and running about twice as fast as normal. We're also under time pressures, of course.

Throughout all the circus mayhem the owner, Senator Seamus Dolan, strolls about smiling – probably at himself for letting us invade his sacred privacy. He is a tall, spare, elderly man in a dark blue suit and with a thick head of grey-silvery hair. He looks like a cross between Beckett and Yeats. All his life he represented Cavan in parliament and still takes an interest. Formerly a schoolteacher, he met his wife Brid in the classroom. Years younger, she married him and had eight children. She must have been a beautiful girl then, because she's a beautiful lady now. She spends most of the day smiling and doling out hospitality. Peter Yates is terrified of this hospitality. When we came here originally, location hunting, usually early in the morning, Seamus and Brid would immediately dish out huge tumblers of whiskey and there we'd sit, getting slowly, politely sloshed. Very funny seeing Peter desperately looking round for a plant pot. But there was no way out. He had to drink the lot. Especially when he told Seamus he was a Scot. However, on subsequent visits I noticed he'd taken to wearing wellingtons.

In front of the house is an immensely tall, thin pine tree. I stood looking up at it at one point. Brid came over and said, 'Yes, it is, isn't it? Tall. Way, way back our youngest son climbed up to the very tip-top. We came running out. I was terrified. He cuckooed down at us. I said to Seamus, "What are we going to do? What are we going to do?" "Leave him," he said, "he'll come down of his own accord." We went back inside. Eventually, down he came. If we'd shouted he might have panicked and fallen.'

All day as we shoot, Seamus ambles about chatting, remembering, talking politics. His rooms are full of books and Dáil reports. 'All the bull they gave us in this country about religion. It was all money. A priest told me one time that in Maynooth they were taught how to keep the minds of the people occupied. If a slate was missing on the chapel roof, make them collect until you got the entire roof done. Keep them at it. That's what he told me. Do you remember the time when it was a mortal sin to go to a Protestant funeral? I was a teacher in those days. If I'd gone out with a Protestant girl I'd have lost my school. Like Master Gleeson before me. They sacked him. He joined the RAF after and was killed in the war.' Making a comb of his fingers he pushes his hair back and stares dreamily down the lake.

'How, why, did we swallow it all?' I asked.

'If I knew the answer I'd be able to walk across that water.'

'Do you think we're brought up as bigots?'

'Do you think you were?' He looks at me. Calmly waiting for reply.

'At times I feel I'm a bigot, yes. Especially about Ulster. The old drums beat in my head. I'm ashamed of myself then. I have to catch myself on. When you see debates on TV . . . Protestant writers, Catholic writers, politicians . . . all pretending to be wise and sophisticated. But when you work it out

217

none of them are giving an inch. Do you know what I'm saying?'

'Oh, I do rightly. But political progress *is* possible.' He's got the air of a man no longer in the hurly-burly. He's seen it all, thought it all out, no longer can do a lot about it. Besides, what's the point of torturing your brain when on such a glorious day you can lean across a gate and look down on Lough Oughter, misty in the sun?

Nikki Clapp sits on a tiny collapsible canvas seat, typing into her computer. She looks up from her labours. 'I don't want to go back to London. How could you ever leave here?'

'You know what they say? It's not bad on a good day. But it's no good on a bad day.'

'That goes for everywhere. What did you think of poor Marie dying?'

'I don't know what to think. She was alive . . . and now she's dead. God, that sounds banal. It's a mystery. That's what it is.'

'Well it proves we weren't all imagining things. Cancer.'

'Yes. The bad lad.'

'Pardon?'

Out on the narrow country road the ADs try to sort out the traffic problems. Farmers on tractors, milk tankers, locals driving to the shop: they all have to squeeze carefully by our parked trucks. At the back of a truck, one of the men from Belfast is having a loud argument with a Dubliner. It's about boxes that haven't been moved properly or something. The Belfaster is Tommy Hamilton. There are no Noël Coward tones now. He is effing and blinding away in his sharp Ulster accent. The Dubliner is effing and blinding back in his nasal, guttural twang. The look on their faces would curdle milk. A Cockney carpenter tries to calm them.

'Oh come off it, Tommy, ever since you lost out in the Karaoke contest, you've 'ad it in for everyone.'

'Fuckaff, you prick. I got bloody flu.'

All through filming McMahon's have run a Karaoke competition. All the crew entered. It's reached the semi-final stage. The other night Tommy, the hot favourite, got knocked out. By the Cockney carpenter . . .

To have such good weather when we so desperately need it, someone must be smiling down on us. We're shooting the scene where Annagh comes out of her house and sees Danny's father waiting for her at the garden gate. The way they're doing it is, I think, the wrong way round. They have her going into the house, the camera on both of them. But if she were coming out of the house, the first shot would show her *and* her house – such a stark contrast to the barracks. Albert, Vicki, Peter and Mike Southon discuss the set-up, the action. It's not working. I can no longer hold my tongue.

'Do it the other way. Have Vicki come out of the house.'

Immediately Peter sees what I'm saying. 'Good thinking, WRITER!' he booms happily.

They do it. It works. I watch with pompous satisfaction. But I think Peter deliberately lets those involved work things out for themselves at first. This way they feel organically connected with the working of the material. He gives them their heads for a bit. Then he steps in and sorts it all out. He probably knows all along the way it's to be shot. It's interesting watching talent at work. Albert, Matt, Vicki, Mike Southon . . . they all have completely different ideas. With a camera, two actors and a house in the background, you wouldn't think there'd be so many ways to shoot it. In the end, though, there's only one way. Sometimes I think getting the story across depends on luck. The whole business hangs on a thread. Luck and threads. In my novel and in the script there are constant images of abandoned cars, machinery, animals . . . When Peter and I saw the two tractors on the hill behind the house, we thought it would make a great image. But today I find we're not shooting it. We can't fit it in. I beg Mark Geraghty, the production designer, to get an old plough and place it in shot somewhere.

'I did see an old plough round here somewhere,' he says.

'There it is – lying in the hedge.'

'Done.'

Minutes later he's trying to lug it over to the outhouses where it'll be seen in later shots. I tell Peter. But Peter says that when we get to the outhouses all those scenes are at night. The plough will be invisible. 'Don't worry. We shot loads of abandoned stuff at Scud's.'

Peter has the flu. The lurgy is spreading. He's on antibiotics. Unlike me, he can't nip off somewhere. The good thing about being the writer is you can have maximum input without the responsibility of having to hang around to see it executed.

After lunch we all assemble outside for the traditional unit photograph. We laugh and cheer when the camera clicks, but secretly most people are nearer to tears. Albert makes a farewell speech. 'It was wonderful. No, no, it was . . . Seeing old faces from other pictures. Meeting new people on this one. This, after all, is our life. This is us. I won't forget you all. You were all wonderful. Thank you all very much.'

He is finished. Wrapped. I want to say goodbye to him, but I can't. I walk away through the orchard and when I come out the other side bump into him as he makes for his trailer. I can't find the words to tell him thanks. I wanted to say, 'Albert, if I were a bricklayer I'd build a wall from Cavan to Salford with your name on every brick. If I were a poet I'd write you a boat-load of sonnets. If I were a singer I'd serenade you every time it rained. If I were Vincent O'Brien I'd breed you ten Derby winners. At least. If . . .' We stopped and embraced.

I repeated to him the words Paddy Martin said: 'Yon's one of the finest gentlemen ever come about this country.'

'Did he say that? Really?'

You can't tell what makes people tick. It's a mystery where an actor gets his talent but, like a good spring well, in great actors it is there near the top and way down deep. One way or the other, Albert is the greatest of the great.

Anthony Brophy is wrapped as well ... No, I don't like saying goodbye. I take off for Clones and go round to the court-house to see Shamie McCabe. The gates into the yard off which he lives are chained up. He's not at home. This yard was where prisoners took a walk awaiting trial. It's been transformed into a garden. A strange garden. On a lawn with long grass are rows of jam jars stuck into the ground. The jars are painted white. In each jar is a white or blue artificial flower. Looks a bit like carnations. At the back of the yard is a wall. Ivy hangs down. Some of the wall is painted in daubs of colour. The daubs might be representations of butterflies. Black ones. The yard/garden is tiny. The jam jars, artificial flowers, the wall, make the place look like an altar. There's something Mexican about it. Once a handballer, maybe Shamie is now a different kind of artist. But the gates are locked.

Back at the filming, the day is turning dusk. In the sky the moon appears. Faintly at first, then as clear as a peeled orange. The lake lies like a dark mirror holding the trees, the fields in sleep.

Breda Walsh from the production office stops in her tracks and looks down at the lake. 'Cavan is a dreamy country, isn't it?'

'Like Venice – a wet dream.'

Up the gravel path leading to the house walk Tommy Hamilton and the Dubliner with whom earlier he was having the row. They have their arms around each other's shoulders. Tommy is in Noël Coward mode.

'We're *terribly* attracted. *Must* we be parted so *prematurely*?'

'Yes,' replies the Dub, 'I'll never fucken' work with you again.'

'No, no, dear heart. You musn't *say* that. I shall die.'

The whole scene is like something out of *A Midsummer Night's Dream*. Driving back to the hotel, in all the dark rivers and lakes along the way, smidges of moonlight lie on the water, floating like dead sprat.

In the hotel bar, sat on a high stool, had a pint. A young fellow sat beside me. 'When the winter comes in, like now, the suicide rate goes up. They can't face another winter alone. But then again, suicide is almost a fashion. I came across a motorbike accident two weeks ago. The pillion passenger was lying dead on the road. Like a fox or a hedgehog. He wasn't supposed to be on the back at all. The young fellah who was got all guilty and killed himself. I meself was in a class of thirty-five. Two of them are dead already. Suicide.'

'Have you got any other funny stories? No, seriously. Well, you know what Seneca said: "The highway to freedom is any vein in your body."'

Day 51: Tuesday 11 October

I spent the morning with Shamie Connolly down at Drumlaney lake. We were going to go out on the boat, but we couldn't find the oars. They're hidden in a hedge, but we can't remember where. The day is, yet again, stunning. The morning mist has melted, the water is still, the air is warm. On the far side of the lake, swans do what they do best – nothing. And are beautiful. On the scrubby drumlin sloping down to Drumlaney, three wild white goats eat all they can see except stones.

Connolly and I enjoyed ourselves looking for the oars, cursing the man who hid them, lost them. 'The hoor. That his boils may never burst.' Even as I looked for the oars I thought of Marie Conmee. Her death notice was in the paper. No family mentioned . . . We looked in every scrub and bush, but couldn't find them. 'Ah now, fuck him from a height. Go aisy or you'll rip the jersey off your back.' I crawled into a bush and came out with wool hanging out of me.

All the time we searched, Shamie kept up a stream of talk about football, politics, current news. 'I've seen the vit give blood transfusions to cattle several times. Over the same red water. Man dear, they pour the blood into the cow's vein through a tundish. You have to watch your cattle every day. Count them, look for red water. You don't get red water in Dublin or Meath. Dry land, you see . . .

'I seen me one morning going out to hunt duck. In this very lake. In the middle of winter. Parts of the lake was frozen. I got three teal duck. Didn't they fall into the water. Too far out to reach. What did I do? I stripped to the buff and out I went. Ah, now, the cold. I got two and I was just reachin' for the third in amongst the reeds when he flew up and landed further down. He was winged only. When I come out of the water I was shivering something ojus. But when I put me clothes on and was walking home my skin was tingling. Man dear, I felt great. I was a lot younger then, mind you. I come back later with the dog and I found his nibs dead in the water. I ate well, I'm tellin' you . . .

'We got to the semi-final in 1945. Agin' Killeshandra. I scored a goal. McGrath scored a goal from a twenty-one-yard free. A blaster. It ended up a draw. In the replay we bate them. I was put off. And couldn't play in the final. I never felt as bad in me life before or since. They won be a point. Francie Dolan and a Munterconnaught player went for the same ball, each of them gave it the boot at the same time – the ball burst. That'll give you some idea. Peter Hearney took my place in the final. Where the fuck did we put them hoors of oars?'

I would have been happy to search all day listening to him. I don't know from where he gets his energy. He hasn't aged in a whole lifetime.

'I don't know so much about that, lad. I think I'm slowin'.'

This evening we're back at the Dolan's. Six o'clock start. The first of our all-nighters. The first shot is of Matt and Vicki under a tree. Mike Southon wants to include the moon. Sure enough, there it is full and high in the sky. 'Yeah, but it's at the wrong angle.' A new artificial moon is made. A plastic one stuck in the middle of a big black piece of cardboard and held up behind the branches of the tree and lit from behind. It takes three hours to set up this first shot. By now I've learnt from Peter. My heart doesn't rock'n'roll any more. I just sit and watch, or wander about drinking tea. Tommy Hamilton comes out from behind the tree. He is sweating profusely. I ask him why. Absolutely seriously he replies, 'I've been holding up the moon.'

The first shot is done and then they rehearse a much more complicated one. Intense discussion between Peter and Mike – angles, tracks, lights . . . Lighting at night is even more complicated. Everyone is stumbling around in the dark, tripping over stones or fence wire. Shadowy figures are caught in the arc lights. On top of a very high crane, lights blare down brighter than the sun, never mind the two moons. Because it's the first night shoot, the unit are padded up against the cold and are in a comradely 'going over the top' spirit. Thousands of strange insects beat into the lights. Insects gone from the cities. Weird moths as big as sparrows.

The mist comes down; it gets colder, damper. I can smell the damp rising up from the trampled ground. I can feel the freezing mist going down my lungs.

Because this is the second-last day/night, there is tremendous pressure on the unit to complete everything that's been scheduled. Conversations are low and urgent. Nigel arrives out of the production office. 'How the devil are you?' he calls out cheerfully. Peter sits in front of a monitor. Waiting. Waiting. He is well-wrapped in blankets. His cigar glows in the dark.

Young Donncha O'Brien, Matt's stand-in, waits under the tree. They are lighting him. Donncha wears special high-heeled boots to take him up to Matt's height. The boots look ridiculous. At the start of the picture when we saw him wearing them we thought he was some kind of nutter with a hang-up about his size. He's about the sanest guy on the shoot, calm and smiling, with a Buddhist philosophy to get him through the day. And night.

'OK – get the actors. Quiet please. PLEASE!'

Vicki and Matt stand under the tree and moon ... with Tommy Hamilton in attendance. There is something heroic about Tommy. War and mayhem all about him for the last twenty-five years, but here he is smiling and holding up the moon ... 'This man with lanthorn, dog and bush of thorn, Presenteth Moonshine ...'

I have a bet with Mike Southon that at the end of each set-up I will recite a poem for him. No, it's not a bet. It's just to keep the two of us cheerful. By the time I've got through a couple of Shakespearean sonnets – LX, XXXIII, XXX, XVIII – I'm wilting from the effort of remembering and from the cold. I feel it going through me. Most people have had the flu. Bet it's my turn. Just one day to go and my body is caving in. Dawn to midnight for two months ... Maybe it's because my hair's been skinheaded. Cissie could be right after all.

Nip to the hotel. My car's parked away down the road for a quick getaway. Bed. Bed.

Day 52: Wednesday 12 October

Wake up wheezing, spluttering, sweating. Damn. I've got the dreaded lurgy. I stagger about the room, get all my gear down into the car. Say goodbye in Redhills, go out to the Dolan's house, say goodbye to the gang there ... then head for Dublin. But I feel dreadful. I can hardly move.

Redhills first. In to Phyllis in the post office. She's been a constant in the village for donkey's years. A friend in need. When we were making *The Playboys*, President Robinson came to the village. It was a unique occasion. No one so important had ever visited us. Never in history. All the dignitaries arrived in a village packed with people trying to shake the hand of a woman shaking Ireland. Kathy Durcan, daughter of Eugene Leddy and a famous singer in Ireland, entertained the crowd while we waited in the brilliant sunshine. And the Bunnoe Brass Band marched in from Drung and played the

Presidential Salute. And Phyllis put out the flags, opened her doors and served wine and salmon to all her friends. An educated lady, she has worked and lived in the village ever since she finished boarding school. 'I always knew,' she said that Sunday, 'one day the world would come to us.'

Now I sit with her in the kitchen over a farewell cuppa and cake. She's given me a big envelope with an LA postmark: the photographs taken by Lisa at the drag hunt. She's enclosed enlarged copies for everyone. The one of Ned Crudden's dog, Coiner, coming through the winning gap is splendid. The raw, wet, green field, the massive blackthorn hedge, the judges crouched hiding either side of the gap, Coiner bounding up the hill puzzled at the disappearance of the scent, and an encroaching crowd of cheering people.

'I must show you someday the telegram your father and the men in the barracks sent when Paddy and I got married. Are you sure you don't want something stronger?'

'No, Phyllis. I'm choked. I've got to get to a chemist's.'

We keep the goodbyes brief. See you soons. Good lucks. Goodbyes . . . Phyllis is a jewel of a person.

Up the street to see Deirdre and Seamus Kelly. Since I got my hair cut Seamus laughs every time he sees me coming. Like Phyllis, Seamus came back from boarding school and never left. He ran the family bar, first with his widowed mother, then with Deirdre after they married. One summer's evening in the early fifties a fire broke out in the oil house at the back of the building. Seamus wasn't there. All the men in the village ran to put the fire out. They threw water on the flames. A river of fire ran down the yard in seconds. At the bottom of the yard was a full hay shed. Old Mrs Kelly stood in the window at the rear of the pub, rosary beads in her hand, praying that disaster might be averted. I remember as we watched the flames leaping from the oil house and dancing across the ground, one of the men saying, 'Can you imagine how hot it must be for the Divil and his wife sittin' on the hobs of hell?' I tried to imagine and was terrified but subsequently could only come up with domestic images of Mr and Mrs Satan sitting by their fire, chatting and reading the *Irish Independent*.

As if in answer to Mrs Kelly's prayers, my father arrived on the scene. In the yard he noticed a pile of sand. The fire was quickly defeated. The entire community went into the bar to celebrate. Seamus arrived home at two o'clock in the morning to find the place packed. The first sight he saw as he came in the door was a man holding up a weight with the hook of his little finger, showing how strong he was.

In those days Seamus drove a maroon-coloured Zephyr Zodiac. A big thrill for us kids was to be taken for a ride in it. It was one of only four cars in the village. Seamus was a fine footballer, but had to retire early after a severe injury he received in a match against Scotshouse. Until recently, Redhills and Scotshouse never played each other since then. Not for forty years. Now his days are spent behind the counter of the grocery shop once owned by Alfie Kells. When Alfie moved up North, Seamus bought it. Children run in and out for sweets and ice-cream. Local people come for provisions.

Seamus looks at the world with an amused eye. He told me once there was nothing happening in the world that wasn't happening in the village: war, shady dealings, passions, partings ... 'It's all on our own doorsteps. All in our own backyards.'

'Did you ever wish you could have gone abroad? To work, I mean, not on holiday?'

'No I was too busy. Never had time.'

In a corner of the shop he watches the world on a TV. The world comes to him. Sometimes I envy men who were able to stay at home. Not leaving ever is better than leaving and then coming back. But staying or leaving, it's the same old drums beating wherever you go. Passions, partings ... The world or the village – they're the same in the end. The world *is* a village. Cities are villages with art galleries.

Seamus and I don't shake hands. Deirdre comes in and

looks at me. I know what she's thinking: 'You don't look well.' 'I know. I'll see you soon. I'll let you know how it's going. I'll ring.' I don't shake hands with Deirdre either. I don't want to risk even a hint of finality. As I go out the door Seamus says, 'This place will be like a morgue after you've all gone.'

Many people I wasn't able to see – they were out or at work. I saw John James North talking with the men on the government-relief scheme, rebuilding the demesne wall. I gave him one of the photos taken by Lisa. John James's wife, when she was young, worked for the Whyte-Venables in the Big House. When he was courting her, each evening after work John James met her at the demesne gates. As kids we'd watch him going down the road, all spruced up after his hard day in the forge. On warm summer evenings he'd take her an ice-cream from Sharkey's shop. 'Give us a lick, John James!' we'd shout after him. He'd smile then and he's still smiling. And so is his wife. The great are gone. The good are still going strong.

Driving out of the village, kids and babies play on the green, happily lost in a big world of their own. I make straight for Cissie's house. Shamie is on the hill at the back, hammering up a barbed-wire fence. 'Cattle bruk out last night.' He looks at me as I cough and splutter. 'I know why you caught it. You had the thatch taken off.'

In the house the kettle hangs on its crook over turf flames. Cissie heaps burning turf on to the lid of an iron pot in which is a round of baking bread. 'Ah now, it's only a wee dod.' On the table is an apple pie and homemade jam. She told me she bakes every day of her life. Has done since she was a girl. She's been to America several times and at the height of the Troubles worked in a college in Belfast. Everywhere she's been, everywhere she goes she has the same effect on people – she lifts their spirits. She has an infectious laugh, great electric energy, tremendous generosity. In this Border house she has fed the world and his wife. She's the loveliest person I've ever met. I was ten when I first came into her kitchen. She's never changed. Maybe it's hardship makes people great.

Shamie goes down to his room. 'I've got something will fix Mr Flu. Leave it to Dr Bonzo.' He comes back with a bottle of potheen. I lash some down and feel it travelling all the way to my toes. Theirs is a house hard to leave.

On the way to the location I go into a chemist's in Belturbet. A teenage girl serves me. She recommends something called Flunova. 'I was badly stuffed last Sunday and I took it and I was flying then.'

Out at Senator Dolan's house the unit are hard at it. This is the last night. The end of the picture. Someone says that Albert is coming out at the crack of dawn with a case of champagne. Having flu when the weather is beautiful is doubly annoying. I stand in the road and feel the sun on my face. The hedges are full of haws, blackberries, fern. And birds singing away at the dying sun. Seamus Dolan wanders over and we talk, leaning on a big double-gate into the farmyard. The gate topples over. He doesn't let me lift it up. He lifts it up by himself. He's over eighty-five. With a phenomenal memory. Doggerel, poems, people, places, debates . . . He seems to remember everything he's ever seen or heard.

'The greatest parliamentarian I've ever seen in action was James Dillon. He was the finest. Great speaker. Great authority. He was on his feet one day in the Dáil. Talking away. Someone behind him – probably had too many ice-creams during lunch – kept barracking him. It wasn't the done thing to look behind you. So when he sat down he asked the Deputy next to him who the heckler was. "Barren. From Meath." "It's a pity his mother wasn't." '

As a Member of the Dáil Seamus was on various visiting boards of prisons and mental homes. 'Desperate people in asylums. Desperate because they shouldn't have been in there at all. Locked up in cells and the doctors in big, plush houses. One woman I knew of was in dispute with her brother over a will. The brother wouldn't give her her due. Eventually she went round to his house one night and broke his window with her high-heel shoe. He called the Guards. Eventually they had her locked away in the mental home. She started writing letters. She wrote and wrote to her TD. He decided he'd visit her. He listened to her tale. "How can I get out of here? I'm not mad." "There's only one way. And that's if you'll marry me." Begad, that's what she did. They had two lovely daughters.'

Every time I cough I turn away and try to muffle it. I wouldn't want to give him my lurgy. He stares into the distance, leaning on the gate. In politics all his life, he's done a lot, seen a lot. Looking at him I think of the Yeats poem: 'Everything alters, And one by one we drop away.'

Peter arrives. In his caravan he prepares for the night – jumpers, jackets, coats. He's had the flu for days now. We say goodbye. 'I'd embrace you but I've obviously done that too much already.' The caterers have already cooked up a vast amount of hot food. Can't even look at it. I really must be ill. There are signs pinned up around the kitchen, bus and tables: 'Please wash hands before eating.' There is a case of Hepatitis A.

Someone says, 'Does that mean I could catch AIDS?'

'The world wouldn't be that lucky,' a voice replies.

'Ooh. Thanks very much. Bitch.'

Peter sips a cup of tea. 'Now it's all down to the cutting. And what sort of performances the boy and girl give. Have they delivered?'

'You're not worried are you?'

'No. Are you?'

'Me? I've not stopped. See you in London.'

He walks away, cigar in hand, smiling.

Conor, the clapper loader, has his board marker poised. Then he writes: 'Roll 280. Slate 651. Take 2.'

The sun's drowning in the lake. Flamingo colours bleed across the water.

So what can I learn from the suicide sun? What have I

learnt from the past few months? Nothing ... I go to bed knowing everything and get up knowing nothing ... And have to start all over again. Which is what the circus is all about. I think.

I gave a thumbing girl a lift outside Cavan town.

'Got to warn you – I've got flu.'

''Sokay. I'm going to Kells. You know, as in "Book Of"?'

'Sure.'

'Funny that. The Book Of isn't *in* Kells. It's in Trinity College, Dublin. My auntie came from America. Had a whole party with her. She took them to see the Book Of. But it wasn't there when they got there.'

'Well, I doubt you'd find a 1623 Folio of Shakespeare's plays in Stratford.'

'What? The bloody Leaning Tower of Pisa's in bloody Pisa.'

'Why are you going to Kells?'

'I'm meeting a guy there.'

'Your boyfriend?'

'No. He gives me stuff.'

'Stuff?'

'Begins with C and ends with E and you put it up your nose.'

'Yes?'

'Yeah.'